Postmodern Semiotics

Postmodern Semiosis

POSTMODERN SEMIOTICS
Material Culture and the Forms of Postmodern Life

M. Gottdiener

BLACKWELL
Oxford UK & Cambridge USA

The right of M. Gottdiener to be identified as author of this work has been asserted in accordance with the Copyright, Designs and Patents Act 1988.

First published 1995

Blackwell Publishers, the publishing imprint of
Basil Blackwell Inc.
238 Main Street
Cambridge, Massachusetts 02142
USA

Basil Blackwell Ltd
108 Cowley Road
Oxford   OX4 1JF
UK

Library of Congress Cataloging-in-Publication Data
Gottdiener, Mark.
    Postmodern semiotics : material culture and the forms of
postmodern life / M. Gottdiener.
        p.   cm.
    Includes bibliographical references and index.
    ISBN 0–631–19215–8 (alk. paper). — ISBN 0–631–19216–6 (pbk. :
alk. paper).
        1. Material culture.   2. Culture—Semiotic models.
    3. Postmodernism.   I. Title.
    GN406.G67   1995
    306—dc20   94–14114
                                                              CIP

British Library Cataloguing in Publication Data

A CIP catalogue record for this book is available from the British Library.

Typeset in 10.5 on 12 pt Stempel Garamond
by Graphicraft Typesetters Ltd., Hong Kong
Printed in Great Britain by T.J. Press Ltd, Padstow Cornwall

This book is printed on acid-free paper

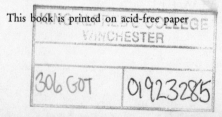

Contents

Preface

Several decades ago an important approach to cultural studies was developed by a number of poststructuralists in France, among whom Roland Barthes was the most influential. Called "semiotics," this perspective extended the work of Ferdinand de Saussure and applied linguistic analysis to the study of culture. After enjoying considerable attention, semiotics entered a period of decline as some of its major adherents abandoned its premises for deconstruction and textual analysis.

This book seeks a revival of the semiotic approach. But it does so within a particular vein. The limitations of structuralism in general and semiotics in particular preclude a return to foundations and classical origins. The subject of this book concerns the relation between symbolic and material culture. It subscribes to a variant of semiotics called "socio-semiotics," which explicitly relates symbolic processes to social context and, in addition, seeks to "socialize" the domain of culture by linking it to the exo-semiotic realms of economic development and political conflict.

Over the last two decades I have published several papers applying the socio-semiotic approach to cultural studies. This effort was also an opportunity to work out a number of long-standing problems in the application of a new, synthetic perspective. I labored at the same time that postmodern cultural analysis became increasingly popular. It seemed to me that while developing important insights, postmodern approaches ignored the relation between symbolic and material culture and privileged, instead, consciousness alone. This idealist bias led to impressionistic accounts which lacked the rigor of earlier semiotic efforts. In a certain sense, my work carries out an implicit dialogue with postmodernism dealing with the ideas of Jameson, Derrida, Baudrillard, and Barthes, among others, and travelling over similar ground – the theme park, the mall, fashion, rock subcultures, identity, image-driven culture, late capitalism, and so on. At each point of comparison the socio-semiotic perspective emulates the insightful power of postmodern cultural analysis but provides an alternative for those interested in a materialist approach to culture and semiotics.

Portions of chapter 1 appeared in *Postmodernism and Social Inquiry*, edited by David Dickens and Andrea Fontana (New York: Guilford Press, 1994), reprinted by permission of the publisher; chapter 2 in *Jean Baudrillard: A Critical Reader*, edited by Doug Kellner (Oxford: Blackwell, 1994); chapter 4 in *The City and the Sign: An Introduction to Urban Semiotics*, edited by M. Gottdiener and A. Lagopoulos (New York: Columbia University Press, 1986) reprinted by permission of Columbia University Press; chapter 5 in *Urban Life*, 11, 2 (1982): 139–62 reprinted by permission of Sage Publications, Beverly Hills, Calif.; chapter 7 in *Espaces et Societes*, 47 (1985): 57–77 reprinted by permission of Jean Remy, Louvain and the Hellenic Semiotic Society, Thessaloniki; chapter 8 in *American Journal of Sociology*, 90, 5 (1985): 979–1001 reprinted by permission of the University of Chicago Press, © 1985 The University of Chicago; chapter 9 in *Qualitative Sociology*, 8, 1 (1985): 29–41 reprinted by permission of Human Sciences Press, Inc.; and chapter 10 in *The Semiotic Scene*, 1, 3: 13–37 (1977).

I would like to thank Doug Kellner, Alexander Lagopoulos and Talmadge Wright for helpful comments when first planning this book. Special thanks go to Simon Prosser of Blackwell Publishers for his astute and patient management of this project.

Part I

Theoretical Considerations

1

Semiotics, Socio-Semiotics and Postmodernism: From Idealist to Materialist Theories of the Sign

An understanding of semiotics is essential for an appreciation of postmodernism. Not only do the arguments of well-known post-modern thinkers, such as Derrida, rely on a knowledge of semiotics, but the entire trajectory of thought that began with poststructuralism draws on the internal critiques of semiotic models. Because the debates surrounding the demise of structuralism and the rise of postmodern ideas were centered in France, particularly in the milieu of the Parisian intellectual, taking up popularized postmodernist ideas whole cloth without an understanding of this context can result in serious blunders. This is so even if the difficult written texts can be read in the original French. Many of the commentaries on post-modernism in cultural studies that have appeared recently lack just such a contextualized and informed understanding of semiotics.

Postmodernism as depicted by academic practitioners in the United States and the UK is almost exclusively about deconstructionism and the problematic of representation. On the one hand, literary criticism and philosophy are concerned about the erosion of foundations where truth claims lack validity because philosophy is writing and all writing is only a mode of representation. On the other hand, cultural studies are now preoccupied with the disappearance of the real and its replacement by simulation, hyperreality and models. These versions of postmodernism either follow the epistemological critiques of Derrida and Lyotard leveled at western philosophy, or the writings of Baudrillard in the realm of cultural studies. In the case of Derrida and Baudrillard, however, such arguments are based by way of critique on a particular version of semiotics, namely the approach of Saussure, whose model of the sign is absolutely central to the postmodern attack on knowledge and representationalism. Social and cultural critics seeking to connect with the postmodern turn follow this anti-Saussurean tradition.

The arguments of the French postmodernists should really be called "post-Saussurean." It may come as some surprise that the deconstructionist or post-Saussurean semiotic tradition is not the only model of the sign or understanding we may possess regarding representation and its problematic. There is another tradition, based on the work of the American philosopher Peirce, which follows a different semiotic model of the sign and holds greater promise for a materialist approach to culture. Analyses of representation based on the post-modern critique of Saussure may be limited simply because that critique did not do away with the importance of the real and its signs in daily life. Cultural analysis based on the Peircian tradition leads us in a different direction, one that can contemplate the relevance of material culture.

This book addresses the subject of cultural semiotics and traces developments that eventually spun off in France in the direction of what is commonly viewed as postmodernism. In addition, however, by keeping the focus on semiotics itself, I shall discuss alternative approaches to the analysis of culture which stand, for the present largely ignored, in relation to the received orthodoxy of deconstruction and the Saussurean tradition. In subsequent chapters of this book I shall discuss how semiotics can be used in the analysis of culture despite the problematic of representation and its various epistemological critiques. After initial introductory material, the discussion proceeds using case studies based on empirical research.

The Origins of Semiotics: Saussure and Peirce

Ancient civilizations possessed medical practitioners, some of whom were successful because the penalty for failure in the case of treating royalty was usually death. Ancient physicians lacked a germ theory of disease and treated all illness by their symptoms. For every sign of distress – coated tongue, skin pallor – there were certain prescribed remedies which apparently had some effect. From this ancient practice arose the first definition of the Greek notion of semiotics – the study of medical signs or symptomology.

Semiotics, then, is a mode of knowledge, of understanding the world as a system of relations whose basic unit is "the sign" – that is, semiotics studies the nature of *representation*. As Eco[1] has observed, the sign is "a lie"; *it is something that stands for something else*.

At almost precisely the turn of the 20th century, two academics on two separate continents began independent investigations into the relation between knowledge and signs. Ferdinand de Saussure (1857–1913), a professor of linguistics at Laussane, and Charles Sanders Peirce (1839–1914), a philosopher at the University of Chicago, developed, quite independently, the basis for the modern study of semiotics, or the "life of signs in society." Both men explored the problem of knowledge arising from the idea that our modes of understanding the world depended on language, an organized system of signs. However, their respective formulations of semiotic dynamics were quite different. As I shall argue below, Saussure privileged the act of communication which makes cultural analysis based on his semiotics limited. In contrast, Peirce was principally concerned with knowledge and the development of language systems that would be instrumental in the acquisition and accumulation of knowledge, such as the specialized vocabularies of natural science. Peircian semiotics, then, relates to the general articulation of signification and culture, unlike Saussure's approach. In this sense Peircian semiotics provides a basis for the development of a mode of cultural analysis that is an alternative to the postmodern approaches based on the Saussurean tradition and its critique, such as deconstructionism, Baudrillard's cultural criticism, and postmodern textual analysis.

Saussure

Ferdinand de Saussure, as a linguist, was concerned with developing a general theory of natural language. While each spoken language uses different words, they all are used to *denote* much of the same things. That is, all societies have culture in common, even if their languages differ. Saussure used the concept of the sign to specify a means of studying these commonalities. According to Saussure, a sign consists of two separate components: a *signifier*, or the acoustic image of the spoken word as heard by the recipient of a message; and a *signified*, or the meaning called forth in the mind of the recipient resulting from the stimulation of the signifier. The sign is three things: the signifier, the signified, and the unity of the two, as he states,

> I call the combination of a concept and a sound-image a *sign*, but in current usage the term generally designates only a sound-image, a word, for example (arbor, etc). One tends to forget that *arbor* is called a sign only because it carries the concept "tree," with the result that the idea of the sensory part implies the idea of the whole.
>
> Ambiguity would disappear if the three notions involved here

were designated by three names, each suggesting and opposing the others. I propose to retain the word *sign* to designate the whole and to replace *concept* and *sound-image* respectively by *signified* and *signifier*; the last two terms have the advantage of indicating the opposition that separates them from each other and from the whole of which they are parts.[2]

The sign, for Saussure, is a bifacial unity of signifier and signified. Unity is effected by culture. That is, the assignment of some signifier, such as the word "chair," to some signified, what a particular community of users "understands" to mean a chair, occurs by cultural prescription. The system of meanings and their words, along with general rules of combination and protocols of usage, are known as language. Hence language is a structure which codifies words and their meanings. Saussure called this structure, which exists *outside* the individual, "la Langue." Through training as children we learn, or are socialized into, a language which we then call on to convey our thoughts. The individual act of discourse Saussure called "la Parole," or speech.

Saussure discovered that language possessed structure and that it was a phenomenon of culture. This led to several other discoveries. The structure of language was *doubly articulated*. That is, there were two distinct ways meaning was conveyed via structure.[3] On the one hand, any utterance consists of a chain of words which unfolds over time or *diachronically*, according to the *syntagmatic* axis. Each of the words conveys the meaning of the sentence by existing within a context of other words. The set of rules governing the placement of words is known as *syntax*, and the meaning that emerges from juxtaposition of each word in the sentence occurs *metonomycally*, which is another way of referring to the relations of the syntagmatic axis. The collection of words: boy, dog, the, the, fed, possesses meaning when we arrange them metonymically as "The boy fed the dog," for example, according to socially prescribed rules of syntax.

In addition to the syntagmatic axis, each use of a word is an occasion to choose from a string of associated words. The presence of any given word, such as "boy," implies the existence of many absent words that could similarly have been deployed, such as "youth," "male," "tike" and so on. The absent but associated words constitute the *paradigmatic* axis of meaning. Correct usages of words are governed by the rules of *semantics*. Furthermore, because the meaning of words arises in part by contrast to what is absent as well as present, by what each word calls forth according to its associations, this axis is also known as the *metaphorical* dimension, or the *synchronic* aspect, i.e. it involves distinctions frozen in time.

For Saussure, all language is based on relations. These are structured through difference or contrasts according to the separate axis of syntagmatic and paradigmatic relations. In turn the syntagmatic structure and the associations in the mind called forth by each of its units are always related to each other, so that they are mutually interdependent. According to Saussure:

> Our memory holds in reserve all the more or less complex types of syntagms, regardless of their class or length, and we bring in the associative groups to fix our choice when the time for using them arrives. When a Frenchman says *marchons!* "let's walk!" he thinks unconsciously of diverse groups of associations that converge on the syntagm *marchons!* The syntagm figures in the series *marche!* "thou walk!" *marchez!* "you walk!" and the opposition between *marchons!* and the other forms determines his choice; in addition, *marchons!* calls up the series *montons!* "let's go up!" *mangeons!* "let's eat!" etc. and is selected from the series by the same process. In each series the speaker knows what he must vary in order to produce the differentiation that fits the desired unit. If he changes the idea to be expressed, he will need other oppositions to bring out another value; for instance, he may say *marchez!* or perhaps *montons!*[4]

For Saussure, then, language is a phenomenon of structural relations and difference, as is also true of the phenomenon of communication through speech. Meaning is created diachronically and synchronically by precisely the same mechanism – namely, *difference*. What is juxtaposed word by word and what is chosen and what is not chosen, or deferred and associated, is defined by difference. Later on we shall also see how this assumption is important for deconstructionism.

The syntagmatic and paradigmatic axes comprise the *structure* of language, and their presence constitutes a *system of signification* which arises due to the combinatory rules of association and juxtaposition. These socially appropriate but arbitrary rules of combination are called the *code*.[5] From the semiotic perspective all cultural phenomena are systems of signification because they are structured according to the relations and contrasts of both the syntagmatic and paradigmatic axes. Semioticians have shown how other cultural manifestations, such as cuisine, can also be considered systems of signification because they possess a structure like language.[6]

Saussure's approach was concerned with the problematic of communication as it was based in the speech act. However, he was also concerned with the phenomenon of language as a manifestation of culture. For all languages, the unity of the signifier with the signified is a cultural convention. This unity is instantaneous in the mind of the receiver but is a conditioned response to the stimulus of the acoustic image. Saussure's sign, then, is conditioned by cultural processes. One of the most important aspects, for Saussure, is the *arbitrary*, conventional nature of the sign. There are no universal, transcendent causes that compel the assignment of a particular signifier to a signified. Rather, in language, the social process of interaction among a community of speakers defines appropriate signifiers for every signified and also regulates the range of meanings for each signifier, because of the presence of redundancy or synonyms. According to Saussure,

> The bond between the signifier and the signified is arbitrary. Since I mean by the sign the whole that results from the associating of the signifier with the signified, I can simply say: *the linguistic sign is arbitrary*. The idea of "sister" is not linked by any inner relationship to the succession of sounds *s-i-s-t-e-r* (sor [soeur]) which serves as its signifier in French; that it could be represented equally by just any other sequence is proved by differences among languages and by the very existence of different languages.[7]

A second feature of Saussure's scheme is that signs are used for communication – that is, they are *intentional*. As Eco remarks:

> ... according to Saussure, signs "express" ideas and provided that he did not share a Platonic interpretation of the term "idea", such ideas must be mental events that concern a human mind. Thus the sign is implicitly regarded as a communicative device taking place between two human beings intentionally aiming to communicate or to express something.[8]

Finally, Saussure also suggested that culture is a pan-linguistic phenomenon. That is, that semiotics, or what he called "semiology," was a way of studying all cultural forms, because they are also structured as a language. In brief, the features of axiological structure – the syntagm and the paradigm, metonymy and metaphor, conventionality, and the sign as the unity of the signifier and the signified – could be applied to all aspects of culture, such as fashion, architecture, cuisine, and so on. Although he did not develop this argument, others, such as the anthropologist Claude Lévi-Strauss and the literary critic Roland Barthes, did, as we shall see below. For Saussure, all culture was structured as a language and, hence, as a mode of communication.

Charles Sanders Peirce

Peirce was a philosopher at the University of Chicago during a time when American pragmatics became a new and important philosophical force. Peirce had several things in common with Saussure, whom he did not know. He, too, developed an approach to the study of signs, which he called semiotics – the name that came to define the field (as opposed to Saussure's "semiology"). Like Saussure, he never systematized his writings on the subject in the form of a book. We receive the work of both men through their collected papers and notes from students: in Saussure's case, the famous *Cours de linguistique generale* published originally in 1915; in Peirce's case, his collected papers (six volumes edited by Charles Hartshorne and Paul Weiss, 1931–5).

Beyond the rather amazing coincidence of contemporaniousness and the minor commonalities listed above, their work was very different. Peirce was not a linguist but a philosopher and he was concerned, not with language, but with how people think. In particular, his interest was in the concept of truth claims and he realized that the understanding of language was essential to any study of truth. He, therefore, sought to classify language as a mode of information, rather than as a mode of communicative interaction between two or more active subjects. In this sense he was concerned less with the social phenomenon of language than with the metalanguages of logical systems, such as natural science, which require precision in writing. Peirce's semiotics was a theory of logic that depended on language structure.

For Peirce, truth claims, or meaning, arise through language only when an idea or concept can be related to by something else already existing in the mind of the interpreter. This is very much like the notion of the signified in Saussure. Unlike Saussure, however, Peirce conceived of the sign as a *three*-part relation: a vehicle that conveys an idea to the mind, which he called the *representamen*; another idea that interprets the sign, which he called the *interpretant*; and an object for which the sign stands. As Peirce suggests: "A sign stands *for* something *to* the idea which it produces, or modifies. Or it is a *vehicle* conveying into the mind something from without. That for which it stands is called its object; that for which it conveys its meaning; and the idea to which it gives rise, its interpretant."[9]

Saussure was concerned with language as a mode of communication and he did not consider, in his system, whether or not an objective world was essential to language. Peirce, in contrast, was no idealist. He believed the real world existed and played a role in signification. It was, after all, the attempt to understand reality that characterized all the sciences. Peirce took this for granted, but saw language as problematic in the quest for knowledge. In particular, he sought to establish conditions for the success of truth claims.

For example, Peirce states immediately after his definition of the sign that "The object of the first representation can be nothing but a representation of which the first representation is the interpretant."[10] But, behind the series of interpretants, according to Peirce, there always existed an "absolute object." Technically speaking, that is, according to semiotics, signification, or the production and consumption of signs, is always a mental process. Thus, the objective world is not a direct part of the sign. This can be illustrated most clearly for imaginary signs, such as the "unicorn." However, in Peircian semiotics, the material world is always implicit in the process of semiosis. Thus, we understand the sign "unicorn," only because we have seen or *experienced* some material manifestation of that imaginary sign – say, the Unicorn Tapestry, for example – and can formulate an *interpretant* or referent with which our understanding of the sign is based. Thus, our experience of the material world and our cognition both play a role in the interpretation of signs. As Zeman observes of Peirce's conceptualization,

> I would suggest that the participation of an object in semiosis as a sign implies a dual nature for that object. On the one hand, the sign – and this includes interpretants – is an object "in the world"; it is empirically describable in terms of its effects in a variety of ways as is any object in the world – it exists, so to speak, in a "public forum." Insofar as it is in this forum, it is as accessible to you in the same way that it is accessible to me. But as a sign, it also stands in a "private forum." It is accessible to me in a way which by its very nature is cut off from you – it is an "element of my consciousness" (of course, I infer that it is accessible to you too in this unique way – unique in this case to *you*).[11]

This duality of signs as being both objects in the experiential world with consequences for our behavior and also cognitive artifacts of consciousness is a fundamental aspect of socio-semiotics (see below) as it is so for Peirce and semioticians such as Prieto (see chapter 8).

In this very significant difference from Saussure, who privileged consciousness alone as well as communication, we are able to specify why Peircian semiotics grasps the more global relationship between modes of representation and culture, including material forms, while Saussurean semiology is limited to the distinction between language and speech and, therefore, possesses formidable contradictions when applied to non-linguistic aspects of culture as exemplified by post-modern cultural criticism. According to Eco:

> I suggest that the essential lesson of Peirce is that the Object is never obliterated; it is only absent (effaced?). And this provisional absence or effacement of the Object is in turn the aspect of Peirce's semiotics which motivates the distinction between language and culture – which makes language/culture dialectically complementary – just as Saussure would have wished, had he persisted in investigating what enabled him to posit *langue/parole* not just as a distinction but an integrated distinction, as organic solidarity.[12]

Peirce was a thinker who arranged his concepts according to threes. His model of the sign, as we have seen, encompassed three entities, although strictly speaking, as Eco, Zeman and others have pointed out above with regard to Peirce, the object world lies in the background and semiosis consists of the cognitive relation between the representatem, which is very much like the signifier, and the interpretant, or Saussure's signified.

For Peirce, however, the sign "stands for" some object only because the relation between representation and the object world is mediated by the interpretant. Peirce conceived of the interpretant as a "psychological event" in the mind of the interpreter. It is an idea, or another sign, which helps understand the first sign by way of contrast. But as a sign, it too can be dissected into its triadic elements. Hence semiosis, for Peirce, was a process of potential infinite regression. The latter idea was taken up by the deconstructionists in their own critique of Saussure. Meaning is always deferred, always becoming through contrast between sign and sign (its interpretant). Later on I shall show how socio-semiotics critiques deconstruction because the latter ignores the social mechanisms that reign in meaning and cut short the *regressum infinitum* of the deconstructionists sign. In fact, one of the central aspects of the socio-semiotic approach to culture, as it also was for Foucault and the early Barthes, is the identification and analysis of mechanisms that constrain knowledge and limit or manipulate meanings through the deployment of power relations.

As Eco notes, Peirce's model of the sign relates language to culture in a global way, unlike Saussure's. One aspect of this distinction is manifested in their respective classification of signs. For Saussure, there is only one sign – the unity of the signifier and the signified. Saussure's sign is part of a system of communication and is motivated (intentional), even if it is arbitrarily fixed by social convention. Peirce, in contrast, considered *nine* aspects of the sign.[13] Of these, following Peirce's passion for triads, three forms of the sign have become most important.

1   A *symbol* is "a sign which would lose the character which renders it a sign if there was no interpretant".[14] It is closest to what Saussure meant by the sign – a vehicle that stands for something else which is understood as an idea in the mind of the interpretant. For Peirce, too, the symbol is conventional and regulated by culture, it is a sign by virtue of some law or rule.
2   An *icon* is a sign that conveys an idea by virtue of its very close reproduction of the actual object or event. International traffic signs, which must transcend particular languages to convey an idea directly, such as a circle with a bar across it to represent negation, are examples of icons, as are the religious pictures used in the Orthodox Church. Icons are weakly motivated or un-motivated – that is, their meaning is only weakly fixed by social conventions. These differentiating qualities are foreign to the system of Saussure, as is also true of the next sign, the index.
3   An *index* is an unmotivated sign. Its meaning is not a product of social conventions or codes. Rather, it is established as a sign in the mind of the interpretant through experience or pragmatic understanding of the material world. The association of lightning and thunder is an index. We see the lightning and anticipate the thunder. We "understand" the meaning of this index as "a storm." Conditioned responses, such as the ringing of a bell and the presentation of food, are also indexes. Through the concept of the index Peirce showed how daily practice or a pragmatic understanding of the material world created meaning through experience rather than through cultural codes.

Peirce's index, unlike Saussure's concept of the sign, allows for the non-human evocation of signs, as in animal–human communication, and also defines systems of signification, such as those built on icons and indexes, that are not systems of communication – i.e., that lack the intentionality of the emitter. A functional system of objects, such as dress, may be a system of signification and not communication in the Peircian approach (see below), because in many cultures the primary purpose of garments is to shield the body from the elements rather than intentionally communicate meaning (although the first function never precludes the existence of the second). Hence, not all cultural systems are true languages as is claimed by the "translinguistics" of the Saussurean system. Furthermore, Peircian semiotics allows for the understanding of behaviorly oriented stimuli that are encoded in material forms as manipulative environments which operate through the power of the index and its experiential basis. The latter characteristic will become important when we discuss in subsequent chapters material forms, such as theme parks or shopping malls, that are environmentally engineered to control or influence behavior.

Peirce's triadic system of semiotics is more powerful than Saussure's, but it is not without its own problems. Peirce did not make clear, for example, what happens to the triadic conception when the object of a sign does not exist, such as the sign "a unicorn," or in the case of an actual lie.[15] That is, Peirce's formulation is as limited as Saussure's for the case of the imaginary relation between thought and its signs, including the case of the simulation or virtual reality as analyzed by Baudrillard,[16] but see the next chapter for a discussion of Baudrillard's postmodernism.

Saussure understood the unity of signifier and signified as a mechanism of culture. Ultimately, these rules were grounded in a cultural code which Saussure called language and which was the rule-bearing structure that produced a system of signification. Codes are the most important aspect of semiosis for the production of meaning through signs.[17] Peirce's rules of correspondence are culturally conceived only with regard to symbols. It is less clear what the function of social codes becomes in the Peircian system. That is, Peirce was not an analyst of culture and it is wrong to make too much of his interest in the "real" world, although he is not a Cartesian idealist in the manner of Saussure. In contrast, Saussure explicitly dealt with the importance of codes and social context in his semiotics, a feature also centrally important to socio-semiotics.[18]

Another limitation concerns Peirce's attempted elaboration of signs which were meant to deal with the subtle problems of inference, but his classifactory scheme is so complex that it hasn't been used by subsequent logicians or even Peircian semioticians. The set of correspondences that would allow for a codified system of signification requires further refinement than that provided by Peirce.

In sum, however, Peircian semiotics improves on Saussure's in the following ways. It acknowledges the existence of the object world, thus avoiding idealism. Peircian triadic analysis avoids simple dichotomies. It provides a powerful classification of signs which includes unmotivated signification and, hence, deals with all of culture, not just language or systems of communication. That is, Peirce's three fold classification of signs allows for the analysis of all systems of signification – i.e., all cultural forms possessing axiological structure (the articulation between syntagmatic and paradigmatic axes). Finally, because all symbols are interpreted by another idea which is itself a sign, there is no clearly defined signified correlated specifically to a signifier. Meaning is always a volatile process of interpretation. As we shall see, this Peircian idea became a central tenant of deconstructionism and the critique of Saussure which Derrida calls the "metaphysics of presence."

Applications and Elaborations of Semiotics

Since the 1920s there have been hundreds of semioticians that have labored to improve on the ideas of Saussure and Peirce. It is simply not possible to review this material, but see Eco[19] and Hervey[20] for examples. Semiotics became an *international* field, with important schools in Prague, Greece, Italy, and Canada, as well as in France. In this section let us consider some of the main applications of the method. For the most part, Saussure had a profound influence on French intellectual life, while Peirce did not enjoy, until recently, much of a following, although I can mention the brilliant University of Chicago semiotician Charles Morris who was influenced by Peirce.[21] Saussure's concept of *la Langue* influenced Durkheim, particularly with regard to the latter's concept of the "collective representation," and became, after its encounter with marxism and Freud's theories, the basis for the French version of structuralism. Unlike Durkheim, however, Saussure was not a structural functionalist. His concept of language/ speech is more dialectical than is Durkheim's notion of the collective representation and it allows for the free-play of cultural forms in daily life.

Among the French the two most important applications of semiotics are found in the works of Roland Barthes and Algirdas Greimas.

Roland Barthes

Perhaps the most influential post-Second World War book on semiotics was Barthes' *Elements of Semiology*.[22] In this elaboration of Saussure, Barthes developed an extremely influential theory of the sign. According to Barthes, a sign, as articulated by Saussure, is principally a form of denotation. That is, the signifier names directly a particular object or marks out plainly to what it is referring. In addition, however, signs can also refer to culturally determined implications, or connotations which have additional meanings. Thus, the word "axe" *denotes* a particular tool for chopping wood. The possession of an axe in some cultures, however, may also *connote* a high social status. Hence the meaning of objects involves higher order levels of connotation that are linked in more substantive ways to cultural processes than merely through the mechanisms of denotation implied by Saussure. For Barthes, the sign can itself become a signifier of another sign, a connotation, or *second order* sign, which signifies a cultural value, such as status. In this case the sign becomes a "sign vehicle" for connotative aspects of culture, such as the status structure of society.[23] In an earlier example using the system of dress, it was noted that this system possesses the non-communicative function of bodily protection. According to Barthes, however, the same objects can also connote status and serve as the basis for ideological aspects of the social order, such as status differences.

For Barthes, systems of signs articulate with cultural values or ideology as connotative codes. These produce richer structures of meaning than was assumed by Saussure. The importance of connotation or second order signs is central to the approach of socio-semiotics. Barthes, in particular, called attention to the ability of signs to build on themselves in second, third, and higher orders of association, much like the infinite regress of Peirce. In this way, a sign can become a hypostatization that condenses an entire ideology in a single word or image.

Barthes' pathbreaking work on the semiotics of culture, *Mythologies*,[24] elaborated on this tiered view of signification or hypostatization and became a model for the analysis of ideologies as cultural forms. In this work he introduces the notion of the myth. Just as a sign, or the unity of the signifier and the signified, can itself be a signifier of another, connotative signified, the levels of connotation can develop further. In a special case, the connotation becomes its own referent and we reach the level of myth. So, for example, as the sign "axe" passes to the connotative level of high status, it can become linked with a state of being connoted by an ideology of high status living or "statusness" which would include other associations through condensation and hypostatization – technology, modernization, progress, social change, mastery of social change, etc. In this case the axe represents the myth of modernity with all its connotations to industrialization, wealth, or privilege, and it endows the possessor with the power of mastery over this myth.

When myths are powerful forces in social organization, as both Durkheim (collective representations) and Marx (ideology) observed, material objects are less important than their connotations. Thus, the axe – what kind it is, how sharp, its utility in the field, etc. – no longer matters in the myth of statusness. What counts is mere possession or the *image* of possession of the axe. All ideologies are also hierarchical symbolic systems which encode both material objects and social actions with preference relations and a prestige ordering. Barthes' concept, therefore, enables us to study the relation between ideology and cultural differences in a new light.[25]

Barthes' fondness for the role of myth as image led him to produce several masterpieces of cultural criticism, including case studies of professional wrestling, food, the face of Greta Garbo, and the promoting of automobiles,[26] and, eventually analyses of images themselves, as in his work on fashion photography[27] and architecture.[28] In a classic example from *Mythologies*, Barthes discusses a picture on the cover of *Paris Match*, a popular magazine, of an African soldier saluting the French flag. The scene denotes an act of national allegiance and connotes military discipline, even suggesting patriotism or nationalism. Thus, the image has several levels. But, for Barthes, what was most relevant about the photo was that this sign of allegiance by an African in the French army was itself a sign of many connotations, or hypostatization of colonial subservience and imperialism. That is, the photo of soldier saluting a flag as a sign could be joined with other associations to constitute still another sign at the higher level of myth – namely, the personification of colonialism and the French subjugation of African people. The image encapsulated "colonialism" with all its connotations, while the material reality of a staged salute – a relation between one individual and a flag – was rather insignificant next to the myth. Later on, Jean Baudrillard was to do much with this discovery of Barthes, to the point of questioning whether reality itself existed in a society driven by such ideologically loaded images (see next chapter).

Algirdas Greimas

Greimas is not widely known in the US, but he is the premier semiotician in France, having recently retired from the Sorbonne. Greimas absorbed the criticisms of structuralism which became essential to any Parisian intellectual's work after the 1970s, but he retained his fondness for Saussure. He pursued the latter's project to develop a *general* theory of semiotics[29] which would include linguistics, the analysis of natural and artificial languages – i.e., all systems of signification, and also metalanguages of scientific discourse that were of interest to Peirce. Greimas' general semiotic theory, therefore, is a tool of interpretive or textual analysis. It was used widely in France until the critique of deconstruction took hold. Today Greimas is less influential because of his reliance on Saussure's model of the sign and his vulnerability, therefore, to Derrida's critique.

The key to Greimasian analysis is the identification of oppositions in a text. According to Greimas, it is precisely through oppositions, or well-defined differences, that meaning is created in writing. These oppositions, in turn, are structured by codes which contain the rules regulating the structure of meaning and difference in systems of signification. If the sign is most important to a Saussurean semiotic analysis, binary oppositions and the identification of codes are essential to Greimas.

Greimas extended his interpretive paradigm to include the structure of social action,[30] creating a general semiotic approach to all of culture. While maintaining ties with structuralism, Greimas' theory acknowledges the role of individual volition. Action produces a sequence of interactions in social situations which he considers a "narrative." The "actant" is a formal role in any sequence of action or narrative, and the whole is regulated by an "actantial grammar," which is the structure of acceptable behaviors and interactions, regulated by the overarching social code.

For example, Greimas[31] analyzes urban space according to spatial oppositions, some of which are: expanse vs. space; here vs. elsewhere; enclosed vs. enclosing. Every particular place, or "topia," has a meaning only because it can be contrasted by the inhabitant with a place that exists elsewhere, even in fantasy, or a "heterotopia." Elaborate fantasy worlds, of course, are called "utopias." These place oppositions articulate with various social *values* or judgments of meaning, or even ideologies, which can themselves be ordered by oppositions such as: sacred vs. profane; private vs. public; superior vs. inferior; masculine vs. feminine. Finally, the value oppositions which articulate with place can constitute *codes*, or what Greimas calls *axiological isotopes*, by ordering the syntagmatic plane, such as:

The aesthetic (beauty and ugliness)
The political (social and moral "health")
The rational (efficacy of functioning, economy of behavior)

which structure environments and their interpretation by users.[32]

Using the above scheme Greimas is able to analyze the meaning of an urban space and its semantization by isotopes or codes. Analogously, his approach is extended to other forms of culture. However, like Saussure, his semiotic analysis is confined to the sign, or the unity of the signifier and the signified, and only the universe of signs exists so that reality is a metaphysical concept, if it is considered at all. In this sense he differs from Peirce and Barthes and from *sociosemiotics* (see below).

Most examples of semiotic analysis today are closest to Greimas' structuralism, even if they do not follow his scheme. Thus, the text is taken as the object of analysis in isolation from society and the independent interpreter is privileged as the sole source of distinctions and observations. Much of this work remains a static, academic exercise giving rise to the objection that anyone's interpretation is just as good as anyone else's, because the synchronic bias of semiotics seals itself off from connections to social practice and social context. Furthermore, those familiar with deconstructionism can see how closely Greimas' approach is echoed in the work of Derrida, in particular. Deconstructionism also seeks to identify the oppositions in the text. Derrida, however, argued that all oppositions are really forms of logocentrism. That is, they are never true oppositions. The authors of texts always bias one term over another. In this way subtle modes of manipulation are introduced in any form of writing. Derrida suggested that this logocentrism (or biasing of terms and concepts) could be "deconstructed" and revealed as a hierarchy. In short, the method of deconstruction attacks the biases of the text through the exposure of its arbitrary oppositions and hierarchies. There are other aspects of deconstruction which will be discussed in the course of these chapters.

Polysemy, Postmodernism and Post-Saussurean Semiotics

The statement "The horse is brown" combines subject and predicate to denote substance. It is the kind of straightforward example of what Saussure meant by meaning conveyed as a string of signs. Few examples of communicative discourse among humans, however, follow this simple universe of denotation and substance. Statements such as "The horse is agitated" which impute subjective and even pejorative states to subjects are complex utterances that open up meaning to interpretation. A receiver of such a message, for example, may observe the same horse and disagree. The truth value of the statement can be questioned. When truth values are thrown into doubt by language, an epistemological crisis can result. This issue was precisely the concern of Peirce, who labored hard, as did other philosophers such as Wittgenstein, to establish conditions under which language could convey absolute knowledge, assuming that absolute knowledge can be attained in some sense.

The complexity of language and the relation of utterances to truth claims was not a concern of Saussure. The latter posited the existence of a structure, *la Langue*, which existed in the minds of socialized residents of society, that could instantly link signifiers with signifieds. Meaning was a simple matching game. Structuralists, such as Lévi-Strauss, took such correspondences to great heights in explaining social phenomena.

The Saussurean model was utterly demolished in a brilliant critique by the French philosopher Jacques Derrida[33] who, by so doing, also helped bury the structuralist enterprise. Derrida was not concerned specifically to critique Saussure alone. His interest was to question all of western philosophy, which he felt had substituted writing for knowledge. For Derrida, in particular, all of philosophy was writing or representation. Western philosophy failed to question the relation between mind, modes of representation, and the study of reality. Instead, it assumed that analytical texts can simply stand in for reality. The text in western philosophy was only a short cut to the comprehension of the real world. Derrida called this a "metaphysics of presence," by which he meant that philosophy fallaciously assumed that reality was immediately grasped through representation, especially writing. He suggested that in fact reality did not enter into writing at all, because the text was always only a mode of representation. In short, as Derrida maintained, "there is nothing but the text."

Among several thinkers that Derrida sought to critique, he found

Saussure particularly vulnerable. The latter's assumptions about language and correspondences were a specifically graphic case of the "metaphysics of presence." Saussure committed the fallacy of conceiving of signs as the simple unity of signifier and signified through the mechanism of *la Langue*. For Derrida, there are no one-to-one correspondences, and signifiers are always open to interpretation. More specifically, Derrida asserted that Saussure's assumption of some facile correspondence between signifier and signified performed by the mind of the listener implies that there exists a "transcendental signified" which can circumscribe the meaning of any signifier. Thus, semiotics, like other modes of western philosophy, was only metaphysics. Paradoxically, Saussure ignored the problem of representation and the volatility of meaning in his theory of signs.

Recall the example of the infinite regression in Peirce's model where one interpretant always led to another, one sign was always interpreted by another sign, and so on (see above). Derrida was influenced by this Peircian conception of semiosis at a time when the attack on Saussure and all of structuralism was raging in France. As he states:

> Peirce goes very far in the direction that I have called the deconstruction of the transcendental signified, which, at one time or another, would place a reassuring end to the reference from sign to sign. I have identified logocentrism and the metaphysics of presence as the exigent, powerful, systematic, and irrepressible desire for such a signified. Now Peirce considers the indefiniteness of reference as the criterion that allows us to recognize that we are indeed dealing with a system of signs ... The thing itself is a sign.[34]

Actually, Derrida was voicing a complaint against Saussure's model of semiotics that was commonly dealt with by other semioticians. As early as the 1950s, Roland Barthes, for example, discussed the problems raised by the presence of *polysemy*: namely, the ambiguous nature of the signifier and the possibility (likelihood, actually) that any given signifier would be interpreted as linked to a different signified by different people. Circumstance and context in communication counts for so much that meaning is always volatile and any putative suggestion of a transcendental signified, as in Saussure, seems ignorant of the basic facts of human discourse.

It was for this reason that Barthes turned his attention to the social techniques that constrained meaning, that roped it in according to well-defined codes of interpretation which, for Barthes, were forms of ideology. Prior to his conversion to deconstructionism in the 1970s, Barthes, like Foucault, was more concerned with the issue of power and how it operated to constrain the volatility of polysemic discourse. He called the ideological mechanisms of normalization and control of language, *logotechniques*. In his study of fashion,[35] for example, he showed how the incredible variety of appearance choices were constrained by the tyranny of fashion as operationalized in the language of fashion reporting. Using aleatory mechanisms, fashion advertising linked signifiers of appearance with signifiers of status and desirable psychological states. Such writing utilizes the chain of signifiers observed by Peirce for a very distinct purpose, by channeling the flow of meaning through logotechniques to make associations desired by the clothing industry between the image of a commodity and the social codes of status or even sexual desire (see next chapter for a more detailed discussion of Barthes' theory). Thus, the system of dress was appropriated by capitalism through the manipulation of the social pressures that comprise the dynamic of fashion.

Lévi-Strauss[36] was also not immune to the problem of polysemy. He discovered its operation as a phenomenon of status. In a study of the tribal settlement space of the Native American Winnebagos, he observed that although there was a dominant conception of their home location which interpreted it as a meaningful cosmological entity, there was also a second competing conception of settlement space which belonged to the lower class of the tribe. In short, the same signifiers possessed different signifieds and these in turn were structured by the class–status division of the society. Very much the same source of polysemy exists in advanced societies and, of course, the divisions are even more complex, making interpretive schemes highly fragmented.

The discovery of polysemy, or what eastern European semioticians, such as Bakhtin,[37] called the *multivocal* aspect of the sign, was the undoing of formal, structural semiotics. In fact, Mikhail Bakhtin anticipated the central thrust of Derrida's critique of Saussure. Bakhtin[38] noted that in Saussure's model the signifier and signified possessed *equal* status in an exchange relation. This means that the sender and receiver are linked in a static, univocal relation where the message simply passes from the sender and is unmodified by the receiver. The receiver's role is simply the decoder of messages, according to Saussure (working, no doubt, with the transcendental signified). In contrast, Bakhtin's view was similar to Peirce's: all signs are mediated by receivers using the cognitive interpretant which is a dynamic and problematic process of association. Meaning for Bakhtin is polysemic or "multivocal," and does not lie within the sign (Saussure), but in the relation between signs (the choice of interpretant). Thus, signification is a social process which involves polysemy and an active search for meaning among participants. There is no transcendental signified nor one-to-one exchange relation in semiosis. Unlike Derrida, who promotes deconstructionism in place of semiotics as a form of textual interpretation, Bakhtin retains an interest in the global relation of culture which he conceives as a *dialogic* relation of multivocity involving an active sender and receiver, or producer and consumer.

Among pure semioticians, only Greimas, Eco, and Bakhtin have attempted to deal with the challenge of polysemy, and socio-semiotics adopts the Peircian-Bakhtinian framework. Virtually all other semioticians and literary critics, like Barthes, who worked from the model of Saussure, quickly abandoned semiotics for deconstructionism after the critique of Saussure.

For deconstructionists and postmodern philosophers, polysemy undermines all grand systems of meaning and interpretation. Philosophy as a system of substantiating the truth claims of language could never be anything more than writing – i.e., individual interpretation – and all epistemological foundations are merely systems of representation. This position ignores the role of speech and language in everyday communication and indeed, for Derrida, the issue is not the relationship between everyday meanings and social practice, but of articulating a philosophy of consciousness independent of social context. Such a position, although challenging to philosophy and the sciences that depend on textual interpretation, has limited value in the analysis of material culture. Thus, we do not embark on the path to deconstruction, but follow a different direction.

Ideology, materialism and postmodernism

The discoveries of Barthes regarding the role of myth in society took a particularly acute turn with postmodernists in the work of Baudrillard. According to Barthes, every object of use becomes encoded with its social function, so that the object itself is a *sign function*. In a society where an axe signifies status in addition to being used as a tool, even if that status is simply "tool user," the axe becomes a symbol or sign function of status. As discussed above, Barthes was principally concerned with the layering of meaning in hypostatizations. He called the second and higher order sign functions "myths." In this case, the object itself was unimportant compared to the image and how it functioned as a condensation point for some ideology.

Baudrillard developed Barthes' idea to an extreme. For him, the media has so pervaded our everyday life with the ideological myths of advanced capitalism that reality itself does not exist. We are all trapped in a *hyperreality* which is defined as a universe of images. Every object, every image merely operates as a second or higher order sign function of mythical proportions. How we label people and objects is now what counts rather than the things themselves or their functional denotations. Within this idealist world, we live by feeding off the images that the media constantly produces.

In the postmodern image of culture, meaning is encapsulated in an immense post-Saussurean world of self-referencing signifiers that make sense only because they define some difference with other signifiers, as the deconstructionists claim. In Baudrillard's world, signifieds no longer exist. For example, in fashion, what is popular today – say, longer hemlines–is so only because its image differs from the fashions of yesterday–shorter hemlines. The intrinsic utility of a hemline length has long since disappeared from social consciousness. Today only the image counts, only the signifier created by difference in the giant system of signification known as "fashion," while deep-level signifieds have disappeared.[39]

Baudrillard, Barthes, Derrida, and other deconstructionists accept Peirce's concept of infinite regress – i.e., meaning arising from the endless play of signifiers – because signs are defined by other signs. But none accept Peirce's epistemological position that, in the end, we confront the "absolute object": that we must acknowledge reality in our daily experience. Furthermore, for Peirce and other pragmatists, our experience of reality produces knowledge that is ultimately *useful* knowledge which involves, in part, the useful manipulation of the object world. As Eco argues, there is a *contextual* basis to truth claims (see below). All utterances and actions have contexts and consequences. Our understanding of the world is built upon such feedback.

In contrast, according to Baudrillard, we have passed from the real to the hyperreal and our understanding of reality comes from a culture based on images. Between Derrida and Baudrillard, therefore, there seems to be little left of the semiotic enterprise. Small wonder that insightful analysts like Barthes ran for cover and abandoned the semiotic project for postmodern literary criticism.

Eco,[40] however, disagrees with the deconstructionist conception of meaning as the free play of signifiers. He suggests that this is a form of idealism, and that meaning must always, in the final analysis, be linked to signifieds, or meaning systems operating as codes. To assert otherwise, as the deconstructionists have done, is to suggest that the

entire universe of all meanings would, through unending infinite regress, be contained in every text, and there would be no point in
writing or creating anything new. Postmodernists following Baudrillard
seem to suggest as much with claims that reality has disappeared and
been replaced by the hyperreal.

The most important observation of Eco in contradistinction to
deconstructionism is his insistence that all connotations of signs are
understood only in specific relation to other signs *within* a particular
semantic field. That is, the interpretation of signs depends on context.
These contexts are structured by particular codes. The combination
of codes and contexts constitutes the semantic field. Thus, for example, as Eco points out,[41] the word "bachelor" is read as "young male
seal" only in the context of the science of marine biology. The latter
constructs a context and a code, or semantic field, for its own meta-
language. The semantic field is bounded and hence constrains the
operation of unlimited semiosis. A practitioner of marine biology
could conceivably ignore the codes and context of its semantic field
and indulge in the free play of signification when interpreting scientific reports, but can only do so at her/his professional peril.

There are other modes of understanding that work against the
deconstructionist critique of semiotics. In psychoanalysis, for example, during a Rorschach test, the doctor provokes the associational
chain of an ink blot image in the mind of the patient. But the psychia-
trist is not interested in the entire, infinite chain of associations, only
in the first few impressions (if not the very first, itself). This is so
because psychiatric practice or experience demonstrates that the first
associations are the most revealing, the most *meaningful* to the patient him/herself. In another example, students with experience taking
multiple choice exams can attest that their first answers are usually
the best. Academic counselors will usually suggest just such a test-
taking strategy. Perhaps the most systematic attention to the critique
of Saussure, however, has been paid by the revised branch of semiotics known as socio-semiotics. I shall return to the analysis of this
approach, which is the one adopted in this book, in the next section.

In short, despite the dilemma of polysemy, there are constraints to
meaning that reign in the free play of signifiers, and perhaps the most
formidable of these is the presence of the material world itself. In this
sense, deconstructionism and Baudrillard idealism are opposed by
pragmatism. Or, as Lenin suggested many years ago, if you doubt the
reality of the automobile, if you think it is only hyperreal, then lie
down in its path. Socio-semiotics addresses the issue of polysemy
from a social context and one of its features is a passionate concern

for the study of all those social mechanisms that reign in meaning. One precursor of this approach is Barthes, whose study of the fashion industry identified the logotechniques of discursive control. Another precursor is Foucault. For him, one obvious set of constraints on the erosion of semantic fields derives from the varied manifestations of power. As Foucault has shown, knowledge and technique controlling the mind and body are engineered into cultural forms (see chapter 3). Deconstructionists have little to say about power, just as they ignore social interaction. Hence, Baudrillard's symbolic reductionism ignores both the material world and our reflexively assessed experience of social context. It is quite surprising how many academics in the United States have been willing to accept this extreme position of postmodernists in the analysis of material culture.

Postmodern cultural critiques are a form of idealism that ignore both the Peircian assumption regarding the final constraints on sign value as arising from the material world and, as Foucault points out, the constraining of meaning by hierarchical structures of power. Myth and the hyperreal complex of the consumer society, which is modulated and controlled by power and agency, cannot obliterate everyday life. The latter still retains enough degrees of freedom for use values to reassert themselves and for subjectively defined actions to reorder the relation between the individual and society.[42] These propositions and others are addressed by an alternative approach, *socio-semiotics,* that takes as its object of analysis the articulation between sign systems and exo-semiotic processes of politics and economics while recognizing the power–knowledge articulation. This book sets out to illustrate the new approach.

Socio-Semiotics

The basic premises of socio-semiotics are as follows.

1   Signs capture the articulation of universes of meaning and the material world. Behind the infinite regress of meaning there exists an objective referent, as Peirce suggested, even if that object is a constructed and reproducible element of fantasy, such as a unicorn, which exists as part of a text or material image. That is, one has to at least have seen some image of a unicorn, or some lexicographic description, to "know" what a unicorn is. Deconstructionism has never been anything more than a philosophy of consciousness. Postmodern analysis of culture based on it only deals with the *conception* of culture –

i.e., the mental image. Socio-semiotics, in contrast, accounts for the articulation of the mental and the exo-semiotic, the articulation between the material context of daily life and the signifying practices within a social context.

2   Systems of signification are multi-leveled structures that contain denotative signs and, in addition, the particular cultural codes that ascribe social values to them, or the connotative ideologies of culture, as Barthes pointed out. For socio-semiotics, all meaning arises from this more articulated, codified dimension. The principal epistemological position of socio-semiotics is that connotation *precedes* denotation. Both the produced object world itself and our understanding of it derives from codified ideologies that are aspects of social practice and their socialization processes. The latter articulation constitutes the object of analysis for socio-semiotics. Codified ideologies, or the codes and contexts deemed important to semiosis by Eco, serve as constraints that structure semantic fields. Without such fields, communication can never occur. These universes of meaning are, according to socio-semiotics, structured by the articulation of knowledge and power, as Foucault suggests. Furthermore, they are reproduced and restructured through pragmatic understanding which is based in the reflexive experience of everyday life, as Dewey, James, Peirce, and Mead suggest.

In contrast to socio-semiotics, deconstruction relies on the critique of representation by an independent interpreter of culture without the need to connect with social context or daily practice. Much postmodern analysis is precisely comprised of these often impressionistic observations by single, and therefore privileged, observers, as in the case of Baudrillard or Jameson, for example. Open up any postmodern analysis of a cultural form – the telephone, a theme park, the mall, Madonna – and you will find the impressionistic analysis of an independent observer, however insightful, without benefit of either a depth analysis of the sign or its social context.

3   Although there is a level of everyday life that is encapsulated by the complex connotations of the hyperreal, the modes of representation that focus on the image and its manipulation by the media, as Baudrillard claims, this does not imply that signifieds no longer exist. Meanings are themselves grounded in everyday life experience. Experience is the encounter with the material world that gives rise to and supports the value systems or codes of culture. New signifieds are constantly being created by people through social interaction and

lived experience (see chapters 8 and 9). Deconstructionism, in contrast, ignores social interaction and the dynamics of communication that both produce and reaffirm/reproduce deep level signifieds.

4   Signs circulate in advanced societies between the level of lived experience, their creation through use values in everyday life, and their expropriation by the hierarchical systems of power, including their use for exchange value in the marketing of commodities (see chapter 8 for a more detailed discussion). Thus, signs are not only symbolic expressions but also expressive symbols that are utilized as *tools* to facilitate social processes. Signs are really sign vehicles that constitute the media of social interaction.

The socio-semiotic model of the sign

The socio-semiotic approach utilizes a model of the sign which deconstructs the articulation between sign value and material life. This perspective borrows from the work of Eco,[43] who extended the ideas of Peirce, and the decomposition of the sign devised by the Danish linguist Hjelmslev.[44] The sign is composed of a signifier and a signified, or what Hjelmslev called the "expression" (signifier) and the "content" (signified). Each in turn can be divided further into a "substance" and a "form," as indicated in figure 1.1.

With this model it is then possible to describe the way cultural codes articulate with material forms. Ideology is defined according to socio-semiotics in a non-totalizing manner as the value systems of social groups. Value systems are correlated to the content of the sign and materiality correlated to the expression of the sign in figure 1.1. This model is an abstraction of the relation between ideology and material forms. It is *not* meant as some dichotomy between either the production and consumption of meaning or the signifier and signified. It expresses a dialogic relation (see chapter 3) where both the sender and receiver of signs are free to interpret meanings in any way they wish. The purpose of the model is to illustrate how ideology

Figure 1.1   The decomposition of the sign according to Hjemslev (Eco)

$$\text{The sign:} \quad \frac{\text{Signified}}{\text{Signifier}} = \frac{\text{Content}}{\text{Expression}} = \frac{\dfrac{\text{Substance}}{\text{Form}}}{\dfrac{\text{Form}}{\text{Substance}}}$$

articulates with material forms. Each aspect has its own social dynamic. However, material forms are never simply matter. They are encoded by ideological meanings which are engineered into form. Similarly, codified ideologies do not exist as mere discursive relations. They are materialized in the social order as interactions, modes of appearance, design of environments, and commodified cultural objects. This conceptualization of the cultural sign will be illustrated by the analyses in subsequent chapters. With these provisos, the decomposition of the cultural sign according to the synthesis of socio-semiotics is as follows (see figure 1.1).

1   The *substance of the content* is over-articulated, over-determined culture, i.e., the culture of the society as a whole which constitutes both the well-spring and the backdrop for specific codified ideologies belonging to particular cultural practices. The *form of the content*, in contrast, is the specific ideology that has been codified in practice and can be materialized in the object world through social interaction and symbolic behavior.

2   The *form of the expression* refers to the specific morphological elements that correspond to the codified ideology, while the *substance of the expression* refers to objects themselves, which correspond to codified ideology and which exist materially, even if that materiality is simply a text in the case of fictitious objects. These levels of the sign are indicated in figure 1.2.

Figure 1.2   The decomposition of the sign according to socio-semiotics

		Substance	Non-codified ideology
	Content	Form	Codified ideology
Sign:	=	=	
	Expression	Form	Morphological elements
		Substance	Material objects, text

3   Finally, every sign is part of a system of signification, which is structured by the syntagmatic and paradigmatic axes. Polysemy involves the intersection of several forms of codified ideology for any given cultural expression. Polysemy produces several signs for any given material object and these would belong to different sign systems, or axiological isotopes, according to Greimas. The understanding of

difference comes from an understanding of the social codes that produce different value systems or connotative relations with material objects.

Socio-semiotics can be used in textual analysis as explored by deconstructionists, but its main purpose is to analyze the phenomena of material culture, such as the interplay between advertising, Baudrillard's sign values, and the objects of everyday life – cars, electronic commodities, houses, shopping centers, malls, fashion, and so on.

For example, the phenomenon of Disneyland has been analyzed using semiotics and in structural terms.[45] Marin's analysis is typical of semiotics in that it is a static rendition of sign oppositions uncovered by the author himself. According to Marin, the oppositions nature/machine, past/future, reality/fantasy, and so on structure the space of the theme park. These oppositions commit the fallacy of structural analysis well documented by Derrida in his critique of Saussure. They are logocentric and hide biases of the "independent" observer, namely Marin. They also assume the presence of a transcendental signified, since they are based on one-to-one correspondences between signifiers and signifieds. In contrast to this approach, a socio-semiotic analysis of Disneyland would try and uncover the production codes used by the designers of the park (mainly Walt Disney) and the social context of the park experience itself (within the context of everyday life in Los Angeles) – see chapter 4.

The premise of socio-semiotics is that any cultural object is both an object of use in a social system with a generative history and social context, and also a component in a system of signification. The basis of socio-semiotics is polysemy and the need to analyze the articulation of several sign systems for any given cultural object. Furthermore, the meaning of cultural objects and their use as expressive symbols in society remains a function of cultural context and interactive process, of particular semantic fields and of the knowledge–power articulation. The meaning of material culture is discovered not through the logocentric textual analysis of some independent observer, but from an analysis of the articulation between codified ideology and material forms illustrated in the socio-semiotic model of the sign. Analysis captures the point of view of both the *producers of culture* and the *consumers of culture*. Often this entails the study of printed documents or historical accounts and, in some cases, personal interviews, as the case studies in this book illustrate.

Conclusion

In the United States a particular brand of postmodernism has achieved
orthodoxy. It is strongly influenced by Derrida, among those engaging in textual analysis, Lyotard, among those concerned with the
philosophical issues of epistemology, and Baudrillard, among those
academics interested in cultural analysis. This orthodoxy derives from
the internal critique of French intellectuals laboring within the
Saussurean tradition and eager to break the bonds of structuralism.
Americans who have dabbled in postmodern cultural criticism seem
overwhelmingly enraptured by this particular French tradition. A great
deal of attention has been lavished on the alleged affects of the disappearance of the signifieds, the polysemic basis of textual interpretation, and the fallacy of foundationalist analysis.

One purpose of this chapter has been to lay the foundation for an
alternative, socio-semiotic approach. Subsequent chapters will amplify
these ideas and illustrate the perspective through empirical studies of
cultural forms. In concluding this chapter, let me briefly sketch out
the ways in which socio-semiotics specifically constrasts with
postmodern cultural analysis and the received orthodoxy of the French
postmodern school.

1   Culture is not simply understood as a system of signification, but
as a sign system articulating with exo-semiotic processes – in particular, economics, and politics. Semiotic analysis that confines itself to
the sign alone (the "left side" of the Peircian triad), can only describe
symbolic relations. Socio-semiotic analysis which includes the symbolic–material articulation – that is, the study of signs and social context – helps *explain* symbolic relations.

2   Meaning is not produced through the free play of signifiers alone.
Rather, signification is constrained by the forces of power in society,
or what the early Barthes referred to as the "logotechniques" of symbolic control. As Deleuze[46] suggests, it was Foucault who demonstrated conclusively how the "substance of the expression" is the
mechanism of power which constrains the play of signification (see
chapter 3). Understanding this point and its importance in cultural
analysis is an essential aspect of socio-semiotics. Material forms, such
as the theme park or the shopping mall, for example, are engineered
for effect just as is Foucault's prison, clinic, and hospital. Material
culture is the condensation of past knowledge and ideologies that

have materialized technique, modes of desire, and knowledge for social control.

3 Postmodernist criticism should not be confined to textual analysis alone, or the critique of forms of representation alone, but should be an inquiry into the ways forms of representation structure everyday life. To forget everyday life and the users of culture is to neglect the formative aspect of culture itself. Furthermore, forgetting the role of power in society, as indicated in point 3 above, compounds postmodern ignorance. In particular, this means that it is necessary to pass beyond critiques of representation, and textual criticism, to engage in critical discourse regarding the articulation between media, or mass cultural forms, power, and material culture (see chapters 5–6 and 8–10).

Notes

1 Umberto Eco, *A Theory of Semiotics* (Bloomington: Indiana University Press, 1976).

2 Ferdinand de Saussure, *Course in General Linguistics*, edited by C. Bally and A. Secheehaye and translated by W. Basking (New York: McGraw-Hill, 1966).

3 Ibid., p. 67.

4 Ibid., p. 130.

5 Eco, *Theory of Semiotics*, p. 8.

6 See below, and Claude Lévi-Strauss, *Structural Anthropology*, translated by Claire Jacobson and Brooke Schoepf (New York: Basic Books, 1963).

7 Saussure, *General Linguistics*, p. 68.

8 Eco, *Theory of Semiotics*, p. 14.

9 Charles S. Peirce, *Collected Papers*, edited by P. Weiss and C. Hartshone (Cambridge, Mass.: Harvard University Press, 1931), p. 1.339. Peirce's collected work, which amounts to eight edited volumes, is referenced in the following manner: the first number corresponds to the volume and the number succeeding the decimal corresponds to the paragraph. Thus 1.339 above refers to volume 1 and paragraph 339.

10 Ibid., p. 1.339; see also 2.227 for a similar definition.

11 J. Jay Zeman, "Peirce's Theory of Signs," in *A Profusion of Signs*, edited by T. Sebeok (Berlin: Mouton Publishers, 1976), pp. 22–39.

12 Eco, *Theory of Semiotics*, p. 58.

13 Charles Pearson and Vladamir Slamecka, "A Theory of Sign Structure," *The Semiotic Scene*, 1, 2 (1977): 1–22.

14 Charles S. Peirce, *The Philosophical Writings of Peirce*, selected and edited with an introduction by Justus Buchler (New York: Dover Publications, 1955).

15 Eco, *Theory of Semiotics*, p. 58.
16 Jean Baudrillard, *Simulations* (New York: Semiotext(e), 1983).
17 Eco, *Theory of Semiotics*, p. 58.
18 Ibid.
19 Ibid.
20 Sandor Hervey, *Semiotic Perspectives* (London: Allen and Unwin, 1982).
21 Charles Morris, *Signs, Languages and Behavior* (New York: Prentice-Hall, 1946).
22 Roland Barthes, *Elements of Semiology*, translated by A. Lavers (New York: Hill and Wang, 1967).
23 See also Erving Goffman, "Symbols of Class Status," in *Sociology and Everyday Life*, edited by M. Truzzi (Englewood Cliffs, N.J.: Prentice-Hall, 1968), pp. 21–32.
24 Roland Barthes, *Mythologies*, translated by A. Lavers (New York: Hill and Wang, 1972).
25 Pierre Bourdieu, *Distinction: A Social Critique of the Judgement of Taste* (Cambridge, Mass.: Harvard University Press, 1984).
26 Barthes, *Mythologies*.
27 Roland Barthes, *The Fashion System*, translated by M. Ward and R. Howard (New York: Hill and Wang, 1983).
28 Roland Barthes, "Semiology and the Urban," in *The City and the Sign: Introduction to Urban Semiotics*, edited by M. Gottdiener and A. Lagopoulos (New York: Columbia University Press, 1986), pp. 87–98.
29 Algirdas Greimas, *Semiotique et science sociales* (Paris: Seuil, 1976). See also *Semantique structurale* (Paris: Larousse, 1966), *Du Sens* (Paris: Seuil, 1970).
30 Greimas, *Semiotique et science sociales*.
31 Algirdas Greimas, "For a Topological Semiotics," in Gottdiener and Lagopoulos, *The City and the Sign*, pp. 25–54.
32 Ibid., p. 34.
33 Jacques Derrida, *Of Grammatology*, translated by G. C. Spivak (Baltimore: Johns Hopkins Press, 1976).
34 Ibid., pp. 48–9.
35 Barthes, *Fashion System*.
36 Lévi-Strauss, *Structural Anthropology*.
37 Mikhail Bakhtin, *The Dialogic Imagination*, translated by M. Holquist and C. Emerson (Austin: University of Texas Press, 1981).
38 Ibid.
39 Baudrillard, *Simulations*.
40 Umberto Eco, "Function and Sign: Semiotics of Architecture," in Gottdiener and Lagopoulos, *The City and the Sign*, pp. 55–86.
41 Umberto Eco, "Social Life as a Sign System," in *Structuralism: An Introduction*, edited by D. Robey (Oxford: Clarendon Press, 1973), pp. 57–72.
42 Michel de Certeau, *The Practice of Everyday Life* (Berkeley: University

of California Press, 1984); Henri Lefebvre, *The Critique of Everyday Life* (London: Verso, 1991 [1947]); see also chapters 8 and 11.

43   Eco, *Theory of Semiotics*.
44   Louis Hjemslev, *Prolegomena to a Theory of Language* (Madison: University of Wisconsin Press, 1969).
45   Louis Marin, *Utopics: The Semiological Play of Textual Spaces* (Atlantic Highlands, N.J.: Humanities Press, 1984), pp. 239–59.
46   Giles Deleuze, *Foucault* (Minneapolis: University of Minnesota Press, 1988).

2

The System of Objects and the Commodification of Everyday Life: The Early Work of Baudrillard

The preceding chapter focused on theoretical issues which justify the socio-semiotic approach. The remainder of this book consists of case studies that elaborate on that perspective. Examples of socio-semiotic research are not necessarily new. In fact, some of the best early studies which explored the ability of semiotics to investigate culture are also precursors of the socio-semiotic approach. In the sense in which the analysis of material culture is understood by this book, perhaps the consummate analyst was Roland Barthes. His early studies are an inspiration. There have been other equally important practitioners during the late 1950s and early 1960s in France. Of these the two best are Raymond Ledrut and Jean Baudrillard.

The aim of this chapter is to satisfy a need to illustrate the socio-semiotic approach to material culture before proceeding with additional theoretical considerations and my own case studies. I choose to consider, by way of illustration, the early work of Baudrillard for two reasons. It is, on the one hand, a substantive example of the socio-semiotic method that has never been translated into English, and, on the other, in the hands of its author, the ideas in this early work were refashioned and retailored into postmodern cultural criticism later on – an outcome that may be lamented for its switch from socio-semiotic analysis to impressionistic observations and sweeping generalizations.

The System of Objects and the Commodification of Everyday Life

Examination of the earlier works of a writer brings with it interesting observations, perhaps surprises, but is it the way authors want to be read? What they mean today may differ from what they meant in the past. Academic work, unlike novel writing, represents both the development and the clarification of ideas. In this essay I am less concerned with Baudrillard the subject than with using his first major text[1] to interrogate the semiotics of material culture, which is the purpose of this book. This essay, then, seeks to retrieve some significant insights from Baudrillard's still untranslated first writings on the semiotics of objects and the study of material culture. By so doing, I hope to advance that inquiry.

In recovering his early work on the semiotics of objects, however, there are some interesting observations that can also be made about Baudrillard's later writings. I find a critical disjuncture between the early effort to study the relationship between semiotics and the commodification of everyday life, and the later effort which abandons that project and replaces it with an impressionistic, idealized, and jargon-laden discourse on symbolic exchange and the orders of simulacra[2] that has come to be known as "postmodern" cultural criticism. The early work of Baudrillard stands out as a "reality-based" analysis of the quotidian changes that are facilitated by material culture, changes in the ideology of daily living and the symbolic images of consumption. Many of the concepts for which Baudrillard is known – such as "hyperreality" and "simulation" – which float ungrounded through his later discourse as general conditions of humanity, are specified in concrete, useful ways in his early work. In sum, for those interested in the relation between ideology and material culture, rather than postmodernism per se, Baudrillard's *System of Objects* ranks as one of the most important books of post-structuralist cultural criticism.

Antecedents: The discovery of structure and the study of culture

The influence of the Swiss linguist Ferdinand de Saussure was at its height in France during the 1950s. At this time the anthropologist Claude Lévi-Strauss[3] had already applied the essential ideas of Saussure to the study of culture. In this tradition, all of culture was discovered to be structured as a language. By this was meant that cultural meanings possessed the double articulation of language and were structured according to two dimensions: the synchronic and diachronic axes, as discussed in chapter 1. Language possesses meaning not only because the sentences we use follow strict laws called syntax (a diachronic dimension), but also because our choice of words follows another set of strict rules, called semantics (the synchronic dimension).

According to the great discovery of semiotics, meaning itself was a product of the articulation or juxtaposition of these two axes as we discussed in the previous chapter.

According to semiotics, for example, the system of cuisine or cooking structured the meal, in one way, according to diachronic rules. Dishes of the meal are served one after the other according to custom. In the "formal" meal, for instance, the hors d'oeuvres come first, followed by appetizers, soup, sorbet, entree, salad, and so on. Violation of the syntax of the formal meal means a dish served out of turn or omitted. Such a *faux pas* would threaten group or social interpretation and sanction of the meal as "formal." In addition, meals are also structured a second way, according to the synchronic or semantic dimension. Each particular dish can be prepared in a variety of ways: boiled, fried, raw, cooked, parboiled, baked, broiled, and the like. At each stage of the meal choices are exercised regarding what to serve: a hot or cold soup, a green or Caesar salad, chicken or beef, and so on. Each of these synchronic choices must also conform to the diachronic dimension – i.e., the choices have to fit together as an ensemble in the normative sense, such as picking the appropriate wine to go with a particular dish. Hence the two dimensions are related to each other and together bring about a realization, regulated by custom, of that social act known as "the meal."

Saussurean linguistics as semiotics was applied to the general phenomenon of culture and became popular in France during the 1960s. As a structural method it allowed for the analysis of all cultural forms as symbolic systems. Indeed, Saussure himself conceived of semiotics as a pan-linguistics, as we have seen in chapter 1. Early work by semioticians gave the impression, following Saussure, that all cultural systems structured as a language could also communicate meanings as a languag.[4] Thus, it was once believed that non-verbal, body language, or kinesics and proxemics, could communicate meanings as vividly as spoken speech. As semiotic studies matured, however, this "linguistic fallacy"[5] of Saussure (and the early Barthes) – namely, that cultural systems structured as a language could also communicate as a language – was exposed and a much more modest approach to the semiotics of culture adopted.

Semioticians today follow Eco[6] and distinguish between cultural complexes that communicate intentional meanings, or *systems of communication*, and complexes that do not necessarily communicate intentionally but are structured as a language, or *systems of signification*. All systems of communication are also systems of signification, but not the other way around. All systems of signification and, by implication, systems of communication possess synchronic (paradigmatic) and diachronic (syntagmatic) axes. Thus, for example, cuisine is a vehicle for the expression of culture and is structured as a language, but it is not a system of communication. Hence, we no longer subscribe to the linguistic fallacy of Saussure. As discussed in chapter 1, it is the approach of Charles S. Peirce, that offers a better grasp of the differences between signification and communication. Socio-semiotics follows Peirce and his analysis of the sign which includes the unmotivated manifestation he called an "index." The theoretical aspects of these ideas will be developed further in chapter 3.

Barthesian cultural criticism

In the 1960s Roland Barthes, the French literary critic, produced some of the most important and enduring semiotic analyses of culture. In literary criticism the two axes of meaning corresponding to the paradigmatic and syntagmatic dimensions are also known as the metaphorical (associative) and metonymical (juxtapositional–contiguous) axes. Using this distinction, Barthes extended the concept of "trope," or figure of speech, to the system of signification. By speaking of literary texts using these concepts he emphasized the importance of the play of difference in the creation of meanings, because both metaphorical and metonymical tropes rely on contrasts or difference – the one associative, the other contiguous. This distinction became a core idea of deconstructionism (see below).

Barthes' work has two main periods. In the first he proposed a translinguistics of culture a la Saussure,[7] by which all cultural phenomena were analyzed as language. In his latter period he acknowledged the limitations of the linguistic approach. During this time he joined the literary critics of the *Tel Quel* journal group, including Julia Kristeva, among others, who were influenced by structuralism and post-structuralism. Eventually this group and its journal abandoned semiotics for deconstructionism.

Socio-semioticians consider Barthes' early period as more important. During this time he was particularly interested in the way systems of signification were overlaid by ideology in the form of written texts or discourse. He distinguished between cultural phenomena per se – systems of objects which did not represent communication or language – and ideologies linked to cultural processes which were discourses that manipulated the users of culture for specific purposes, such as the sale of commodities. The discourse surrounding the use of objects, such as the language of advertising, *was* a system of communication filled with the intentionality of ideology that constituted a text. By distinguishing between systems of objects which constitute modes of signification from ideological discourse involving the use of those objects, Barthes distinguished between material culture and the mode of communication used to manipulate consumer choices.

In 1967 Barthes published one of his most comprehensive semiotic analyses of a system of objects, the fashion system (*Systeme de la mode*).[8] Barthes showed how bodily adornment is structured as language – that is, as a system of signification (see chapter 10). But Barthes made the distinction between the system of dress, which functions as a mode of signification, and the system of fashion, which is a mode of communication, or ideology, that possesses intentionality. In particular, the system of fashion is an ideology propagated by the fashion industry and advertising for the control of appearance in order to sell commodities. This distinction between signification and communication is central to the socio-semiotic approach and, among other things, insulates it from the critique of deconstructionism (see chapter 3).

For instance, each area of the body from the top of the head to the toes can be a location for the articulation of styles of dress. At every location of the body, the individual has a choice regarding how to articulate with styles of adornment – whether to wear a hat or not, a necktie or not, a skirt or pants, and so on. These choices are regulated by the paradigmatic axis of the society's particular dress code. As a system of signification, the dress code regulates all fashion alternatives, such as size, shape, color, and style.

In addition, when any individual chooses body adornment, attention is usually paid to how well the individual choices of head covering, shirt, skirt, and shoes, for example, fit together as an ensemble. These contiguous items are also regulated by the society's dress code and constitute the syntagmatic axis. People can commonly violate the dictates of fashion by inappropriately mixing different combinations of clothing or adornment. In short, the dress code, which regulates appearance alternatives, is structured as a system of signification. Societies use the power of the dress code to make distinctions between men and women, young and old, caste or class differences, states of joy and mourning, and so on. These distinctions in some societies are formalized as "sumptuary laws".[9]

The dress code, however, despite its regulatory power, is not a text nor a system of communication (see chapter 10), i.e., a language, although *it is structured as a language*. Barthes suggested that superimposed on this code in capitalist society, is a second system, the fashion system, which attempts to control the everyday decisions of individuals regarding appearance for the purposes of selling the commodities of the fashion industry. According to Barthes the instrumental manipulation of the fashion system, which accompanies the commodification of daily dress, operates through the texts of talk shows, magazines, advertisements, designer shows, and everyday discourse. For Barthes, the fashion system as an ideology attempts manipulation of appearance choices through a variety of semiotic methods which he called "logotechniques." This term specifies the use of ideology for the control of consumption and refers to the general phenomenon of consumer manipulation by the commodity industries principally operating through advertising. Logotechniques are examples of the knowledge–power–culture triple articulation.

The fashion overlay that colonizes daily life utilizes semiotic properties of language. For example, an everyday necessity, such as waiting for a commuter train to go to work, would be metonymically conflated with the wearing of a particular fashion object, an overcoat, for example, in a visual magazine ad. The text which accompanies the ad would compound the logotechnique of visual metonymy with associations, such as the statement "A perfect coat to wear while waiting for the train." The logotechniques of fashion discourse supercede the dress code in an attempt to manipulate consumers to buy specific products not because of need, but in order to "look fashionable." Their intentionality makes the texts of fashion a system of communication. The logotechniques of fashion have been somewhat successful in regulating consumer choices (see chapter 10). As a result, the phenomenon of fashion, as a cyclical prod that stimulates consumption, has now spread to other consumer choices, such as the purchase of cars and electronic equipment. This new consumer logic, based on rapid changes in appearance as a means of boosting the turnover of consumer purchases and, therefore, the rate of capital realization, is equated with the effects of postmodernist, late capitalism.[10]

The System of Objects

There is little doubt that Barthes' work on the fashion system provided the model for Baudrillard's early books. In *The System of Objects*, Baudrillard concerns himself with the way home furnishings and interior decoration have passed from an ersatz, subjective, and personalized activity to one that is highly regulated by a code of design and appearance based on the commodification of household interiors. Baudrillard introduces ideas similar to Barthes' but he also generalizes his concerns by connecting to other issues popular at the time in France, such as the role of technology[11] and urbanism[12] in changing everyday life.

In contrast to Barthes, in this early book Baudrillard provides a basis for his later postmodern musings, because he explicitly raises the issue of modernity (conceived as an historical epoch) and its affects on the regulation of household interiors using the design concepts of modernism (conceived as a form of art or design), a subject which Barthes ignores in his work on the fashion system. That is, Barthes was concerned with the articulation between culture and power as circumscribed by the role of ideology in consumption and as an extension of capitalism. In contrast, Baudrillard is sensitive to historical change. He views the culture–power articulation as an historically changing complex. Thus, Baudrillard is less concerned with the power of ideology to control everyday life, and more interested in the general effect of cultural change under the sign of modernity (later postmodernity) which he sees as an inexorable and pervasive shift to the commodification of all cultural objects. This theme is closer to Karl Marx's analysis of the effects of capitalism than is Barthes' emphasis on ideology.

At the very same time in his early work, however, Baudrillard lays the foundation for his transcendence of marxism (which he fully accomplished in his books later on) by demonstrating the power of cultural, as opposed to economic, change (conceptualized here as the movement of modernity) in the alteration of daily life. The commodification of quotidian existence proceeds as modernist ideas attain hegemony. This cultural movement is manifested in daily life as a subset of the fashion phenomenon, in particular, as part of an effort to keep up with others and be "modern." In short, the forms of modernity causing social change operate through the logotechniques of fashion and design, through the coercive power that Saussure, Barthes and, also, Durkheim, understood to be a power of any language, just as they do through changes in "political economy" which are most often taken to be primary by marxists.

The System of Objects is an exemplary exercise in materialist semiotics. Unlike Baudrillard's later writings, assertions are backed up by concrete examples, theory is explicitly stated, and connections are made between the author's observations and the work of others. As Baudrillard wanders through the typical middle class household, he concretely demonstrates how a modern system of signification articulates with common everyday objects and commodifies daily life. The set of household furnishings determined by modernist design practice is a system of signification, not communication. But the ideologies which valorize particular modernist designs, especially at the expense of pre-modern or traditional and ersatz modes of home decoration, constitute a system of communication or logotechniques of consumer manipulation.

The book consists of three parts. The first analyzes what Baudrillard calls "functional objects," which are consumer goods associated with home furnishings. He then considers commodities as projections of the future, such as gadgets and robots, which are advertised as either "the latest" in home furnishings or projections of the future of decor. The latter was a common activity in the 1950s under the spell of the modernist ideal of progress, along with projections of the landscape for the future city, in world fairs and the like. Finally, he discusses "nonfunctional objects," the antiques, anachronistic marginal commodities and collections that are also found in the middle-class home. For each of these areas, Baudrillard describes the social shift from a traditional to a "modern" way of life which is part of a "new social order," or "hypercivilization." This is also conceptualized as a process of the disenchantment of the traditional world through the hegemonic intrusion of abstract systems of signification tied to fashion and modernist design practices. In other words, Baudrillard's interesting thesis explored in this book is that the commodification of everyday life takes place through the hegemony of the generalizing and differentiating tendencies of the fashion system, commodification and technological innovation that are hypostatized under the sign of "progress."

The functional system

The configuration of the home and its furnishings in the traditional mode represented the domination of paternalism. We access this configuration through childhood memory of the family home which depicts "not an objective world, but the boundaries of a symbolic relation of family life" (p. 26).

The contemporary home is configured by the disenchanting effects of modernity. Each room of the house is a target for the articulation of fashion and modernist home furnishings. The traditional configuration is eradicated by new consumer purchases. Each room is commodified as a separate unit. There are kitchen "sets" for the kitchen, living room "sets" for the living room, and bathroom "sets" for the bathroom. Decor and appearance are structured metonymically, as an ensemble, as well as metaphorically, as a syntagm.

As with the conceptualization of "postmodernism," which came much later in Baudrillard's writings, the metonymical relation dominates this system of appearance. Thus, in the latter Baudrillard, all of culture consists only of the play of signifiers structured by the metonymical relation. In the present case, the modern decor of home furnishings is structured by the opposition "milieu/position" which is typified according to the general concept of "ambiance," or organized under the sign of ambiance (p. 28) – i.e., structured as a relational milieu according to the logic of interior design.

Baudrillard notes that the modern objects remain familiar. They are still chairs, tables, lamps. Only their design has changed. What counts most is the way they now fit into the organizing system of modernist fashion. Thus, the liberation of objects from traditionalism and the emotional, subjective context of daily family life by modernity "is only a liberation of the function of the object, not the object itself" (p. 26). Hence the system of household objects organized under the sign of ambiance constitutes a functional system. Modernist design's emphasis on pure form, on line, on shape, on the fit of the ensemble or decor liberates the object from the sentimentality of traditionalism through the emphasis on function. Functionality, for example, is expressed in the shift from a "grandfather clock" or the clock as heirloom, to the abstract, functional clock designed according to a particular fashion.

As Baudrillard remarks, however, when objects are freed from affect and reduced to function, people are freed from sentimentality but become only "users" of objects. The transformative shift of modernity creates a set of functional objects as commodities and a status of humans as users or consumers. This transforms the house from the hearth of tradition and historical continuity to a showcase for consumerism and status.

Here Baudrillard draws on earlier work by the planning critic Françoise Choay.[13] The milieu of modernity reduces all meaning to the sign of function. The modern environment is "hyposignifiant;" i.e., its symbolism is attenuated. But he pushes this idea further by showing how the functional space is dominated by the metonymical (i.e., contiguous) relation "which is the basis of modernity" (later, for him, postmodernity and the hyperreal culture of simulation). Ambiance is constructed through difference and relation. The modern decor signifies not through sentimentality and affect (i.e., metaphor), but through inter-relation, or intertextuality, by creating a milieu or space. The "meaning" of objects in the home passes from the code of traditionalism, with its deep-level signifieds, to the self-referencing, hyperreal system of appearances based on the play of signifiers alone. The production of meaning through metonymical differences is the mechanism by which the space of the home is structured according to modernist ideology.

Baudrillard comments on what has been lost in the shift from tradition to modernity. The 19th-century bourgeois home was filled with mirrors. All images were reflected back to the center, reinforcing the unity of space while also amplifying space. Today the use of mirrors in the home has largely disappeared. Modern decor emphasizes separation according to the ensembles of each room. The unity of the home is broken up by modular construction, partitions and blank walls. Along with the break-up of interior space, clocks have also disappeared. "In the petite bourgeois home the clock often crowns the mantle piece, itself often dominated by a mirror . . . The tick-tock of a clock consecrates the intimacy of a place – it makes it resemble the interior of our bodies" (p. 33). The home as metaphor, as body of the family focused towards the center through mirrors, loses its heart, the clock, as the framing piece of the living room.

Modernity transforms personal space not only through the logotechniques of interior design but also through the effects of technology and the desire for technology under the sign of progress. The practice of consumption is altered into a technological practice of the manipulation of objects. We turn things on, adjust them, calibrate them, gauge their output, and arrange them according to specifications. The arrangement of the home changes from the celebration of possession, as among the 19th-century bourgeoisie, to the management and manipulation of objects or, as Baudrillard suggests, "a praxis" of location.

Gadgets and the technological society

The system of objects is ruled by the articulation of the logic of interior design and the products of technological society.[14] For Baudrillard, the domination of a technological logic in modernity means the eradication of nature and its historicity or connection to the past. "The goal of a technical society is the bringing into question of the very idea of genesis, the omission of origins, of a given meaning and 'essences' of which old furniture was the concrete symbol" (p. 38). Home furnishings are no longer meant to signify continuity with the past. They are meant to be controlled, managed, manipulated, and inventoried. They can also be sold or junked when "out of style." The old, traditional order is based on the oral structures of historicity – every object has a story. The new technical, modern order is a phallic environment of calculation, functionality, and control: "everything must go together, be functional – no more secrets or mysteries" (p. 46). This phallic order of calculation disenchants the world and privileges the metonymical relation of ambiance or arrangement.

The abstraction of objects in high-tech designs brings to an end "the age old, anthropomorphic status of objects" (p. 66). Technology is an elision of the human gesture which can no longer be perceived in the design of the gadget. Traditional society produced objects that conformed to the use by the human body and were an extension of human physical abilities. Like the ancient scythe or basket, these objects were extensions of the body. Technological gadgets erase all connection to the body. Buttons are pressed, dials are turned, and the work gets done through electronic and mechanical means.

Baudrillard suggests that the functional logic of modernity is amplified by the dominance of technology in its displacement of the humanizing attributes of traditional home furnishings. He states,

> Household appliances, cars, etc., require only a minimal participation. Almost as much as the workplace, the home is ruled by regularity of command gestures. The whole body used to be needed for gripping objects, but now only contact (hand, finger or foot) and control (sight, sometimes hearing) are needed. In brief, only people's "extremities" participate actively in the functional environment. (p. 68)

In short, the desire for gadgets helps propagate the social changes of modernity. This desire becomes one powerful way individuals are attracted to the new fashions in objects, thus guaranteeing their participation in modern society. Once introduced into the home, gadgets redefine the logic of use. Their forms and deployment are divorced from the morphology of the body. The technological object helps transform decor to abstraction and calculated ambiance. According to Baudrillard, the humanized world of the traditional home is transformed into a functional milieu of technique.

The nonfunctional or marginal object

"A whole category of objects seems to escape the system we have just analyzed – the unique, unusual, folk, exotic or antique object [objet ancien]" (p. 95). According to Baudrillard, these objects are also part of modernity and they are most often acquired recently according to the practice of interior design rather than inherited as part of continuity with tradition. As Olalquiaga[15] observes, the "memento mori" has a place in the (post)modern milieu.

The antique stands outside time, hence it has the special function of signifying the passage of time. This is not "real time," according to Baudrillard, but the signifying time of fashion. It is time as cultural index. The antique object, like the system of modern objects, is subjected to a logic of interior design, but it is a separate one that structures the marginal or nonfunctional elements within the home.

Folk art is a variation on the antique object. The folk object stands outside both time and space. It signifies historicity and otherness. Acquisition of folk objects is the reverse phenomenon of the desire for technologically sophisticated objects by the underdeveloped world (p. 106).

The marginal object is not synchronic or diachronic, it is achronic. It represents a transcendence of the fashion system. "These objects are less objects of ownership than of symbolic intercession, like ancestors. They are an escape from dailyness, and escape is never so radical as in time, it is never so profound as in its own infancy" (p. 106). The marginal object stands outside the myth of progress embodied in modernity.

Baudrillard extends his comments on the marginal object to an explanation for the significance of the "second home." The successful, modern bourgeois purchases a second home in the country. The country home possesses a country decor. Every effort is made to preserve the image of rustic nature. The country home stands outside the time line of modernity, of progress. "In a civilization in which *synchrony* and *diachrony* tend to organize a systematic and exclusive control of the real, a third dimension appears, that is, anachrony" (p. 114). The acquisition of the country home by the successful modern contrasts with the desire for a modern home by the less fortunate working classes.

The marginal system: The collection

The anachronistic object stands outside the system of objects to signify the dimensions of space and time. The "collection" represents a separate, contrasting dimension to the system of objects. According to Baudrillard, every object possesses two functions: to be used or to be possessed. Modernity tries to reduce the object to its abstract function of use. When technology prevails we have the extreme case of the machine – pure function or pure use value. In opposition, certain objects are important because of their value as possessions. The pure object stripped of its function becomes an object in a collection.

As Baudrillard suggests, the objects of a collection are all equal. They are not distinguished by their function, only their value in the collection. The logic of collection is metonymical – we have only a succession of objects which can always be increased incrementally. You "add" to a collection, the single object never suffices. It is the same when sexual practices are transformed by the logic of possession. "The relation of love dotes on one loved one, while possession is only satisfied by a series of lovers" (p. 116). The activity of collection is a kind of promiscuity of possession and it is always pursued passionately by the collector.

Baudrillard likes the analogy between collecting and a certain kind of sexuality. In fact, he sees collecting as a stage of latent sexual evolution or transition. The formidable phase of collecting is usually during the years between seven and 12. This corresponds to the latent period prior to puberty (p. 122). According to Baudrillard, the activity of collecting declines after puberty. But it then re-emerges after the age of 40. This personifies the regression to the anal stage "which is expressed by behaviors of accumulation, order, aggressive retention, etc." (p. 122). In short, with the advent of middle age, when a diminution of the sex drive is experienced by the neurotic adult, the behavior of collecting appears as a passionately pursued substitute.

The section on collecting in this book is quite entertaining reading. Baudrillard makes a succession of interesting observations about collecting and collectors. He remarks that the collector reaches the heights of passion, not through the acquisition of objects with an intrinsic worth, but through fanaticism. Furthermore, the collected object is the perfect domestic pet. It is an other that is totally controlled. Baudrillard also suggests that, because the collection is animated by the displaced sexual desire of the collector, the ultimate object of the collection is the collector him/herself. Hence, "it is better never to complete the collection always desiring another item" (p. 134). Finally, Baudrillard observes that "The deprivation of the possessive game would be as de-stabilizing to the individual as the denial of dreams. Objects help us to resolve the irreversibility of birth towards death" (p. 134). The collection, like hyperreal simulation, is a never-ending chain, like the chain of signification – the indefinite displacement of one object with another.

A Brief Note on Postmodernity

Baudrillard develops several ideas in this first book which figure prominently later on in his postmodern writings, especially the concepts of model and differance. The reduction of affect through the hegemony of interior design as ambiance is accomplished by consumerism which emphasizes decor. The integrating logic of the ensemble expresses itself through the model – the kitchen set, the model room, the model house. Commodification and consumerism imply mechanical reproduction of the object. The model is generalizable to any social status. Consumption as an act becomes the consumption of the model. It is, in short, a simulation.[16]

The hegemony of ambiance means the domination of the metonymical figure in the system of objects. To follow modern decor means relating object to object through the abstract practice of interior design. When meaning is dominated by the paradigmatic axis, it is produced by contiguity. This relation is always one of deferral. In place of the sign conceptualized by Saussure as the unity of the signifier and the signified, we have the sign of deconstruction, the endless deferral of signification – i.e., the relation of signifier to signifier to signifier, and so on. This infinite regress is more difficult to demonstrate for the paradigmatic axis, a subject that Baudrillard ignores, although it is covered by postmodernists with the issue of "intertextuality."

Difference as *differance* is always produced by discourse. This is both the discovery of deconstruction and its great limitation, since it is a form of idealism (see chapter 1). We leave the system of objects and deal with the system of language: writing or speech. The process of differance or the production of meaning through the chain of signification lies at the heart of all logotechniques. Baudrillard illustrates this with regard to the expropriation of colors by the system of interior design. All colors are signified by affective states – warm, cold, cheerful, gloomy – through the discourse of fashion. Yet, the warmth of a color is a functional warmth. Its warmth does not derive from a warm substance but from its difference with other colors. It is not "warm" but only a signified warmth that can never be realized or materially experienced, because it cannot change the characteristics of its own matter and be "warm." "What characterizes this warmth is the absence of any heat source" (p. 51). In short, its warmth is a discursive relation, or simulation. As part of the chain of signification, the discourse of decor belongs to hyperreality.

In Baudrillard's analysis of the system of household objects he shows how a fashion aesthetic that is calculating, phallic and abstract invades the home with the commodification of everyday life through modernity and converts signifying objects into hyperreal signifiers belonging to a system of interior design. This cultural system is ruled by ambiance and it replaces the sentimentality and paternalism of the traditional family home. The modern system of objects supercedes the traditional system in three respects: (a) a change in the primary function of the object from affective associations and use value to ambiance; (b) a change in primary needs from tradition to consumerism; and (c) a change in the symbolic relation between (a) and (b) from historicity and paternalism to phallic-centered calculation and control under the sign of ambiance (p. 88).

Baudrillard sees the system of objects as being dominated by the logic of metonymy and differance. Unlike Derrida, however, he does not equate reality with the chain of signification. At least, not in this first book. Given time, however, Baudrillard fashions a vision of postmodern life that is equated with the hyperreal and which is constituted, like the conceptualization of the text by Derrida, through the metonymical play of difference. As in the case of Barthes, something happens to Baudrillard in the 1960s, and he moves to a deconstructionist position, not because of the critique of Saussure, as in the former case, but because of an extreme vision about the commodification of daily life under new conditions termed "postmodern."

In this sense, does the belief that there exists a material world of use values which grounds the symbolic world of sign values in the system of objects belong to modernity alone – that is, to the period analyzed in this first book of Baudrillard? I think not. Material culture and its systems of signification exist in the present conjuncture as well (see chapters 3 and 8). To be sure, by not subscribing to this premise we reach the postmodernity of the later Baudrillard of *Simulations*.[17] Even if the present is postmodern, in the sense that the interplay of sign value dominates cultural logic, it nevertheless still depends on the deployment of material objects within the subcultural context of everyday life. That is, sign value, or the status of objects as expressive symbols, remains linked to both the status of objects as possessing use value in daily practice and exchange value in the exo-semiotic system of capitalist accumulation. (See the chapters below for more detailed discussion of these assertions.)

The process by which cultural hegemony is expressed as the reduction of all objects to sign value does not eliminate either the practices of daily life, which are based on use value, or the system of capital accumulation, which relies on exchange value. Rather, cultural hegemony is characterized best by the way use values and exchange values are exploited by the postmodern culture of consumption which privileges the image over substance.[18] As in the case of home furnishings, the commodification of everyday life creates a certain space in addition to deploying a sign system. In fact, the former is the material vehicle of the latter. Baudrillard captured this fundamental relation between ideology and materiality in his first book, only to abandon it later.

Postmodernists see only a world of signs; they miss the material culture that acts as sign – vehicles for signification and its relation to everyday life. As Baudrillard shows in this book, the relation between signs and material objects is not a simple dichotomy. Ideologies, like modern styles of furniture, are engineered into material forms. Socio-semiotics takes this as its fundamental analytical understanding of social life. As we shall see in the next chapter, this means that the "substance of the expression" – the material vehicle of ideology – is as important to cultural hegemony as is the "content of the form," or codified ideology itself.

In Baudrillard's first book we see that modernity commodifies everyday life. This is accomplished through the articulation of ideology and material home furnishings according to an integrated system of signification. Postmodern culture, I contend in the following chapters, operates in a similar way. Neither the sign nor its material sign vehicle, neither ideology nor material culture, are privileged. Both aspects articulate together in social relations. According to socio-semiotics, the free play of signification, of which much has been made by postmodern cultural critics, deconstructionists and Lacanian analysts of identity, is constrained and reigned in by important mechanisms of power, capital accumulation, and social convention. We seek to study the latter mechanisms and its relation to the former – i.e., the circulation of sign value. In later work Baudrillard abandoned the style of analysis, following Barthes and socio-semiotics, which emphasized the articulation between ideology and material life. However, we do not have to travel that same road, which involves a journey towards idealism and reductionism in pursuit of a fatalistic vision – the reduction of all life to the hyperreal in the culture of postmodernity.

Baudrillard's *System of Objects* describes the specific way commodification of daily life proceeds through the transformation of the home by the practice of interior design. But he fails to distinguish, as Barthes did in *The System of Fashion*, between material culture as a system of signification and the ideological discourse which regulates consumption. By conflating the logic of home decoration as use value, which grounds the *modern* system of signification, and the logotechnical discourse of interior design as fashion, which constitutes a hegemonic system of communication and an ideology of the modern, Baudrillard opens the way for the reductionist vision of postmodernity contained in his most recent writings where the real implodes and disappears in the ideology or hyperreality of the image.

By way of conclusion, it is interesting to extend Baudrillard's analysis and consider some of the current changes in daily life that might be considered harbingers of postmodernism. Taking as one dimension of postmodern change the increasing hyperdifferentiation of people's lives, I can briefly suggest some aspects of household commodity use and new technologies that may be significant. These would lead to greater flexibility in individual schedules and represent a kind of everyday correlate to the flexible arrangements of production and distribution characteristic of the postmodern economy.

First, the video tape recorder and player, or "VCR," has liberated individuals from the structured and controlled regime of the media industries. People now have the capability of recording shows to be watched at their own convenience. They can also rent or buy tapes which they can view instead of normal TV programming. Added to this flexibility is the widespread use of cable TV which can feed worldwide channels to the home. The cornucopia of channels on the family TV set leads to a new kind of freedom and hyperdifferentiation of viewing habits which is further enhanced by the use of VCRs. In response to this variety a new practice called "channel surfing" has emerged, which involves using a remote control to switch from one offering to another when things get dull or when commercial breaks come on.

Second, the family meal time has been restructured by the introduction of the commercial microwave to the home. Microwaves enable people to cook food fast without long preparation time. They also enable the easy use of leftovers. Members of households are no longer dependent on one parent – traditionally, almost exclusively the mother – to make meals. Use of the microwave liberates individuals from this dependency and hyperdifferentiates both meal choices and meal eating times. The microwave has been so effective that it has given rise to a whole order of marketed foods that are prepared for microwave use. Snacks and dinners are offered usually frozen in an incredible variety of cuisine styles and formats which further amplify the extent of hyperdifferentiation. Increased flexibility of meal preparation may aid and may be a concomitant effect of flexible or extended work schedules for people with flexible labor demands, such as commuting long distances or shifting work arrangements and part-time jobs.

Computer modems and "home" work stations may be considered a further development of postmodern tendencies. Connection through the information "net" between home and office allows for greater flexibility in work schedules and leads to increased hyperdifferentiation among individuals. While the shift to home working may be overrated as a general tendency of corporate business, it has been effective in nurturing a variety of new professional circumstances, such as flexible and dispersed work in publishing, legal services, business management services, home education, systems analysis, and information processing.

If VCRs, home computers, microwaves, and other electronic gadgets may be considered postmodern technological innovations, it could also be argued that the electric light bulb provided the foundation for hyperdifferentiated everyday life. The light bulb clearly belongs to the modern, not the postmodern, phase of industrial development. Yet its introduction was instrumental in allowing for the increasing differentiation of work, family, and leisure-related daily schedules. The light bulb liberated people from the diurnal rhythm of agriculture and made 24-hour urban life possible. Without electricity, for example, Las Vegas could not exist. Recently, astronauts circling the globe claimed that Las Vegas is the brightest spot on earth. What is the significance of the nighttime maps that are taken by satellites and used by the state? They show the electricity trace of human activity. This trace is becoming more regionally dispersed – through the rain forests or across entire regions, for example – and more differentiated in the present, postmodern period.

It should be emphasized that Baudrillard's analysis privileged the structural dimension of modernist changes in the home. Along with the new regime of household furnishings, however, also came a new kind of social status – the modern homemaker. Structural changes are linked to the creation of new types of subjectivities. Modernism articulating with the culture of paternalism produced the woman as "homemaker." The new technological advances in keeping house were aimed at the "housewife" and advertised as "labor-saving" devices. The home was designed, in part, around the new regime and social status of the woman housewife and the logic of commodification presupposed the emergence of this new subjectivity, at least for the middle class who could afford the new conveniences.

With postmodern changes in the home including the new modes of flexible cooking, work and leisure arrangements, we can rightly wonder if there is an emergent sensibility being produced among people who must interact within the hyperdifferentiation social world. This question remains one for future work. I can observe, however, that family life and housework are being restructured because of the increase in divorce, commuting times both of adults and of children, and participation of middle-class women in the full-time labor force. Household coping strategies today should reflect both the restructuring of daily schedules and the development and refinement of new technologies for home needs. At this moment they may also be producing new subjectivities that enable men, women, and children to cope with greater flexibility and continuing differentiation of all social tasks.

Notes

1   Jean Baudrillard, *Le Système des objets* (Paris: Denoel-Gonthier, 1968).
2   Jean Baudrillard, *Symbolic Exchange and Death* (London: Sage, 1993).
3   Claude Lévi-Strauss, *Structural Anthropology*, translated by Claire Jacobson and Brooke Schoepf (New York: Basic Books, 1963).
4   Roland Barthes, *Elements of Semiology*, translated by A. Lavers and Colin Smith (New York: Hill and Wang, 1967a).
5   Martin Krampen, *Meaning in the Urban Environment* (London: Methuen, 1979); see chapters 1 and 8.
6   Umberto Eco, *A Theory of Semiotics* (Bloomington: Indiana University Press, 1976).
7   Barthes, *Elements of Semiology* and *Mythologies* (New York: Hill and Wang, 1972).
8   Roland Barthes, *Système de la mode* (Paris: Seuil, 1967b).
9   Rene Konig, *A La Mode: On the Social Psychology of Fashion* (New York: Seabury Press, 1973).
10 Stephan Crook, Jan Pakulski and Malcolm Waters, *Postmodernization: Change in Advanced Society* (London: Sage, 1992).
11 Jacques Ellul, *The Technological Society* (New York: Alfred Knopf, 1964).
12 Henri Lefebvre, *Critique of Everyday Life*, Vol. 1 (London: Verso, 1991).
13 Françoise Choay, "Urbanism in Question," in *The City and the Sign: An Introduction to Urban Semiotics*, edited by M. Gottdiener and A. Lagopoulos (New York: Columbia University Press, 1986), pp. 241–58.
14 Ellul, *Technological Society*.
15 C. Olalquiaga, *Megalopolis* (Minneapolis: University of Minnesota Press, 1992).
16 Baudrillard, *Symbolic Exchange*.
17 Baudrillard, *Symbolic Exchange*; Fredrick Jameson, "Postmodernism, or

the Cultural Logic of Late Capitalism," *New Left Review*, 146 (1984): 53–92.

18 Robert Goldman, *Reading Ads Socially* (New York: Routledge, 1992); see also chapter 8, below.

3

The Substance of the Expression: The Role of Material Culture in Symbolic Interaction

The ancient Etruscans built cities in a particular way. Before the walls were erected, an ox was hitched to a golden plow and led around in a great ellipse that circumscribed the area of the new settlement. This "sacred furrow" defined the space within which people would live and marked the exact location of the city walls by separating the sacred area of habitation from the profane universe of the outside. Etruscans located within such environments lived a town life that not only involved the usual buying and selling, or raising of families, but also one that was imbued with the symbolism of the sacred furrow and its cosmological status. Other ancient towns, from Catal-Huyuk to Beijing, also had similar cosmological codes by which their space was conceived.[1]

Ancient cities are excellent for illustrating the fundamental premise of socio-semiotics – namely, that the articulation of ideology with material objects constitutes a non-reducible social process. The codified ideology of the Etruscans, which allowed them to make sharp symbolic distinctions between the sacred and the profane, had to be deployed within a certain space that was constructed. Materiality and spatiality were produced by that codified ideology. However, once constructed, this symbolic space also became the environment of everyday life and, as a certain space, possessed use value as well as functioning as a sign vehicle. This relation between the material and the symbolic is not a dichotomy. The constructed space of the Etruscans, as is the case with all material culture, embodied codified ideology and was, in fact, the *material expression* of ideology, just as their codified ideology presupposed its expression in material forms. There is, then, a complex relation between semantic fields and material culture, as the discussion of Peircian semiotics in chapter 1 suggests. All sign value implicitly presupposes its material expression, and, in the same way, all material objects exist within socially constructed semantic fields in order for them to be understood and used.

Current approaches to the relation between symbols and material culture ignore this complex relation. They invariably privilege the mental over the material.[2] Among sociologists, for example, the problematic of symbolic communication is the province of the subfield of symbolic interaction. But this approach has been unable to keep up with the developing discussions in cultural studies that analyze the relation between meaning and material life, especially with regard to recent work in postmodernism. According to Denzin,[3] for example, "A behaviorist theory of the sign, symbol and language,[4] unresponsive to Peirce's[5] semiotic of the sign, has given interactionists a weak theory of the symbolic." As a consequence of its limited treatment of material culture, symbolic interaction has failed to develop a viable approach to cultural analysis. Put succinctly by Denzin,[6] "symbolic interactionists have failed to produce an American version of cultural studies. This failure absorbs the majority of the criticisms that have been directed at the theory."

In short, for at least one prominent symbolic interactionist, this subfield's lack of a symbolic theory covering the global relation between language and culture accounts for its inability to develop an adequate approach to cultural analysis. And this lack, in turn, constitutes most of the limitations of the subfield, even threatening its future existence. As we have seen in the discussion of postmodernism and particularly Baudrillard's theory of sign value, however, there are also similar limitations to postmodern cultural analysis. The privileging of sign value by the latter ignores what socio-semiotics takes as fundamental: namely, the non-reducibility and duality of symbolic and material processes.

This chapter addresses the relation between materiality and symbolism, or the socio-semiotics of objects, and the role objects play in meaningful social interaction. Given the fact that semiotics represents a more global approach to communication and signification than does symbolic interaction,[7] I do not seek to argue for the former at the expense of the latter. My goal is not to play a zero-sum game of criticism in the face of two established and useful forms of knowledge, because for both the object of analysis is the process of Symbolic Interaction.[8] Rather, I seek to reconcile what at first may appear to be fundamental differences in order to arrive at a synthesis of semiotics and symbolic interaction that can study, on the one hand, communication through Symbolic Interaction, and, on the other, signification through the expressive symbols of material culture.

In chapter 1 I introduced some of the central concepts of socio-semiotics. One of the key ideas is that semiotic analysis must proceed with a conceptualization of the sign. Simply invoking terms discursively, such as "signifier," "sign," and the like, may give the impression that semiotic analysis is being performed, but this would not be the view of semioticians. Both Peirce and Saussure developed models of the sign in order to specify the process of semiosis. As indicated in chapter 1, the socio-semiotic approach has developed out of internal critiques among semioticians regarding the relative ability to analyze material culture, while also taking into account the deconstructionist critique of Saussure – that is, by avoiding a model of semiosis that commits the fallacy of the transcendental signifier. Socio-semiotics follows Eco, after Hjemslev, and uses the decomposite model of the sign described in chapter 1. According to socio-semiotics, any material object constitutes the intersection between social context and the codified, connotative ideologies of social practice, on the one hand, and the material, objective, production or design practice which produces the object world, on the other. It is the latter's relation to the former that has been neglected by both semiotics and symbolic interaction.

The argument below proceeds in three stages. First, I review the apparent merger of semiotics or postmodern modes of cultural analysis and symbolic interaction in the work of some leading exponents of the latter approach. Second, I critique both semiotics and symbolic interaction from the perspective of socio-semiotics and its analysis of material culture. In a third and final section, I sketch out a synthetic argument which reconciles socio-semiotics and symbolic interaction. This *rapprochement* not only makes a place for symbolic interaction in the analysis of material culture, but also addresses some fundamental limitations of the two approaches in the analysis of Symbolic Interaction which are overcome by the effort of synthesis.

My argument focuses on the conceptualization of a materialist semiotics. As Deleuze[9] remarks, it was Foucault who understood best the essential difference between ideology and material forms and the need for a materialist approach to counter the idealism of marxist ideology critique (the same point is made in Game[10]). The regulation or hegemonic domination of people proceeds through both ideology and the material environment. It is the study of the latter, or the *substance of the expression*, and its articulation with codified ideology, or the *form of the content*, that characterizes the socio-semiotic method and avoids the idealism of both deconstruction and marxism. A final section of this chapter will develop these ideas.

Symbolic Interaction and Semiotics

The established discipline of symbolic interaction has many variants and its practitioners are situated in a variety of graduate faculties in sociology.[11] Most followers would probably agree with the basic premises of the approach articulated by Blumer.[12] As paraphrased by Denzin,[13] first, "human beings act toward things on the basis of the meanings that things have for them; second, that the meanings of things arise out of the process of social interaction; and third, that meanings are modified through an interpretive process which involves self-reflective individuals symbolically interacting with one another."

What is most striking about this formulation to a semiotician is how easily she/he would agree with it. One could just as readily be talking about the one field as the other. But semiotics would never cast its own basic assumptions using precisely this kind of mold. The above formulation by Blumer privileges human interaction; indeed, it locates the process of symbolic interaction in the communication process between socialized and socializing individuals, or, as Denzin suggests above, in a behaviorist approach to the sign. As Eco points out, semiotics is meant to deal with the more global phenomenon of culture and does not restrict itself either to language alone or to the process of communication. Instead, semiotic analysis is concerned with all cultural forms, of which linguistic phenomena constitute only a part. In addition, the basis of semiotics is the constitution of the sign in a system of signification (see below) which does not have to represent an act of communication. In its most basic sense this means that signification does not have to possess an intentional desire on the part of two individuals to convey a specific message, which is, in contrast, the assumption of symbolic interaction (see below).

Over time, symbolic interactionists, while privileging interaction and communication between people, failed to develop the first of Blumer's basic assumptions and articulate an approach to material culture, or the social life of objects as expressive symbols.[14] There are additional limitations of symbolic interaction as a basis for cultural studies, just as there are important failings of semiotics in the same endeavor. These issues will be discussed in the course of this chapter. Most striking is that despite the limitations, symbolic interactionists have remained concerned enough about the problem of Symbolic Interaction to have lately gone outside the parameters of their own field for help. In recent years some of the more prestigious symbolic interactionists have turned their attention to semiotics and seem to treat the commonalities between it and the field of symbolic interaction with a seriousness of purpose.[15] Let us consider this turning towards the semiotic in more detail.

Do excellent symbolic interactionists make good or poor semioticians of culture? I shall argue the latter.[16] But my argument is based on the internal critique of semiotics which has produced a variant, socio-semiotics, to deal with the issue of material culture. In what follows, therefore, I intend to have my critique of symbolic interactionist semiotics meld with a critique of semiotic and postmodern cultural studies, rather than intending to disparage the efforts of important symbolic interactionists to address the limitations of the field.

Symbolic interaction and semiotics: A critique

Among the several symbolic interactionists dabbling in semiotics (see above), I choose to consider the work of one person, Robert Perinbanayagam, as illustrative of the limitations of this effort (i.e., with this part standing in for the whole endeavor). There are several structural and personal reasons for my choice. Perinbanayagam is arguably the most important member of the field practicing today. His two most recent books[17] deal explicitly with both the problematic of Symbolic Interaction and semiotics. Finally, I have chosen to focus on Perinbanayagam because his approach to the field of symbolic interaction is at once accessible and illuminating. It is work I respect.

According to Perinbanayagam,[18] when symbolic interactionists consider the process of Symbolic Interaction they are almost always focusing on the speech act of communication as their object of analysis. This perspective has the following limitations. It reduces Symbolic Interaction to communication; usually this is face-to-face interaction. The type of signifier considered by symbolic interaction is the spoken word, the acoustic image of Saussure, which is regulated by the social dynamics of *la parole* or speech. Symbolic interactionists assume that all Symbolic Interaction is intentional and is based on a social act. Finally, the assumption of intentional communication as the basis of the process of Symbolic Interaction also restricts that process to an idealist conception of communication using an idealist conception of the sign. These failings not only represent limitations of symbolic interaction from a semiotic point of view, but they are also core assumptions which make a synthesis between symbolic interaction and deconstruction, or postmodern cultural analysis, impossible.

A. The signification limitations of symbolic interaction

1 Limitations of the field of symbolic interaction Symbolic interaction limits itself to the social world of communication, usually involving two individuals within the same speech community. It focuses, not on the problematic of signification (see below), but on the problematic of communication asking: what? how? when? and, through what complex process does communication take place?

Semiotics is a more global inquiry into the nature of symbols than is symbolic interaction. According to semiotics, meaning can be created by the relation of all kinds of objects to each other and does not restrict itself to social interaction within a speech community. There are two main ways all systems of meaning produce signification: through syntagmatic and paradigmatic positioning; both of these are based on the operation of difference between cultural units.[19] When a cultural system contains both a syntagmatic (or syntactal) order and a paradigmatic (or semantic) order, we say that it is a *system of signification*. By this is meant the following.

First, the units of the cultural system bear a juxtapositional or contiguous relation with each other, such as the juxtaposition of articles of clothing on the body. This syntagmatic relation is regulated by the laws of culture involving appropriate modes of appearance. Second, however, the choice for each article of clothing is also regulated by culture according to the array of alternatives offered by the paradigmatic dimension of appearance. If the decision to wear a hat is made, that decision must be in conformity with the juxtapositional relation of other parts of the body, but, in addition, the user must decide on the *type* or *style* of hat to wear which is dictated by the normative rules of the paradigmatic axis.

In sum, both the syntagmatic and paradigmatic axes produce meaning through the operation of relational differences. In the former case the relation is juxtaposition and in the latter it is a comparative difference. Any cultural system, such as the fashion system, which structures its meaning according to these two intersecting dimensions, is called a system of signification. This property does *not*, however, imply that communication is present. Symbolic interactionists fail to consider the distinction between signification and communication. In contrast, according to semiotics, when an individual chooses a particular ensemble of clothing according to the dictates of fashion, or, in some historical cases, according to the legal codes of sumptuary laws, they are engaging in a social act of symbolism but may *not be* engaging in communication (see chapter 10). For semioticians, communication is only a special case of signification as the latter is meant to include all manifestations of regulation through culture – i.e., through symbolic forms.

2 The privileging of speech acts in symbolic interaction Most often, when symbolic interactionists are referring to symbolic acts, they mean social interaction and speech. This is not to say that attempts were never made to analyze material culture (see Blumer, and Stone on fashion,[20] for example). Rather, it is speech that is usually privileged and in all analyses a restricted speech model represents the underlying scheme of interaction. There is a sender, for example, a message that is encoded in speech, and a receiver in the social act studied by symbolic interactionists.[21]

Semioticians, in contrast, recognize that even in the case of communication, the act of speech carries with it a multidimensional structure. According to Jakobson,[22] for example,

> The ADDRESSER sends a MESSAGE to the ADDRESSEE. To be operative the message requires a CONTEXT referred to ("referent" in another, somewhat ambiguous nomenclature), sizable by the addressee, and either verbal or capable of being verbalized; a CODE fully, or at least partially, common to the addresser and addressee (or in other words, to the encoder and decoder of the message); and, finally, a CONTACT, a physical channel and psychological connection between the addresser and the addressee, enabling both of them to enter and stay in communication. [See figure 3.1.]

Figure 3.1

```
                         Context
                         (referential)
                         Message
                         (poetic)
Addresser ───────────────────────────────── Addressee
(emotive)                Contact                (conative)
                         (phatic)
                         Code
                         (metalingual)
```

As Jakobson[23] points out, this complex relation requires that six different functions of communication be adequately performed in order for messages to be exchanged, including the referential, poetic, emotive, phatic, metalingual and conative functions (see figure 3.1). For semioticians the appropriate role of these functions is part of the problematic of communication, so too are the various social processes that determine different hierarchies of these functions in the communications act. I know of no works by symbolic interactionists that deal with the inherently complex act of communication with such rigor.

3 Intentionality and like-mindedness in the model of symbolic interaction   According to Perinbanayagam,[24]

> signs originate in one mind as intentional acts and create effects in another. The two people must adopt a common state of mind in order for this to happen ... The sign is double-edged in a double sense: it connects the signifier to the signified, i.e., the vehicle to the concept in the mind of an agent, on the one hand, and the mind of one to another through the signifier, on the other.

Such a statement would be extreme even for Saussure, who at least admitted the possibility that the signifier, or acoustic image, could be created in nature, as in the case of a bird call, for example. The communicative bias of symbolic interaction privileges intentionality. But, as Peirce[25] has shown, not all signs are intentional. According to Peirce, an index is an unmotivated sign. It consists of a stimulus and a response based on the associative mental habits of the receiver. Pavlov's dogs learned to associate the ringing of a bell with dinner, for example. We associate a red light with stopping. Both of these cases are examples of signs that are indexes, and neither is a case of the intentional communication of a symbol.

The suggestion by Perinbanayagam that signifier and signified are joined in one-to-one correspondence, and, in addition, that this occurs through an idealized process of like-mindedness on the part of the communicators, also commits the principal fallacy of signification in deconstruction's critique of representation. For this reason, attempts by symbolic interactionists, such as Perinbanayagam, to synthesize deconstruction or postmodern cultural criticism with their field are doomed to self-contradiction and immanent critique. Let us consider this final limitation next.

B.   The deconstructive or postmodern limitations of symbolic interaction

1 The fallacy of the transcendental signified   In Saussure's model of the sign, the signifier, or the acoustic image, is automatically assigned a corresponding signifier in the mind of the receiver. Thus, the utterance of the word "chair" immediately stimulates the formation of a mental concept: the meaning of the stimulus "chair" in the mind of the receiver. Derrida critiqued this Saussurean model of the sign, and this intervention has become the basis of deconstruction. He suggested that it was a fallacy to believe that signifiers are automatically joined in one-to-one correspondence with a signifiers, because this assumes the presence of some "transcendental signified." Thus, Saussure's semiotics is a form of metaphysics. For Derrida this emphasis on one-to-one correspondences completed in thought is a fundamental failing of all western philosophy, just as modes of interpretation using this model of the sign are merely metaphysical.[26]

As Denzin[27] suggests, one of the most important contributions of deconstruction has been its "rupture of the formulas that equate written words with spoken words with mental experience, and voice with mind." Just as Perinbanayagam privileges the process of communication in social interaction, he also assumes the presence of a transcendental signified in his model of the sign. The basic assertion of deconstruction, however, is that this simple Saussurean model is a fallacy.[28]

2 The fallacious distinction between signification and meaning
Another stumbling block arises when Perinbanayagam tries to mesh Mead with Saussure by distinguishing between "meaning" and "signification". According to Perinbanayagam, Mead used the two terms interchangeably.[29] Perinbayanagam, however, suggests that it is better to reserve the term "significance" for the articulation of a symbol by the initiator of a message, while "meaning" is reserved to indicate "that a successful discourse has been accomplished" when it elicits the appropriate response from the receiver of the message.

There are important ideas here that are muddled. As we have seen, semioticians distinguish between signification and communication (not meaning). Signification arises from structural difference according to the articulation between the syntagmatic and paradigmatic axes. Communication occurs in the special case when intentionality, like-mindedness, social context, and the various functions of the sender–message–receiver model are performed adequately. Meaning, however, can occur in both cases: i.e., we can discuss the presence of "meaning" when considering either systems of signification or communication.

In contrast, Perinbanayagam legitimizes his distinction between signification and meaning without much understanding of semiotics. He relies solely on Saussure when he says about the usage of his distinction that: "Such a usage is congruent with Saussure's intent in his concepts of signifieds and signifier. The former is described as the 'object' that is in fact being indicated or designated, whereas the signifier is the instrument by which such identification is being made."[30]

By relying on Saussure again in such a straightforward way, Perinbanayagam's attempt to update Mead commits the fallacy of the transcendental signified. Furthermore, by failing to clarify the difference between signification and communication, symbolic interaction cannot adequately capture the problematic of culture and the complexity of the process of Symbolic Interaction.

3 The idealistic speech act and idealism in symbolic interaction
According to Perinbanayagam all interaction is social, is based on the "social act" as defined by Mead, and has communication as its purpose. There is a close bond between the initiator and the recipient of interaction. The one tries to pitch meaning in a way intentionally designed for interpretation by the recipient. The latter, meanwhile, adjusts mental responses to be attuned to the sender. This focus on like-mindedness by Mead has been critiqued as idealistic, because more contemporary symbolic interactionists since Mead have discovered through research that communicators seldom try to be so mutually accommodating, even in families.[31] In practice communication is rarely ideal.

Perinbanayagam acknowledges the limitations of Mead's conception and attempts to elaborate on the role of ambiguity in Symbolic Interaction. But, he fails to understand that the perspective of symbolic interactionists is not only idealistic but also idealist. Symbolic interaction privileges the mental process of interaction over the physical. According to Perinbanayagam,[32] establishing Symbolic Interaction requires that "The two people must adopt a common state of mind, in order for this to happen." This assumes a dual state of mental process. Thus, symbolic interaction as a field fails to account for the physical manipulation of the body by forms of signification (to be discussed below). Hence it fails to provide a basis for the analysis of material culture, and, therefore, of all cultural studies. Signification, and even communication, can take place through the mediation of objects as expressive symbols in addition to the direct encounter of like-minded individuals that symbolic interactionists have in mind.

4 The failure to acknowledge the role of power   In Perinbanayagam's reworking of Mead, the failure to address the idealist basis of symbolic interaction also prevents symbolic interactionists from adequately dealing with the role of power in communication.

Perinbanayagam uses the following example from Mead[33] to illustrate the problematic nature of Symbolic Interaction as communication: "You ask somebody to bring the visitor a chair. You arouse the tendency to get the chair in the other, but if he is slow to act, you get the chair yourself."

Then Perinbanayagam[34] provides the following commentary of Mead: "The other, if one is to conclude that a meaningful transaction has been created, must indeed bring a chair sooner or later, other things being constant. If he brings a table, then obviously no meaningful transaction has been concluded . . ."

I am less convinced that no meanings have been conveyed. It is easy to see that, perhaps, the issue of power plays a role in this interaction. If this incident took place among unequals, among people with different levels of power, and, further, if the subordinates were concerned enough about such differences to engage in resistance, then an interpretation other than the one advanced by Perinbanayagam suggests itself. Bringing a table instead of a chair when ordered is not only an effective act of resistance, but it is also a Symbolic Interactive gesture that could be useful to the holders of power by signalling to them that all is not well. As Foucault might point out, all discourse represents an articulation of power and knowledge. In this sense symbolic interaction is less idealistic than simply naive in its promotion of like-mindedness as the basis of interaction.

5 The privileging of a point of reference in Symbolic Interaction   Perinbanayagam is not unaware of the limitations of Mead. On the contrary, he seeks to specify the problematic nature of communication following a critique of Mead as idealizing the communicative act. With Stryker[35] he acknowledges that much interaction fails due to failures of communication which involve not only verbal utterances but the failed thinking and gesturing to the other that is so central to the social act for symbolic interactionists. According to Perinbanayagam,[36] failed encounters can be deliberate (he stops short of acknowledging that they may fail due to deliberate resistance; see above), but they usually miss because of "erroneous perceptions," anxiety, and bad information.

This interpretation is interactor-centric (a neologism coined only for this sentence). That is, it judges failed communication as the personal failure of one or the other party to interaction. Failed communication is, in this view, someone's fault. But, semioticians have long ago had to deal with the problematic nature of communication produced by the structural ambiguity of the sign. This polysemy[37] or multivocity[38] of signifiers constitutes a major issue in the analysis of discourse (see chapter 1). For semioticians, failed communication is not a personal fault. No single point of reference is privileged, such as the truthfulness of the sender or the intentionality of the author. In fact, according to deconstructionists, ambiguity is nothing more than the play of meaning which is the essence of any text. Derrida, unlike Perinbanayagam,[39] would never suggest that during interaction there is a capacity "to mistake the role of the other," because no single participant, even the text, is privileged so that the concept of "mistake" bears relevance.

The Semiotic Analysis of Material Culture

In its own way postmodern cultural analysis, especially the work of Baudrillard and his followers, possesses similar limitations to those of symbolic interaction. Both privilege idealist forms of meaning and fail to specify the relation between individuals and material culture in the process of Symbolic Interaction. Both neglect the object world. In fact, for Baudrillard[40] that world has ceased to exist as a determinant of action and has been replaced by the media images of reality. These are constitutive of a hegemonic, image-driven culture[41] and ultimately, of subjectivity and the basis of human action. This idealism is the soft underbelly of the postmodern critique.[42] It ignores reality. It also ignores the materialist approach of Foucault and other poststructuralist cultural analysts.[43] There are several other limitations of postmodern semiotics that I shall consider: its commission of the linguistic fallacy, the failure to apply an adequate theory of the sign *au-dela* Saussure, and a failure to specify the relation between the material forms of the expression on the one hand, and the discourses of power on the other.

In discussing these limitations I shall argue in favor of a socio-semiotic approach to material culture. However, I shall also indicate places where the approach of symbolic interaction as conceptualized by Perinbanayagam, Denzin, Manning, and others also makes a contribution to our understanding of objects as expressive symbols.

The limitations of postmodern semiotics

1   The linguistic fallacy

In the earlier period of semiotic analysis it was suggested that any system of signification was also, potentially, a system of communication. Thus, people could "speak" through food, clothing, or nonverbal gestures. Several books appeared which suggested that objective cultural systems functioned as languages.

This perspective commits the "linguistic fallacy" (see chapter 1) and contemporary semioticians no longer hold such a view of culture. The confusion arose because of a failure to distinguish adequately between different levels of semiosis – specifically, the failure to distinguish between denotative and connotative levels. While all objects can become signs of their own function, this sign vehicle may only represent the most elementary need of humans for objects. The wearing of a fur coat, therefore, may "mean" nothing more than that the individual is cold. Layered on top of this denotative level, however, social behaviors produce connotations that convey a second meaning which represents a more socially inscribed message. Thus, the wearing of a fur coat can connote social status, wealth, and participation in fashion (see chapter 10).

In semiotics it is as important to recognize the power of first-order significations, which make the objective world meaningful through the creation of sign functions (i.e., in the sense in which Marx meant the "humanization" of the material world), as it is to acknowledge the way social processes layer meaning upon meaning onto material culture through second-order connotations that may convey communication and intentional messages, or the creation of cultural sign vehicles.[44] It is the latter process, as discussed in chapter 1, which requires recognition of the role of social context or the relevance of semantic fields in any semiotic event.

The above distinctions are central to a socio-semiotics of material culture. While it also might be interesting to study the functional relations between objects, their producers, and users as a signifying activity, a more compelling area of inquiry is represented by the articulation between connotations and objects. The latter involves a variety of social processes that are regulated by the mechanisms of status, mass cultural fashions, daily social rituals, and other interactive aspects of modern culture all transpiring within specific social and interactive contexts as both Eco and symbolic interactionists point out. However, according to socio-semiotics, social context includes exo-semiotic processes of economics and politics which are often neglected by both semiotics and symbolic interaction.[45]

Postmodernists such as Baudrillard, in contrast, eviscerate this world, leaving us only the empty shell of sign value. Instead, the three-way relation of exchange, use, and sign value defines an often contentious and manipulated world within which social processes of capitalism deriving from the need for consumerism drive the interaction between connotation building and material objects[46] (see chapters 2 and 8).

2 Peirce and the three-fold nature of the sign

In Saussure's system the sign represents the unity of the signifier and the signified. As discussed in chapter 1, this model assumes a one-to-one exchange relation between the signifier and signified, which is a fallacy (Bakhtin), and the presence of a transcendental signified that can unite signifier and signified automatically into a sign, which is another fallacy (Derrida).

Peirce, in contrast, gave us at least nine different choices for signs, of which three are the most important to cultural analysis.[47] His concept of "the index" is the most relevant to the kind of cultural world depicted by postmodernists, as we have seen in the privileging of metonymy by both Baudrillard and Derrida (chapter 2). The index does not convey symbolic content. It is a stripped-down sign best understood as a stimulus which engenders a response. When an individual sees lightning, she/he most often associates it with the noise of thunder. For Peirce the lightning is the index of thunder, it serves as thunder's sign. For the index, the kind of communication that symbolic interactionists consider as the basis of signification does not exist, yet the indexical sign, for Peirce and Peircian-inspired socio-semiotics, does signify.

Indexes are increasingly important signs in a postmodern world dominated by signifiers functioning as stimuli carefully designed to engender desired consumer response.[48] When a mall shopper encounters the exterior of the mall as an undifferentiated facade and searches for the entrance door, or when the same shopper steps to one side while walking within the mall to avoid a bench or some other obstacle and deviates towards a store entrance, that shopper is responding to objects as indexes (see next chapter) and the mall itself is but a sign function of shopping. Within the mall the symbolic environment is more complex. The material form of the interior is engineered by mall designers to have the desired effect of promoting consumption. In order to use the mall, shoppers have to *understand* the significance of the objects and respond accordingly. Indexicality and signification, not symbolism and communication, are characteristic of this mode of social behavior.

At the same time, hyperreality and signs as expressive symbols are also present. Thus Baudrillard is not completely wrong. These images and simulations have the effect of bridging the symbolic environment between the mall itself and the image-driven culture of magazines, advertising, TV, film, and popular music outside the mall. Social life is saturated by the hyperreality of media and advertising. This media hypersphere conditions individuals to be receptive to certain symbolic stimuli. In addition, the hypersphere provides integration and continuity to daily life by "rationalizing" consumer choices. The purchase of a shirt or blouse at the mall makes sense because an actor in a popular TV show or Madonna, for example, wore it recently. The desire to buy a computer, stereo or car is primed by the hypersphere of simulation to which we are all exposed. Thus, Baudrillard's hyperreality, or image-driven culture, really constitutes one aspect – namely, "the form of the content" – which then articulates with the materiality of the mall, or "the substance of the expression."

The objective world, then, is not a universe that privileges two-way interaction between people and communicative acts in the manner envisioned by symbolic interactionists. Often it is the world of objects that simply manipulates individuals through the latter's ability to read a physical environment, or the individual's desire to "be fashionable" or fit in socially through specific consumer choices. Communication and the cooperative "social act" have little to do with this kind of symbolic interaction; but power and hegemonic domination through cultural forms are more relevant. However, postmodernists are also wrong when they argue that the objective world is a hyperreality that privileges sign value and the image of objects. The objective world expresses the duality of the ideology–material articulation. It contains objects of use which give rise to functional sign vehicles through human practice. It is a world with actions and consequences that requires pragmatic understanding of its users, as symbolic interactionists also maintain.[49] Often, images have little to do with this kind of interaction. Only the effects of signs, in all their pragmatic consequences, are made to count in an increasingly instrumental culture.

3 *Material culture and the limitations of structuralism*

Symbolic interaction privileges communication, as we have seen. In some cases its practitioners have acknowledged the role of objects as "expressive symbols," such as in Blumer's[50] interesting study of fashion.[51] Despite this effort, the objective world remains a dependent, ancillary factor to the autonomous realm of social interaction and the creation of the interactionist subject. Expressive symbols are explained in symbolic interaction by a behaviorist theory that privileges the cognitive, conscious thought processes of the interacting subject. This bias results in a "weak theory of the sign."[52]

Some types of semiotics are equally biased in the opposite direction, and share with symbolic interaction a limited grasp of the symbolic role of material culture. Semiotics is a form of structuralism, and, along with the latter, tends to privilege the synchronic supra-individual aspect of culture. The work of structural anthropologist Lévi-Strauss[53] on kinship, for example, reduces individuals to powerless marionettes pulled to and fro by the action of general laws of marriage and family relations. Similarly, the structural marxist Althusser did away with the relatively autonomous subject entirely by conceptualizing individual action as simply the trace (*traeger*) of systemic forces. By emphasizing systems of signification which are structural forms relatively independent of human action, semioticians expose themselves to the criticism of ignoring both the mental life of the individual and the subjective basis of all action – an objection that cannot be made about symbolic interaction. The latter inquiry has provided us with several interesting accounts of sign-based production of identity and subjectivity combining the work of Mead and postmodernists.[54] Semiotic analysis, as opposed to the socio-semiotic approach, with its emphasis on the synchronic relationship of signs and its de-emphasis of social context and the exo-semiotic articulation, can never be more than a certain kind of descriptive work. Unlike socio-semiotics, it can never provide an explanation for either the production or the consumption of signs.

For all their insights into the cognitive and meaningful basis of society, on the one hand, and the power of systems of signification to structure social interactions, on the other, both symbolic interaction and structural semiotics fail to theorize the relation between social process and material forms. Socio-semiotics tries to overcome this limitation by arguing that adequate analysis must account, not only for the structure of the material environment as a system of signification, but also for the cognitive "reading" of that environment in the constitution of action and the interacting subject.

Material Culture, Symbolic Processes and Socio-Semiotics: A Synthesis

Theorizing the relation between material forms and social process begins with the insights of Foucault and an appreciation for "the substance of the expression," or rather, the articulation between codified ideology and material forms. Despite the label of "discourse theorist" assigned to Foucault by some popularizing writers, he clearly distinguished between the discursive and non-discursive realms of society[55] and considered both equally important for analysis. For Foucault, this was not intended as some Cartesian distinction between speech or cognition and material life. Rather, he sought to separate analytically the articulation of ideology which functioned as discursive practice from the functioning of material culture as produced by knowledge and technique.

Discourse is the force that observes, reflects, and channels energies in social process, much in the same way that symbolic interactionists conceive of this activity. But social activity also produces material forms which are embodiments of social forces even if they are not objective, concrete models of discursive ideas or beliefs. That is, social discourse and social forms are two aspects of regulation and normalization processes. This relation between forces and forms constitutes the most basic aspect of Foucault's approach to society, as Deleuze[56] observes: "Foucault's general principle is that every form is a compound of relations between forces. Given these forces, our first question is with what forces from the outside they enter into a relation, and then what form is created as a result."

By analytically separating the study of discourse and its associated forms, Foucault reached beyond both Weber and Marx, whose respective work on social change stressed the role of ideology (i.e., in different ways, a metaphysics of consciousness). Both Weber's study of rationality and the Marxian focus on the ideology of capitalism emphasize the cognitive aspects of social change. But these same social forces also produced important material forms that were instrumental in societal transformations, including the production of a certain space.[57]

According to Foucault,[58] for example, the social desire to regulate criminals constitutes an historical discourse going back many centuries. Each of several historical periods was marked with its own discourse of regulation or revenge which also labelled the criminal – i.e., produced the "deviant" subject. This ideology of incarceration was then applied to form – the form of the body and its physicality in the body of the labelled criminal, and the form of the punishing machine which disciplined the labelled offender. As Foucault insists, however, the physical form of punishment *cannot* be derived from the discursive force of the disciplining ideology. Torture machines and dungeons in earlier times and the form of the prison today are material objects which have meaning because of ideologies of punishment, but these forms cannot be derived from the discourse of discipline and the social institution of the law, although they are related to the law and derive their aura of legitimation from it. The social forms of punishment and regulation represent a relatively autonomous articulation of knowledge and technique. These social forms are what we call material culture.

In modern society the discourse of the law has produced or created the social category of the "prisoner" – a criminal subject which is the target of regulatory practices. But the design of the prison itself is a mechanism for the regulatory practices that legal discourse as an ideology merely signifies. The text of the law does not specify the material form of punishment, only its duration. The criminal is sentenced to do time, but the physical nature of that sentence is not regulated or specified by the discourse of the law. The design of the prison, the material culture of incarceration, derives from a separate practice.

In the Peircian semiotic system the prison itself, in its materiality, functions as an index as well as a symbol. Its physical environment constitutes the stimulus to the regulated responses of prison behavior. We have all seen the movies – the prison bell sounds and the cell doors open in response, the prisoners all file out, they are all wearing the same clothing, they are all visible because they are bathed in the panoptic gaze of power, they do what is expected of them and follow the prison routine, or they are disciplined. All of this complex behavior is based on prison practice and molded by the material environment; it is not specified in the discourse of law. Yet, both are related to each other, the force of ideology and the form of practice are two aspects of the same carceral social process in the global system of regulating deviant behavior.

Foucault specified the articulation between discourse and material form in the same way with his studies of the medical clinic and the mental hospital. In each case, a professional discourse articulates with knowledge to produce the practice of regulating individual bodies that are either "ill" or "mentally ill" and the material forms that are the objective instruments of that regulation. The birth of the clinic or the mental hospital, like the prison, owes its genesis to this articulation.

Some contemporary sociologists have attempted to deal with the new forms of social life, but they neglect basing their analysis on the relation between material and social forms. Ritzer,[59] for example, calls attention to the "McDonaldization of society," or "the process by which the principles of the fast-food restaurant are coming to dominate more and more sectors of American society" and the globe.[60] Ritzer bases his conception of McDonaldization on Weber's theme of rationalization, because in both cases the desired effect of institutional intervention is greater functional rationality – i.e., efficiency, predictability, quantity, and control through formal rules and regulations. Ritzer's discussion is insightful, but he neglects material culture. For him the force he seeks to study is confined to the conceptual realm of rationalization, while its effects are simply observable signs of success as McDonaldization spreads across the globe. This analysis never leaves the metaphysics of consciousness characterizing the work of Weber.

McDonaldization, however, works not only because of formal rationality but also because it involves the instrumental engineering of material forms for the fast processing of people who are hungry. Much of what Ritzer discusses concerns less the alleged conceptual "rationality" of the theme park, fast food, medical experience, than the effective *regulation* of people through material design for the instrumental purpose of maximizing profit. In fact, this distinction is clear when he, like Weber, is also able to discuss the "irrationality" of rationality. The latter arises in practice; i.e., in the material and social context of instrumental and allegedly rational forms, such as the daily practice of bureaucracy, fast-food outlets, the large hospital, and the like.

The McDonald's form represents the intersection of capitalism, formal rationality, and environmental engineering using available technology. It is the latter process which both provides capital with machines that might successfully accomplish its goals and also provides us with the new forms of mass culture.

The prison, the clinic, the mental hospital, the fast-food outlet, or the theme park are other material forms that articulate with regulatory discourse in society. The adequate functioning of each depends on a complex articulation between ideology, modes of discourse and forms of spatial practice. While Goffman (see note 44) and symbolic interactionists have been most interested in studying the interactive qualities of life in these institutionalized settings, socio-semiotics seeks to show how ideology, interaction, and subjectivity are related to material forms.

Postmodern cultural criticism has, with few exceptions, ignored the interrogation of material forms in this way. Studies of the mall, theme parks, hotels, and other environments, from a postmodern perspective, privilege the symbols and images of consumer culture as thematic sign vehicles. But these image-driven consumer experiences also take place in particular spaces or environments. Designers of the machines for the realization of capital through the consumption of symbolic culture engineer space for instrumental effect. Thus, material forms express ideology, just as codified ideology requires material culture as its sign vehicle. The mall, for example, is designed to stimulate and facilitate the purchasing of commodities (see next chapter). McDonald's is designed to process hungry people fast. People acquire competency in negotiating these complex spaces, even if they do not share the instrumental desires of capital. This competency in negotiating the material environment is an essential aspect of daily life.

Through Symbolic Interaction people become practitioners of mall behavior, theme park behavior, and so on. In this practice they read the sign functions of material space in addition to engaging in Symbolic Interaction with others. While these modes of knowledge cannot be derived from the ideological force of image-driven culture, it nevertheless represents an important component of the overall practice of postmodern life. Sign functions, which serve as stimuli to behavior originating in the great overarching media sphere of hyperreality which encapsulates our daily life, and the material, instrumental objects and spaces of the environment are both constituent components of culture.

Every time we enter a hotel, a theme park, a freeway, a subway, a McDonald's restaurant, or an office building, we draw on a repertoire of gestures and interactive competencies in order to negotiate material space as well as communicate with others. At the hotel, for example, individuals enter the lobby and make their way to the front desk in order to register. They complete the registration forms, negotiate the environment to find their rooms, and settle in. This practice is deployed in a great variety of venues, ranging from disorienting postmodern buildings to simple "bed and breakfast" hotels, and from our own local area to places around the globe. Familiarity with the procedures and environmental materiality of one hotel provides preparation for experiencing all others in a similar way. In addition, the designers and operators of hotels seek out the normalized practices and structure their commodification around them. These uniform practices of daily life become pertinent to all similar material forms regardless of their specific location. That is, once we learn how to work the hotel or the McDonald's in our home town, we are then capable of successfully using our repertoire of actions at hotels or McDonald's in Tokyo, Paris, or mid-town Manhattan with equal success, despite the need to modify behavior according to specific local circumstances. In turn, once the success of one built environment is documented, other built forms will follow this lead.

We negotiate our everyday environment reading the indexicality of material design and through the articulation of our desire with expressive symbols or images. It is this conjuncture of material objects and Symbolic Interaction that is captured by the socio-semiotic synthesis. While symbolic interactionists have shown how these competencies are dependent on communicative interaction and postmodernists have shown how images and symbols are also important to our daily practices, only socio-semiotics tries to account for the entire three-way complex of material forms, Symbolic Interaction and signs in daily life – that is, the articulation of codified ideology (the form of the content), social context (the substance of the content and its "pre-signifiers"), and material forms (the substance and form of the expression).

Notes

1 Ancient cities differed with regard to the kinds of codes that were used to structure settlement space. The earliest cities relied on cosmological/religious conceptions. Sites of power, such as Athens, Rome, and Beijing, were structured by a mixture of these earlier dimensions articulating with the forms of centralized state power. See Alexandros Lagopoulos, "Semiotic Urban Models and Modes of Production," in *The City and the Sign: An Introduction to Urban Semiotics*, edited by M. Gottdiener and A. Lagopoulos (New York: Columbia University Press, 1986), pp. 176–201.

2 See chapter 8; Eugene Halton, *Meaning and Modernity: Social Theory in the Pragmatic Attitude* (Chicago: University of Chicago Press, 1986).

3 Norman Denzin, *Symbolic Interaction and Cultural Studies* (Oxford: Blackwell Publishers, 1992), p. 2.

4 Charles Morris, *Foundations of the Theory of Signs* (Chicago: University of Chicago Press, 1938).

5 Charles S. Peirce, *Collected Papers of Charles S. Peirce*, vols 1–8, edited by P. Weiss and C. Hartshone (Cambridge, Mass.: Harvard University Press, 1931–1958).

6 Denzin, *Symbolic Interaction*, p. xiv.

7 See Umberto Eco, *A Theory of Semiotics* (Bloomington: Indiana University Press, 1976).

8 In this chapter I shall distinguish between a field of sociology called

"symbolic interaction," and a ubiquitous social process that I call Symbolic Interaction which involves the role of meaning in all social interaction and the organization of social processes according to the meaning of action. Since the latter term appears less frequently in the text, I have retained capital letters for it so that it might be more noticeable when used.

9 Giles Deleuze, *Foucault* (Minneapolis: University of Minnesota Press, 1988).

10 Ann Game, *Undoing the Social* (Toronto: University of Toronto Press, 1991).

11 For histories of the field of symbolic interaction, see Herbert Blumer, "Collective Behavior," in *An Outline of the Principles of Sociology*, edited by R. Park (New York: Barnes and Noble, 1939), pp. 219–80, and *Symbolic Interactionism* (Englewood Cliffs, N.J.: Prentice-Hall, 1969); Sheldon Stryker, "Symbolic Interactionism: Themes and Variations," in *Social Psychology: Sociological Perspectives*, edited by M. Rosenberg and R. Turner (New York: Basic Books, 1981); Stanford Lyman and Arthur Vidich, *Social Order and the Public Philosophy* (Fayetville: University of Arkansas Press, 1988).

12 Blumer, "Collective Behaviour," 1969.

13 Denzin, *Symbolic Interaction*, p. xiv.

14 See chapter 8, below; Halton, *Meaning and Modernity*; Denzin, *Symbolic Interaction*.

15 See, for example, Norman Denzin, "On Semiotics and Symbolic Interactionism," *Symbolic Interaction*, 10, 1 (1987): 1–19; Peter Manning, *Semiotics and Fieldwork* (Beverly Hills, Calif.: Sage, 1987), *Symbolic Communication* (Cambridge, Mass.: MIT Press, 1988); Robert Perinbanayagam, *Signifying Acts* (Carbondale, Ill.: Southern Illinois University Press, 1985), *Discursive Acts* (New York: Aldine de Gruyter, 1991).

16 I can say with total assurity that symbolic interactionists, from Blumer to Denzin and Lyman, have important contributions to cultural studies. Hence I am referring specifically to their attempts at integrating semiotics and symbolic interaction.

17 Perinbanayagam, *Signifying Acts, Discursive Acts*.

18 Ibid.

19 Eco, *Theory of Semiotics*.

20 Blumer, "Collective Behavior"; Gregory Stone, "Appearance and the Self," in *Human Behavior and Social Processes*, edited by A. Rose (Boston: Houghton Mifflin, 1962).

21 Perinbanayagam, *Discursive Acts*.

22 Roman Jakobson, *The Framework of Language* (Ann Arbor: University of Michigan Press, 1980), p. 81.

23 Ibid., p. 81.

24 Perinbanayagam, *Discursive Acts*, p. 10.

25 Peirce, *Collected Papers*, vols 7, 8; see also Eco, *Theory of Semiotics*.

26　Jacques Derrida, *Speech and Phenomena* (Evanston, Ill.: Northwestern University Press, 1973); *Of Grammatology* (Baltimore: Johns Hopkins Press, 1976); *Writing and Difference* (Chicago: University of Chicago Press, 1978).

27　Denzin, *Symbolic Interaction*, p. 292.

28　One contribution of this paper is to point out how symbolic interactionists muddle the use of semiotics, while acknowledging that they have been making important contributions to a synthesis of their field with postmodernism. Thus, for example, while Denzin interprets Derrida correctly in the previous quote, he also asserts the following in a recent paper: "Both Peirce and Saussure assume a one-to-one relationship between an object as referred to in language and its meaning. Both give primacy to what is signified by the symbol, or the sign, that is the sound-image, or referent object" (1987: 3). Denzin here conflates Peirce and Saussure. Yet Peirce possessed a different model of the sign (see chapter 1) that has not only inspired aspects of Derrida's deconstructionism, but also Eco's work and socio-semiotics. Derrida's criticism of the transcendental signified is most correctly pertinent to the Saussurean model of the sign.

29　Perinbanayagam, *Signifying Acts*, p. 9.

30　Ibid., p. 10.

31　Stryker, "Symbolic Interactionism."

32　Perinbanayagam, *Discursive Acts*.

33　George Herbert Mead, *Mind, Self and Society* (Chicago: University of Chicago Press, 1934), p. 67.

34　Perinbanayagam, *Discursive Acts*, p. 10.

35　Stryker, "Symbolic Interactionism."

36　Perinbanayagam, *Signifying Acts*, p. 13.

37　Roland Barthes, *Elements of Semiology* (New York: Hill and Wang, 1967).

38　Mikhail Bakhtin, *The Dialogic Imagination*, edited by M. Holquist (Austin: University of Texas Press, 1981).

39　Perinbanayagam, *Signifying Acts*, p. 17.

40　Jean Baudrillard, *Simulations* (New York: Semiotext(e), 1983).

41　Fredrick Jameson, "Postmodernism, or the Cultural Logic of Late Capitalism," *New Left Review*, 146 (1984): pp. 53–93.

42　Christopher Norris, *What's Wrong with Postmodernism* (Baltimore: Johns Hopkins Press, 1990); Douglas Kellner, *Jean Baudrillard: From Marxism to Postmodernism and Beyond* (Oxford: Polity Press, 1989).

43　See Game, *Undoing the Social*.

44　One of the earliest references to the importance of sign vehicles was made by Erving Goffman ("Symbols of Class Status," in *Sociology and Everyday Life*, edited by M. Truzzi (Englewood Cliffs, N.J.: Prentice-Hall, 1968), pp. 21–32). Goffman emphasized the use of objects as expressive symbols (i.e., as intentionally meant to convey some meaning). This is the same sense in which this concept is used by socio-semiotics, although sign vehicles can still unintentionally also signify as well as communicate. For Goffman the sign vehicle was used to signify social status: "Specialized means of displaying one's position frequently develop. Such sign-vehicles have been called *status symbols*. They are the cues which select for a person the status that is to be imputed to him and the way in which others are to treat him" (1968: 22).

Unlike Jeffrey Alexander, in *Durkheimian Sociology: Cultural Studies* (New York: Cambridge University Press, 1988), who sees little difference between the ideas of Saussure and those of Durkheim, Goffman was well aware that the analysis of culture as status required more than the structural functionalism of Durkheim, because of the importance of interaction. According to Goffman, "These status symbols must be *distinguished* from what Durkheim called 'collective representations' which serve to deny the difference between categories in order that members of all categories may be drawn together to affirm their single moral community" (1968: 22).

Goffman goes on, in this paper, to distinguish between sign vehicles that represent structural "categories" of status from those that are more interactively based and function as "expressive symbols." It is the latter that is of special interest to both symbolic interactionists and sociosemioticians. For a reading of Goffman that illustrates the way he anticipated aspects of the semiotics of culture, see H.-G. Vester, "Erving Goffman's Sociology as a Semiotics of Postmodern Culture," *Semiotica*, 76, 3/4 (1989): pp. 191–203.

45 Mark Gottdiener and Alexandros Lagopoulos, eds, *The City and the Sign: Introduction to Urban Semiotics* (New York: Columbia University Press, 1986).

46 Robert Goldman *Reading Ads Socially* (New York: Routledge, Chapman and Hall, 1992); Douglas Kellner, *Baudrillard: A Critical Reader* (Blackwell Publishers, 1994); Jameson, "Postmodernism."

47 Eco, *Theory of Semiotics*.

48 Goldman, *Reading Acts Socially*.

49 Perinbanayagam, *Signifying Acts*, p. 12 see also *Discursive Acts*.

50 Blumer, "Collective Behavior."

51 See also Stone, "Appearance and the Self."

52 Denzin, *Symbolic Interaction*, p. 3.

53 Claude Lévi-Strauss, *The Elementary Structures of Kinship* (Boston: Beacon Press, 1969).

54 Denzin, *Symbolic Interaction*; Manning, *Semiotics and Fieldwork*.

55 See Barry Smart, *Michel Foucault* (New York: Tavistock).

56 Deleuze, *Foucault*, p. 124.

57 Henri Lefebvre, *Critique of Everyday Life* (London: Verso, 1991).

58 Michel Foucault, *Discipline and Punish* (New York: Vintage Press, 1979).

59 George Ritzer, *The McDonaldization of Society* (Newbury Park, Calif.: Pine Forge Press, 1993).

60 Ibid., p. 1.

Part II

The Substance of the Expression: Case Studies

4

Recapturing the Center:
A Socio-Semiotic Analysis of
Shopping Malls

The phenomenon of the mall in the United States can only be understood within the context of the fundamental changes in socio-spatial
organization affecting the urban environment over the past thirty
years.[1] These are summed up by the concept of "deconcentration" –
i.e., the general dispersal of population and economic activities throughout the metropolitan region. This process involves both the restructuring of the central city and the surrounding metropolitan region
according to the new logic of global capitalism and deindustrialization
among the advanced economies.[2] The socio-spatial outcome of changes
since the 1970s is a qualitatively new form of settlement pattern – the
multi-centered metropolitan region.[3]

   In the past the urban phenomenon was restricted to the large city.
They were magnets for investment and population which were concentrated within city borders and which supported vital industrial
economies. At present the specificity of the urban has been superceded
by metropolitan regional growth and the multi-centering of economic
and residential activity. Since the 1950s the massive movement of
population in the United States to the formerly peripheral areas of the
metropolitan region has been accompanied by a general dispersal of
commercial, cultural, political, manufacturing, financial, and recreational activities. This has altered the morphology of late capitalist
space in a fundamental way. At present, we can no longer speak of
the modern or the postmodern as being a city phenomenon. The new
relations are dispersed throughout the multi-centered metro region.[4]

   According to Barthes,[5] the classic city form was organized around
a center which possessed material manifestations corresponding to
each of the primary forces of social organization. Thus, the classic
city had a kind of semantic unity represented by its center within
which the specific social practices of politics, religion, business, and
cultural interaction had their material or constructed correlates. This

historical form of city space included a large town square which facilitated pedestrian mingling, and several adjacent buildings including
a church or cathedral; a civic building, possibly also housing a court
of law; a bank or brokerage house; and, most importantly, a market.
In its purity of integration, the classic city center circumscribed the
forces of social organization within a specific geographical environment. Physical remnants of this form of agglomeration can still be
found in many of the older towns and cities in the United States.

At present the hierarchical and fragmented mode of socio-spatial
organization characteristic of late capitalist society which is not visible but which underlies metropolitan space as a deep structure of
social relations no longer necessitates the convergence of seminal
societal functions in any single place. The basic change produced by
deconcentration and restructuring during the present phase of late
capitalism has been this breakup of the functional unity of the central
city and its underdeveloped hinterland. In its place we have a new
form of settlement space – the multi-centered metropolitan region.

Currently, the metropolitan landscape has been altered to accom-
modate the increasing functional specialization of many different
centers which have been dispersed throughout a sprawling network
of polynucleated realms. Political administration, to take one example, occurs through the medium of a network of decentralized units
of the state: the chain of local jurisdictions, city halls, county offices
of administration, police stations, and so on. These are linked together by electronic modes of communication and computerized
methods of record keeping along with a uniformly acknowledged
administrative practice of expertise and knowledge, despite local
variations.

In another example, the economic structure has been articulated
into progressively more specialized, decentralized units which have
become increasingly independent in their location considerations from
the need for centrality and agglomeration. Thus, chain stores, factories, branch banking, McDonald's-type fast-food outlets, and mass
cultural venues have all been dispersed in the wider space of the
expanding metro region. In short, while the old central cities remain,
their functions have been altered and restructured toward a progressively more specialized role in the global economy while other functions are dispersed in an expanding network of deconcentrated
minicenters throughout the region, the nation, and the world.

Within the growth of massive metropolitan regions, privatized
modes of consumption have prevailed. In this new form of space, often
called "suburbia," but what I prefer to refer to as the multi-centered

metropolitan region (which *includes* the central city as well), there are few public spaces set aside for social communion. Everyday life is structured by the many separations of metro living: the separation of home from work; of schools from the local neighborhood; of sociability and leisure activities from the propinquity of neighbor-hood life. Crime and the pathologies of daily living produced by uneven development prevent enjoyment of the use values of parks, plazas, and city public space. Within such an environment, the residents left to spend time during the day lack a common public ground for socialization, something which the old town square or center once supplied. Increasingly, public spaces are abandoned out of inconvenience or fear. Instead, the place of social communion is now frequently found within the fully enclosed, climate-controlled shopping areas known as "malls."

The first fully enclosed mall was built in Edina, Minnesota, a suburb of Minneapolis, in 1956. According to one developer, "The idea of having an enclosed mall doesn't relate to weather alone. People go to spend time there – they're equally as interested in eating and browsing as in shopping. So now we build only enclosed malls."[6]

The large, fully enclosed mall has become the new "main street" for the bulk of the metropolitan population living outside the central cities in the United States.[7] As Kowinski has observed, in the newer areas of the sunbelt, such as California, Texas and Florida, "Malls *are* the downtown, right from the start."[8]

The retailing power of the mall is almost irresistible. It has become the most successful form of commercial environmental design in multi-centered regional space. In 1977, malls did over half of all retail business in the United States, and their return on gross sales ranged from $100 to $300 per square foot – the highest of any type of commercial building.[9] In many metropolitan regions, suburban malls are competing out of existence those retailers located in the central city. In part, this has caused a crisis of real estate devaluation in the old downtown and has led to government programs and activities of finance capital to rescue the value of central city land through new business schemes which often include the building of the downtown's own fully enclosed malls.

In some cases, for example, blighted industrial sites have been renovated and the mall form imported into the large central city. Ghirardelli Square in San Francisco and Faneuil Hall in Boston are two examples of mall conversions for blighted factory sites. In other cases, such as the Minneapolis downtown mall or the Santa Monica mall, retailers have joined together to rescue their downtown locations by converting individually sited outlets into an aggregation of shops and pedestrian walkways.

The mall is a distinct architectural form that dates back several thousand years to the cities of the Mediterranean. Several hundred years ago, a fully enclosed mall that is quite massive in scale was built as the grand bazaar of Istanbul. The mall form consists of an enclosed area of separate shops integrated by pedestrian walkways, eating establishments and quasi-public mini spaces. They are machines for the realization of capital – that is, the transformation of manufactured goods and services by consumption. As the entire settlement space of late capitalist societies has been restructured by deep-level changes and their social consequences, including uneven development, the mall form has been successful in locating with impunity in all areas, including the old central city itself.

A Socio-Semiotic Analysis of the Mall

A socio-semiotic analysis of any aspect of the built environment begins by taking into account the specific design practices which have articulated with space. In the case of malls, they can be understood best as the intersection sites of two distinct structural principles. On the one hand, the mall is the materialization of the retailer's intention to sell consumer goods at a high volume under present-day relations of production and distribution. The mall, then, is the "substance of the expression" engineered for the realization of capital in a consumer society. As such, it embodies particular design artifacts – i.e., the morphological elements, or the "form of the expression" – which are *instrumentally* designed to promote purchasing.

On the other hand, the mall is also the physical space within which individuals come to participate in a certain type of urban ambiance which they crave. They are consumers of this quasi-public space at the same time as they circulate as consumers for the benefit of retailers. The latter activity is regulated by a second design practice which emphasizes the representations of various consumer ideologies propogated by the media, advertising, and processes of social status, that structure the universe of meaning for consumers. The content of the mall experience, which is the "form of the content," or codified ideology, articulates with the image-driven culture of the larger society and its ideologies of consumption that are propogated by the media.

In sum, the mall represents a double articulation of formal design elements regulating the physical, material vehicle of mall construction and the representations of the consumer experience within the constructed space. Both aspects are orchestrated by the instrumentality of consumer manipulation for the purposes of the realization of capital. Finally, this particular articulation of materiality and consumer fantasies articulates further with the global culture of consumerism primed in daily life by media images, status pressures, and advertising. These articulations produce the sign systems of the mall.

Case study

The following socio-semiotic analysis of malls is based on site visits to enclosed shopping areas within the Los Angeles-Orange County region of Southern California. Whenever possible, published information on malls located elsewhere has also been used to complement these first-hand observations.[10] A reading of the sign systems which can be found at the mall is organized by recognizing that signification occurs with reference to two separate orders of meaning – the one paradigmatic and the other syntagmatic. The first axis of meaning involves the design motif of the mall itself, since the mall is itself a sign. The second consists of the way the separate elements within the mall produce meaning through metonymy or contiguity. I shall consider these separately, provided it is understood that each axis of meaning also depends on each other.

The individual's experience of the mall is dominated by the encounter of representations and the image-driven culture within its walls. By seeking to separate analytically the paradigmatic and syntagmatic elements of meaning, I do not wish to assert that this mall experience can be experientially compartmentalized in some Cartesian dichotomy between mall motif and interior design. Nor do I assert that both the content and the expression of representations are dichotomized in individual experience. These analytical distinctions enable us to isolate the different aspects of the articulation between modes of representation and material forms – the aim of socio-semiotics. But it should always be understood that the individual experience of material cultural forms is an integrated phenomenological encounter that breaks down barriers and melds consumer fantasies of daily life, media onslaughts of the image-driven culture, instrumental advertising representations that prime consumer fantasies, and the free-floating signifiers that become objects of desire through the instrumental practices of capital realization processes.

This functional reason for the existence of the mall, however, is only one aspect of the mall experience. The quasi-public space of consumption is also the staging area for the individual realization of consumer fantasies and self-actualizing personal practices, including possible forms of resistance, that assume particular behaviors within the mall. Thus, the instrumentality of the mall vis-à-vis capitalism intersects with the material existence of the mall as a space of everyday life, as a place of use values and their realization through social interaction, much in the same way that other spaces, such as the prison, the clinic, the hospital (analyzed by Foucault), constitute the articulation between discursive and non-discursive practices. It is this conjuncture of interaction and instrumentality, rather than the emphasis on one aspect or another, which is captured by socio-semiotic analysis. After discussing paradigmatic and syntagmatic semiosis I will consider, in a final section, the behavioral and cognitive aspects of the mall experience.

The paradigm: The motif of the mall

The purpose of a mall is to sell consumer goods. The function of mall design, therefore, is to disguise the instrumental exchange relation between producer and consumer, which is always more to the former's benefit in capitalist society, and to present cognitively an integrated facade which facilitates consumption acts by the stimulation of consumer fantasies. Thus, the mall, taken as a whole, is a sign itself, since it connotes something other than its principal instrumental function. The mall motif is its disguise.

The motif of the mall serves as a code which integrates the particular consumer fantasy that designers have chosen as the overarching associational image they hope will hide its instrumental nature. The mall is determined not by culture, but by the desire for profit taking and the need to design a machine for the realization of capital under current conditions of multi-centered metropolitan and regional development. This complex of factors constitutes the *pre-conditions* for the signifying practices of the mall and also defines its exo-semiotic context.

With regard to the mall as a sign, then, the substance of the content is the ideology of consumerism, or rather, the pre-signifying desire to consume mobilized as a desire in the present culture, as a means of self-realization, and the various ideologies of consumption that both regulate and fragment the population as markets. These ideologies exert an instrumental control over the other aspects of the mall sign determining its elements, so that the "substance of the expression," which is the material vehicle of capital realization – the mall as a built environment – is also a manifestation of consumer ideologies. That is, the formal elements of design existing throughout the mall at the level of the content and also at the level of the expression (see figure 4.1) are all constrained in their respective possibilities by the instrumental function of the mall. It is the job of the former elements of signification to *displace* that instrumental function. But, in order to work, they have to be harmonized and regulated so that they are in concordance.

Thus, by acting as a sign itself, the mall provides the unifying theme of the mall experience. The mall motif is an overarching, instrumental code, which defines the associational or paradigmatic axis of meaning, creates a short circuit between the fantasies of consumerism existing in the larger culture, and the particularized fantasies and representational appeals to consumption within the mall space itself.

The motif of the mall is chosen by the designers and architects who apply the knowledge acquired through years of retailing experience. Trade journals, government reports on retailing, educational institutions teaching marketing, and the like, all help to produce and distribute the knowledge of mall design. When specific elements achieve particular success in one location, they are often tried elsewhere. Thus, there is a kind of iconic mimesis or "standardization" that mall motifs tend to assume over a period of time. Perhaps the best example of a successful motif is the concept of "galleria," to be discussed below. The uniformity of motif choice is the architectural analogue of the media or marketing search for canonical forms that appeal to a mass audience. For the case of the mall, developers replicate design motifs which have proven successful elsewhere in the belief that at other locations the same consumer fantasies will function to attract and hold shoppers.

Recently, for example, a motif, sometimes referred to as Ye Olde Kitsch, has become popular. This follows its success as a retro style in such places as Faneuil Hall in Boston. Orange County, California has a mall which reproduces this motif, called "Olde Towne." As one

Figure 4.1 The decomposition of the architectural sign

Sign:	$\dfrac{\text{Content}}{\text{Expression}}$	=	Substance	=	Social ideology
			Form		Architectural ideology
			Form		Architectural paradigm
			Substance		Morphological units

approaches it, a large sign with the logo "Olde Towne" frames its entrance. But the mall is neither old nor a town. Instead these signifiers float disembodied and detached from their signifieds, a fundamental characteristic of the advertising form. The free-floating signifiers are used to denote a simulation: the interior decor of the mall which is made to represent some fantasy of 19th-century Americana. The signifier provides the code for the interior mall design and denotes the invocation of nostalgia. As Baudrillard would say, the mall is a simulation.

Within this particular mall every store front, including the offices of the security staff or mall police, mimics the "Hollywood" image of 19th-century American towns as envisioned by architectural practice. Stores are connected by antique streets complete with mock gaslight poles spaced every few yards. The entire ensemble is reminiscent of "main street" in Disneyland, a scaled-down version of the type of town which contemporary patterns of development have long since helped to destroy.[11] In fact, malls with unifying motifs, such as Olde Towne, which are simulations after the destruction of their own referents, much like the images of extinct animal life that circulate through late capitalist society, can be understood in the same manner as Disneyland (see next chapter). They thrive on the contextual contrast to the environment surrounding them. The nostalgic yearning for an idealized conception of small-town life is generated within a metropolitan milieu where the actual small town and its distinctive social relations have disappeared. The yearning for the intimacy of quaint wood and stucco structures can be understood as produced by an everyday life situated within environments that negate intimacy through the massive sprawling scale of multi-centered regional development.

In short, the success of the mall motif and its code which integrates the physical experience of the mall depends on its ability to contrast positively with the everyday environment in the surrounding space. Elements drawing on this contrast and the fantasies that successfully make this contrast are then transformed into material realizations by the professional practice of architects and mall developers.

This observation can be underscored by the second, equally successful design motif called High-Tech Urban, which recreates the density of the central city by piling up two and three stories around a large, open space which then displays the names of shops in the high-tech style of steel, plastic and glass. The prototype of this high-density mall is the Galleria of Milan, Italy. This "galleria" form as well as the name has been replicated in places such as Houston (Texas),

White Plains (New York), Sherman Oaks (California) and Glendale (California). Less obviously, the High-Tech Urban code also characterizes multiple-story malls which have been developed with great success in other parts of Southern California, such as Fox Run in Los Angeles County, and the Beverly Center in Beverly Hills (and quite obviously in other parts of the United States, as well).

In places like Los Angeles and the newer cities of the sunbelt, deconcentrated patterns of residential development have reduced population density to levels that contrast with the compact, bounded city form of the past. Thus, malls using this second motif recreate the urban space of agglomeration on a small scale and reproduce in a temporary setting the urban experience of population density as well as the "latent eroticism"[12] of the public space as ludic center. Within such malls a kind of bird's-eye view is afforded to people at the higher levels who are often seen pausing in their pursuits to watch the pedestrian traffic of shoppers below. The constructed space of the multi-storied, high-density mall transcends for the moment the many separations afflicting life outside it in deconcentrated regions of the metropolis. While such malls fulfill other functions and thereby have an appeal for other reasons, the reliance on nostalgia for city environments of the past seems to be a consistent characteristic of currently popular mall motifs – Ye Olde, High-Tech, or otherwise.

In sum, the most important design aspect of a mall is its overarching motif which supplies the code that integrates the sign system of the interior and also articulates with the global culture of consumption in the larger society. The search for a successful motif seems to be facilitated through the contextual relation between the constructed space of the mall itself and a comparison with its surrounding regional environment. Both Ye Olde Kitsch and High-Tech Urban are variants of nostalgia for the urban socio-spatial experience of the past which contrasts distinctly with the design patterns of present-day deconcentrated metropolitan areas.

The syntagm: The articulation of design elements within the mall

The syntagmatic dimension involves the engineering of space within the mall form and the piecing together of appearance alternatives for store front facades. The purpose of intra-mall design is solely instrumental – the control of crowds to facilitate the transformation of production into consumption for the realization of capital. But the success of this purpose depends on the consumption of the ambiance within the mall and the ability of individuals to self-actualize modes of behavior that they themselves deem desirable. As in the case of the mall motif, the instrumental function of the interior must be disguised at the very same instant it is materialized in space. In fact, it is precisely through the effectiveness of disguise that the quasi-public space of the interior enables individual consumption of the use values provided by the encounter with others within the mall.

The "form of the content," which is the overarching code of the mall, dictates the design elements that will constitute the "form of the expression," so that the disguise which is the mall can be finely tuned in all of its parts. In some cases, such as the Olde Towne mall, individual stores must, by the rules of tenancy, conform to the overarching motif of the mall's code. However, all malls have distinct regulations that "normalize" store facades within the mall according to its motif.

Several distinct techniques of design are utilized to bring about the harmony of this associational relation. First, malls have ugly, blank walls on their outsides, as all activities are turned inward. In fact, from the parking lot most malls look like concrete bunkers with an occasional logo of a department store serving as the only break in a monolithic pattern of bricks and steel. The purpose of this design is to discourage loitering outside the mall and to quicken the pace with which shoppers will leave or return to their cars. According to Stephans,[13] this denial of the street or true public space outside the built environment of the mall is called "introversion." The mall design replaces public space with a self-enclosed, besieged and regulated environment, much like the medieval castle. Thus, while the world outside may be filled with the vagaries of urban life in a society characterized by crime, uneven development, and social stratification, the experience within the mall is sheltered by blank, fortress-like walls and by the auspices of its feudal-seeming proprietor, the mall management. In many cases, the gaze of a paternalistic security force is extended to the outside parking lot, with surveillance cameras or guard towers, thereby making the mall an island sanctuary in a crime-ridden society.

A second feature of mall construction often greets consumers as they enter the main area. Designers have recycled the sign function of the city as a ludic center within the mall. In a number of cases the entrance is a large open space, like a town square, which includes some form of special attraction not directly related to shopping itself. For example, the Olde Towne mall (see above) has a full-scale carousel at its center complete with recorded calliope music. For a nominal cost children can ride on it, while parents watch their amused faces.

In a second case, just inside the main entrance of the Del Amo Mall in Los Angeles (one of the largest in the country), stands a massive, two-story clock tower with a special set of chimes that shoppers can enjoy at regular intervals. At its base instructive signs explain the "unique" features of the clock tower so that shoppers are attracted to its performance as a special event. The tower and its surrounding open space also recycle important elements of the old town square, especially recalling the centers of Renaissance cities in western Europe with their own ornate town clocks and chimes.

A highly developed example of the mall as ludic center can be found in the new Mall of America outside of Minneapolis, now the United States' largest mall. This fully enclosed mall is built around a seven-acre theme park modelled after Camp Snoopy in Knotts Berry Farm, California. The park comes complete with a mall-scaled roller coaster ride and other amusements including theme park uniforms for the workers. The combination mall/theme park has been copied by the MGM Grand Hotel in Las Vegas (opened in 1993), which is a combination gambling casino/theme park.

Malls also devote a significant amount of space to fast-food restaurants that are often aggregated into "food courts." These also resemble town square ludic centers, especially reminiscent of Mediterranean-style built environments. Such spaces can be found in almost any mall. They are usually centered around a large area filled with light from skylights which frames the seating area interspersed with plants and perhaps fountains. The entire ensemble captures a charged urban ambiance which draws shoppers to pause, to see, and to be seen. The availability of snacks and fast food is an important feature of the mall. As one well-known developer has remarked, "They come to shop, but they stay for the food."[14]

In any of its manifestations, the recapturing of the traditional ludic center creates the illusion of urban civility. Individuals living in environments with few public spaces and low-density demographics, such as in suburbia, can find something that many of them lack and often crave once they enter the mall – a well-ordered, open space of social communion. Yet, the mall is only a quasi-public space. The management has the legal power to regulate the kinds of people and activities found there. Malls, for example, can exclude political and union assemblies. They enjoy the legal right to prevent workers from picketing a shop with which they are engaged in a job action. Furthermore, unlike the public space in many towns (but not all), pedestrians are discouraged from loitering within malls, except in places designated for that purpose. Thus, the recycling of the town square form within the mall by design practice must be recognized as providing only an illusion of civility, as the urban ambiance is harnessed to the profit motives of privately controlled space which is predicated on the constant flow of a large volume of people.

The most important aspect of the syntagm are the sign systems that are found within the mall. For the most part, denotative and even indexical aspects of the sign take precedence over connotative functions in order to facilitate the flow of pedestrian traffic. When the connotative function is present, it generally signals a particular consumer or commodity status within a stratified society comprised of individuals with variable household budgets. Thus, the connotative signs are sign vehicles of status and social distinction.[15]

Within the mall, for example, the appeal of stores is based on the general convergence of merchandising around the mimesis of current fashion imperatives. Yet, stores are stratified according to the general range of prices they charge. Consumers pick and choose among this variety by cueing in, through experience, to those establishments which offer merchandising within what are judged as acceptable costs, even though items purchased in separate stores at different prices may look alike because of this convergence of appearance alternatives produced by the ensemble of practices comprising the logotechniques of the fashion industry.

The store logo and signs advertising consumption, such as sales, denote a type of budgetary envelope wherein consumers can hope to find a variety of items that fall within their own expenditure limits. The signifiers, then, are sign vehicles denoting status. But, they are also free-floating signifiers that connect cognitively in primed consumers with the more global advertising and media environment of the image-driven culture. The desire for commodities does not begin at the mall. Everyday life is saturated with commercials and demonstrated needs derived from contact with others. Desire is tied to particular brands, logos, signifiers. Consumers entering the mall, therefore, are already primed to purchase specific brands and specific types of commodities. In this sense, the sign systems of the mall are but extensions of the commodity and advertising sign systems in the larger society.

A final aspect of syntagmatic design elements involves the engineering of pedestrian flows among the stores. Malls work principally because of the presence of a few large department stores which pull in customers. Their location defines the overall floor plan, with specialty shops filling up the intervening space between the big draw stores. In fact, malls are classified according to the number of large department stores they contain. Usually there are at least two, as this number enables designers to "anchor down" the mall and orient its paths on a linear axis. With two stores at opposite ends, customers have to walk from one to the other and thus pass all the lesser known shops in between. The very largest malls contain three or more giant department stores, thus permitting a floor plan with intersecting axes and, hence, more space for other stores. The Del Amo Mall, in Los Angeles County, has nine major department stores spread out over a large area. In all of contemporary urban history there has never been a single central city with that many major stores located within one area.

The business volume of the smaller shops relies primarily on the draw of the big stores and the ease with which the floor plan facilitates browsing and impulse buying. Paths are broken up by obstacles, such as large concrete planters and trash bins, benches, the zig-zagging of store layouts, and blank walls that jut out into traffic and require detours towards other shops. These all function to disorient slightly the ambulation of consumers and force them to take some added time in getting from one place to another within the mall.

The store fronts of retailers located along these paths must work to entice the impulse buyer to come in. Here the name of the shop and its appearance, while having to preserve the design elements of the mall's central motif, take a secondary role to the display arrangements in the window of the facade itself. The elements of lighting, window dressing, and commodity display assume great importance for such stores, as do connections to the global sign system outside the mall of media and advertising.

Store fronts and displays exploit the advertising signals engineered by manufacturers into the very objects of consumption, such as: clothing designer labels, records and book jacket covers, and motifs of appliance design, as in the "high-tech" cases of stereo equipment or vacuum cleaners. Such efforts comprise a second way in which the sign systems of the mall link up with and are extensions of mass marketing, media, and advertising in the global culture of late capitalism. In fact, the shop within the mall, as well as the mall itself, constitutes the phenomenal form for the realization of capital. It is precisely that space within which the process of production is transformed into consumption through the mediation of advertising and mass marketing practices and their consumerist ideologies. This intertextuality of mall and the society's image-driven culture of consumption structures the sign systems of the individual shops as much as does the motif of the mall itself.

Within the mall the activity of consumption and its links to spectacular forms of consumerist ideology is often stratified according to the differentiation of income levels among consumers and their markets. The specialization of stores within any single mall enables this constructed space to cater to several different income levels. In some cases malls themselves are distinguished from each other because certain ones cater to the more affluent, while others service the middle class. Higher status malls, such as Fashion Island in Newport Beach, California, bring together elite fashion manufacturers and specialty shops which cater to an up-scale crowd. In such places the name of the retailer or designer indexes status in the same way as the department store logo. At Fashion Island, for example, one can shop at an Yves St Laurent showroom which employs sales people who speak French.

In sum, then, consumption at the mall depends on the strength of intertextual ties with the larger culture of advertising and media. The mall stores mix signs of status with commodities that possess certain exchange as well as sign values. These signifiers connote what is fashionable, what is indicative of a certain socio-economic status, what belongs to the set of commodities associated with a specific lifestyle, or, finally, and quite simply, what signals to others that the particular consumer has shopped at such and such a store or mall and not elsewhere. The mall space, therefore, is designed to provide as much free reign as possible, within the confines of its castle-like introversion, for advertising signals and free-floating signifiers of the image-driven culture to operate on and entice the pre-conditioned minds of the customers to consume.

The experience of the mall

The mall is a functional machine for the transformation of production into consumption and, therefore, for the realization of capital. But the mall is also a quasi-public space which brings together people and the sign systems of image-driven culture. People experience the built environment and a kind of communion of shoppers which leads to open-ended outcomes, serendipity, chance encounters, and the cognitive participation in consumerist fantasies. Because the mall itself is an instrument of capital, it does not follow that all of its users are only manipulated by its constructed space for instrumental purposes. In fact, without the space of communion the mall could not succeed as an alternative to multi-centered regional life. By creating a kind of urban ambiance in a quasi-public space, the mall enables a variety of behaviors not all of which are instrumentally linked to the purchase of commodities.

Studies of malls illustrate the many ways people participate in the experience.[16] It is a place for the gathering of adolescents and old people who go there principally for social reasons. Shoppers also plan time to browse, dwell at the food court, or pause at micro-environments that allow stopping and sitting. In the spectacular Mall of America these elements of sociability are fostered by the large ludic center which is a theme park. Families can entertain themselves for hours within this space. Other attractions include restaurants, bars, video arcades, comic book stores, coffee shops, specialty clothing stores, instructional electronic outlets, game stores, and the like. The mall experience, then, is the articulation of consumerism and carnival or ludic town life.

Entrance to the mall means the actualization of consumerist fantasies that are primed by years of conditioning deriving from exposure to advertising and the mass media. According to Langman,

> Malls as dream-like *fantasies* are places of unabashed contradictions of time, place and subjectivity that exist as much in imagination as reality. Although there have been historical antecedents in the distribution of goods, malls cannot be thought of apart from the mass mediated images of television that stimulate and soothe at the same time. They exist as indoor worlds with atriums of plants and trees from far away climes, marble fountains with multi-colored light shows with lasers, holograms and strobes with backdrops of chrome waterfalls. The design and layout of malls attempts to create a utopia of consumption situated between a mythical past of the pre-automobile Main Street of Smalltown where one walked from store to store, and the future high tech world of neon, holograms, lasers and space travel as malls come to resemble the space station of *2001*, the Starship Enterprise or high tech future cities. They create nostalgic memories of neighborhood and lost community, or at least, Christmas card images of a past abundant with goods and cohesion.[17]

While most venues of everyday life are normalized by surveillance and institutional social codes, malls afford the luxury of unstructured sociability. This is especially attractive to adolescents who are hemmed in by the constraints of family, on the one hand, and school, on the other. However, at the mall it is possible to find a variety of cohort groups, genders, races, and classes interacting in the quasi-public space. Field research on mall behavior uncovers a spectrum of activities that thrive in the atmosphere of minimal surveillance, including the illicit meetings of the opposite sex among married adults as well as adolescents, the phenomenon of "killing time" among all age groups, exercise for the elderly, or "mall walking," and family outings by people who seem to have limited places to go. Many of these activities were depicted in a recent movie, *Scenes from a Mall.*

As capitalist society has shifted from an emphasis on production to consumption, subjectivity is realized through the act of buying and the persona of the consumer. Malls, therefore, allow for the realization of consumerist subjectivity as well as of capital accumulation. But this subjectivity is virtual because it depends for its *meaning* on the free-floating signifiers of the advertising and media culture. According to Kroker and Cook,

> Shopping malls are the real postmodern sites of happy consciousness. Not in the old Hegelian sense of a reconciled dialectic of reason, but happy consciousness, now in the sense of the virtual self . . . the self now is a virtual object to such a degree of intensity and accumulation that the fascination of the shopping mall is in the way of homecoming to a self that has been lost, but now happily discovered.[18]

The mall experience is partly this finding of a self which is the self as conditioned consumer in the ludic, amusement sphere of commodity capitalism. This consumer self is only primed by TV and the advertising media. It becomes actualized within the consumption and quasi-public ludic space of the mall. This sphere is a commodified utopia where the vagaries of daily life and the inhumanity of the production process exist as but faint echoes of the economy. The mall presents a material, built environment that is an amusement space, a carnival center. The self, which is actualized as a consumer self, transports to the mall, encounters the disorienting design features of its architecture, and searches out the region of clear light past the parking stalls, the gangways, escalators, stairs, entrance doors, and into the grand avenues of consumption and consumerist communion. This phenomenology of the mall experience depends on the connotative signifiers of codified consumerist ideology, or "the form of the content" interlinked with an ability to negotiate and be negotiated by the machine that is the mall environment, or "the substance of the expression."

Conclusion

The mall represents the consummate device for the conversion of production to consumption and the realization of capital. But this is so because, for many metropolitan residents, it is the only safe or available place to meet others in unstructured, minimally regulated space. People come to the mall because they are driven both by consumerist fantasies and in order to seek a common ground for sociability in a society with limited opportunities for public interaction. As Jacobs[19] suggests, however, the mall can never satisfy the alienated needs that people seek to fulfill there. In fact, the mall only makes worse the problem of consumerist-directed lifestyles.

In many regions of the metropolis, everyday life and its core of sociability has been usurped by the instrumental space of late capitalism and by the pathological consequences of contemporary society, such as high rates of crime, including random street violence. Instrumental spaces, such as malls, can be contrasted with the ludic city center of the past. In the latter, associational rights were guaranteed by founding city laws, even if they were regulated by a nascent urban government and class distinctions, such as sumptuary (appearance) regulations. Public spaces meant freedom of association, speech and assembly. They produced a public self unfettered by economic imperatives.

The public sphere has evaporated in the multi-centered region and with it the staging grounds for this public self. In its place we have the virtual self of the "amusement society" created and reproduced by the media and advertising. This self exists alone and unfullfilled until it enters the mall. For a brief time, the encounter with the mall brings about a special and partial self-integration, which is the realization of the consumer self. But the moments pass too quickly while the impoverishment of humanity and public life remains in the deteriorating city.

Notes

1   M. Gottdiener, *The Social Production of Urban Space* (Austin: University of Texas Press, 1985); *The New Urban Sociology* (New York: McGraw-Hill, 1994).

2   Barry Bluestone and Bennet Harrison, *The Deindustrialization of America* (New York: Basic Books, 1982); Gottdiener, *Social Production of Urban Space*; Saskia Sassen, *The Global City* (Princeton, N.J.: Princeton University Press, 1991).

3   Robert Kling, Spencer Olin and Mark Poster, *Postsuburban California* (Berkeley: University of California Press, 1991); Gottdiener, *New Urban Sociology*.

4   M. Gottdiener, "Space, Social Theory and the Urban Metaphor," in *Current Perspectives in Social Theory*, edited by B. Agger (Greenwich, Conn.: JAI Press, 1991), pp. 295–313; Gottdiener, *New Urban Sociology*.

5 Roland Barthes, "Semiologie et urbanisme," *L'Architecture d'aujourd'hui*, 153 (1970–1), 11–13.
6 W. Kowinski, "The Malling of America," *New Times*, 10, 9 (1978): 30–56.
7 Jerry Jacobs, *The Mall* (Prospect Heights, Ill.: Waveland Press, 1984).
8 Kowinski, "Malling of America," p. 46.
9 S. Stephans, "Introversion and the Urban Context," *Progressive Architecture* (December, 1978): 49–53.
10 E.g., Jacobs, *The Mall*.
11 See R. Francaviglia, "Main Street Revisited," *Places* (October, 1974): 7–11.
12 Barthes, "Semiologie et Urbanisme."
13 Stephans, "Introversion and the Urban Context."
14 Ibid.
15 Pierre Bourdieu, *Distinction: A Social Critique of the Judgement of Taste* (Cambridge, Mass.: Harvard University Press, 1984).
16 Jacobs, *The Mall*.
17 Lauren Langman, "Neon Cages: Shopping for Subjectivity," in *Lifestyle Shopping: The Subject of Consumption*, edited by R. Shields (New York: Routledge, 1992), pp. 40–82.
18 Arthur Kroker and David Cook, *The Postmodern Scene: Excremental Culture and Hyper-Aesthetics* (New York: St Martin's Press, 1986), pp. 208–9.
19 Jacobs, *The Mall*.

5

Disneyland: A Utopian Urban Space

To all who come to this happy place: Welcome. Disneyland is your land. Here age relives fond memories of the past ... and here youth may savor the challenge and promise of the future.
Dedication plaque, July 17, 1955

Disneyland as a specific place and as a theme park has received attention recently as a prototypical postmodern environment.[1] Baudrillard, for example, sees no difference between Disneyland and the city of Los Angeles that surrounds it, because the built environment in the United States is a simulation pure and simple, as he suggests:

> It is no longer a question of a false representation of reality, but of concealing the fact that the real is no longer real, no longer exists ... Disneyland is presented as an imaginary in order to make us believe that the rest is real, when in fact, all of Los Angeles and the America surrounding it are no longer real, but of the order of hyperreal and simulation.[2]

Other observers, while not subscribing to the extreme reductionism of Baudrillard, nevertheless claim a certain postmodern specificity for Disneyland. They know it was constructed in the 1950s, but they suggest that it is exemplary of a fantasy-based, "postmodern" image-driven culture; hence its popularity.[3] Such a mode of analysis does not deal with Disneyland as a material cultural form, but with the ideology of postmodernism. That is, the subject of analysis is not Disneyland but postmodernism, and the goal of this kind of interpretation is not the illumination of the Disneyland experience but the desire to impute features of postmodernism to this constructed space. In short, this type of writing is a kind of ideology that privileges the cognitive categories of the analyst and ignores both the material substance of the built environment and its articulation with the everyday experience of users. What postmodern interpreters ignore, in contrast, socio-semiotics takes as its object of analysis.

During the 1950s, shortly after its construction, Disneyland had already become the most popular attraction in the United States. Both the original theme park and Disneyworld in Orlando, Florida are now the most popular attractions in the world. The concept of the theme park, developed by Walt Disney, has been imitated in countless other forms that have also achieved success, such as Knotts Berry Farm in California or Dollyland in Tennessee, and, the specific form of Disneyland has been reconstructed in places like Japan and France.[4] There is something universal rather than postmodern that has contributed to the success of this built environment and the experience it offers over the years.

Prior to the attention paid by postmodern scholars, a number of writers had already offered analyses of Disneyland. Real,[5] for example, uses a Marxian phenomenological approach. He sees the park as an extension of capitalism's consumer-oriented culture and the effectiveness of "mass-mediation." By the latter is meant that our culture has reached a stage where all symbolic activities are mediated by the pervasive effects of the mass media. Disneyland works because of its strong connection to the Disney cartoons and Disney television programming of the 1950s, in much the same way that the mall works because it connects with the consumerist priming of the mass media and advertising (see chapter 4).

The first semiotic analysis of the theme park appeared in the 1970s.[6] Louis Marin, a French semiotician, applied a Greimasian analysis to Disneyland. He considered the park as a text and dissected its themes. These were categorized, following Greimas, according to their oppositions, such as nature/machine, past/future, and reality/fantasy. As an example of semiotics, rather than socio-semiotics, Marin's oppositions exist as textual distinctions extracted by his independent analysis of the signifiers. The result is an important *description* of Disneyland as an ideology, but Marin cannot provide *explanation* for either how the park was produced nor why it has remained so popular.

The premise of socio-semiotics, in contrast, is that any cultural object is both an object of use in a social system with a generative history and social context, and also a component in a system of signification which can be interpreted by users. Socio-semiotics studies this articulation between ideology and built, material forms which function as expressive symbols. Due to polysemy, this approach must consider the intersection of several different sign systems and user "readings" for any cultural object. Often this entails researching interviews or the study of printed documents, written discourse about the object or experience, and historical records. In this precise way socio-semiotics overcomes the static, synchronic structuralism that privileges the independent analysis of the interpreter in ordinary cultural criticism.

For any built environment, such as a mall or theme park, with intentionally encoded symbols in its construction, we must distinguish between two separate levels of signification: the *production* or *consumption* of space. Both activities involve spatial forms, on the one hand, and certain symbolic *conceptions*, on the other. The conception of the produced space and the conception or cognitive understanding of the consumed space is often different, due to polysemy. Thus, we cannot say that some projected designed space will convey, as a language, the precise symbolic content intended by the designer to the mind of the user. To do so would commit the linguistic fallacy. "Production" refers to the production of meaning through the built environment, including the construction of a space or relations among built forms where the sender may be an individual or group with or without an intention to communicate a specific message. "Consumption" refers to the "reading" of space or the "image" of the built environment, where the addressee is an individual or "collective synchronic or diachronic subject either known or unknown to the sender".[7] This reading is characterized by temporality because the receiver encounters the spatial message experientially through the use of the built environment.

In sum, the production of meaning is qualitatively different from the consumption of meaning, although it is possible that both functions can be performed by the same individual at the same time – that is, production and consumption are not true dichotomies, nor contrasting processes, where meaning or signification is involved. They are, instead, two parts of a complete whole – the experience of the built environment as a *meaningful* space. The significance of this distinction can be illustrated by the realization that most writing about settlement space, architecture, or the built environment deals exclusively with a "reading" of the space as a text (i.e., only involving the consumption of meaning). This kind of writing tells only half the story about material culture.

The Socio-Semiotics of Disneyland

The place

Disneyland was carved out of the advancing suburban sprawl of Los Angeles by Walt Disney's purchase of a 160-acre orange grove adjacent to the city of Anaheim. The "Magic Kingdom," also known as "the happiest place on earth," or as "D-land" by frequent Southern California visitors, has a "classic" form, consisting of four separate realms: Frontierland, Adventureland, Fantasyland, and Tomorrowland; and three distinct towns: Main Street, New Orleans Square, and the recently added Toontown, which may in fact be considered another realm, due to its size. At the Anaheim site Toontown occupies the space adjacent to Frontierland which once housed Bear Country, an old time country and nostalgic fantasy that failed to be popular among users.

Each of the realms is organized around some central unifying theme, which is manifested in the variety of amusement rides available to visitors. The built environment is illustrated in figure 5.1. Visitors to

Figure 5.1   Disneyland

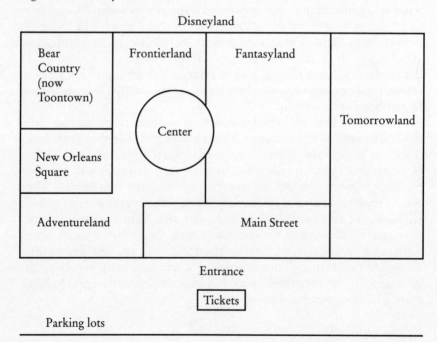

the park leave their cars (virtually their sole means of transport in suburbia) and become pedestrians, making their way on foot through this amusement space. In essence, they return to the city, or at least to an urban-style experience, because they assume the status of pedestrian among a crowd of "others." They make their way on foot through the theme park, some with well-defined destinations and others by wandering through the quasi-public space.

Disneyland, however, is not a true city or urban experience but a simulated urban space that is smoothly run by a major corporation and is devoid of the many pathologies common to actually existing cities in our society. It also is a very sophisticated simulation of mass culture that is made possible by advanced imaging and "imagineering" technologies, computer-assisted administration, and high-tech people-moving devices. Most city planners or politicians only aspire to incorporate such technology, or simply dream about it. As an employees' brochure indicates,

> And with our own postal service, full service bank, security and fire department, Disneyland is almost like a city in itself. James Rouse, highly respected master planner and builder, in his keynote speech before an urban design conference at Harvard University said, "I hold a view that may be shocking to an audience as sophisticated as this: that the greatest piece of urban design in the United States today is Disneyland . . . I find more to learn in the standards that have been set and the goals they have achieved in the development of Disneyland than any other single piece of physical development in the country."[8]

Syntagmatic analysis

Disneyland stands at the conjuncture of multi-valent codes produced by the larger social context within which the park is located. There are at least nine meaning systems converging on this urban space supplied by the larger social context that are important for understanding the experience there. Clearly this reveals the necessarily open-ended aspect of this analysis because there are many more codes actualized in settlement space. However, I have stopped at nine because I find these aspects of the social context most useful for an understanding of the production of syntagmatic meanings through the operation of difference between Disneyland and the surrounding space of Los Angeles. These systems of signification with their own codes are: transportation, food, fashion, entertainment, social control, economics, politics, and the family.

Understanding Disneyland through the plane of contiguity, or the syntagmatic axis, requires that we consider it as a separate part of the social formation that has produced the rest of the Southern California region. Consequently, we can compare Disneyland to what is left behind by visitors – the urban/suburban region of Los Angeles which produces a metonymical contrast or difference that is a source of meaning for the experience of the park itself. The syntagmatic meaning of Disneyland is revealed by its oppositions with the quotidian, the everyday life of residents of Los Angeles. These oppositions exist for each of our nine codes or systems of signification. They are: transportation: pedestrian/passenger; food: celebration/subsistence; fashion: tourist/resident; architecture: fantasy/function; entertainment: festival/spectacle; social control: communion/coercion; economics: the market/capitalism; politics: participatory democracy/representative democracy; and family: child-directed/adult-directed. The summary aspects of these oppositions are indicated in table 5.1, which condenses the contrasts found between Disneyland and Los Angeles.

Everyday life in Los Angeles requires reliance upon the automobile, the rational planning of meals and special trips to suburban shopping centers, housing as property value or equity, clothing as career image, adherence to norms because of compulsion or coercion, participation in competition out of necessity, and limited access to the means of social decision making through representative democracy. Above all else, Los Angeles is the archetypical sprawling urban space where miles and miles separate individuals from each other and the ordinary activities of daily life, such as shopping and recreation. Guy Debord has remarked that such deconcentration represents the end of urban life. While not referring to Los Angeles in particular, he states:

> The present moment is already the moment of the self destruction of the urban milieu. The expansion of cities over countrysides covered with uniformed masses of urban residues is directly officiated by the imperatives of consumption. The dictatorship of the automobile, pilot-product of the first phase of commodity abundance, inscribed itself on earth with the domination of the highway, which dislocates ancient centers and requires an ever-larger dispersion. At the same time, the moments of incomplete reorganization of the urban tissue polarize temporarily around "distribution factories," enormous supermarkets constructed on bare ground, on a parking lot; and this centrifugal movement rejects them when they in turn become overburdened

secondary centers, because they brought about a partial recom-
position of agglomeration.[9]

In contrast to the Los Angeles region, Disneyland is a utopian
urban space. The multi-centered region of Los Angeles aptly fits
Debord's description of a supercession of urban life by something
else driven by the dictates of consumerism and located within an
expanding, poly-nucleated milieu.[10] Disneyland, in comparison, invokes the essential condition of the citizen in classic cities, the status
of being a pedestrian wanderer. It is a built environment that entertains, part of the growing and increasingly pervasive entertainment
culture of our society that is manifested in material forms.[11]

What is most surprising about our syntagmatic analysis is that it
reverses previous criticisms of Disneyland, because the quotidian world
of Los Angeles is far more open to a socio-spatial critique. In fact, the
wholly positive attitude of the Disney corporation about the virtues
of this park as a settlement space, a view also shared by builders such
as James Rouse, now seems eminently reasonable. Thus, my comparison of Disneyland and Los Angeles can be viewed as a critique of the
latter to the benefit of the former. However, the following will also
dwell on Disneyland's own negative attributes. Although it may simu-
late a utopian urban space, the park is also a machine designed to
maximize profit by the manipulation of consumer fantasies and their
desire for a benign space that entertains. Let us detail these comparisons as outlined in table 5.1.

Food

Food in Disneyland becomes part of the festival. It is available whenever one is made hungry by pedestrian activity. It is state fair food,
party food, snacks bought almost anywhere and at any time. Los
Angeles, in contrast, is the space of food as subsistence. It is the
everyday world of planned meals, budgets, organized shopping trips
by car to the "temples of hurried consumption." Food is the housewife's burden and the husband's terminal illness.

Fashion

In Disneyland, appropriate attire is the uniform of play, the valida-
tion of being a tourist. Although the Disney authorities do regulate
appearance by insisting upon the middle-class leisure outfit, nevertheless this is a qualitative departure from the work uniforms of everyday

Table 5.1 Summary of sociospatial codes and oppositions

Sign system	Disneyland	Los Angeles
Transportation	*Pedestrian*: Walking in a group. Wander without a map. A very efficient mass transportation system also exists for fun, as another ride.	*Passenger*: The auto is a necessity. Poor mass transportation. The auto is expensive and dangerous. It requires insurance, licensing, maintenance.
Food	*Celebration*: Festival food, snacks, state fair food, bought anywhere at any time.	*Subsistence*: Food for nourishment, planned meals budgeted, special trips during the week to do shopping.
Clothing	*Tourist*: Outdoor uniform of play, resort wear, people often can be seen wearing the Disney insignias (mouse ears).	*Resident*: Uniform of everyday life, work, career-oriented, subject to fads.
Shelter	*Fantasy*: Architecture as entertainment. Symbolic and/or iconic.	*Function*: Housing as equity, status, protection: design is functional and conformist.
Entertainment	*Festival*: The ludic structure of the classical city. The urban space as fun. Participation with others in a wide variety of activities. Serendipity and freedom.	*Spectacle*: "The organization of alienation and representation in everyday life." Passive, commercialized, few choices. Culture as a commodity.
Social control	*Communion*: The decorum of the crowd the only constraint on behavior. Employees define and constrain	*Coercion*: Coercion of the wage-labor market, of the state and its agents of control; exercised on an

Table 5.1   (Cont.)

Sign system	Disneyland	Los Angeles
	the individual only as part of "the audience" and as a participant in the stage show that is Disneyland.	individual basis, socialization and the tyranny of the group.
Economics	*The market*: Once the initial purchase is made, money is reduced to tickets, choices are displayed as in the market, illusion of cornucopia.	*Capitalism*: Production for profit, pursuit of money out of necessity, the tyranny of the budget.
Politics	*Participatory democracy*: Decisions are made by participants. Individual acts directly on the environment.	*Representative democracy*: Decisions are made for people by their elected representatives in a mystified process of governance.
Family	*Child directed*: Children decide schedule.	*Adult directed*: The hierarchy of home life.

life. (Recently they refused entrance to several "punk rockers" with short hair. In the 1960s they used to prevent long-haired youth from entering the park. Times change but the urge to regulate remains.) People in D-land can often be seen in Hawaiian print shirts or wearing mouse ears and other famous Disney icons. Their clothing signifies their status as workers during leisure time – i.e., during the circulation of people themselves for consumption purposes. In Los Angeles, individuals dress in career-oriented fashions for their roles as part of the labor force; i.e., they "dress for success" or to conform to the appearance expectations of others at work. These styles are dominated by the "logotechniques" of the fashion industry and by class distinctions.

Entertainment

In Disneyland, entertainment is group oriented and presented in a
wide variety of forms, from live music to costumed street theater to
the various rides themselves. In fact, the entire space is a form of
entertainment because it can be read as a motif linked to the entertainment industry of which the Disney corporation is a major part.
Disneyland entertainment captures the feeling of being at the participatory, ludic festival of the medieval city. As a brochure states,

> Up until now, audience participation in entertainment was al-
> most non-existent. In live theater, motion pictures and televi-
> sion the audience is always separate and apart from the actual
> show environment. . . . Walt Disney took the audience out of
> their seats and placed them right in the middle of the action, for
> a total, themed, controlled experience.

The urban cultural element of serendipity[12] thrives in this space, as
live action can pop out at passersby almost anywhere and at any time.
This resurrects the spontaneous, stimulating aspect of the medieval
city because it combines play with independence – the air of freedom.
   In contrast, Los Angeles possesses a pathological form of serendipity: random street violence and one of the highest crime rates in the
country. Several years ago Disneyland had its first shocking crime,
although in the past a few workers have also lost their lives there. A
teenager was stabbed and eventually bled to death. According to news
reports at the time, the park management had insisted that the mor-
tally wounded youngster be taken off the premises to a hospital,
rather than being treated on the scene, and he died en route. Overwhelmingly, however, visitors to the park expect a respite from urban
violence and they are rarely disappointed. As a result, the experience
of Disneyland is manifested, in part, as a deep sigh of relief from the
paranoia and pathology of urban life.
   The culture of Los Angeles, in contrast to the festival of Disneyland, is dominated by the spectacle – i.e., the "organization of alienation and representation in everyday life."[13] The spectacle does not
allow for participation, only passive viewing. Entertainment is the
commercialized commodity of big business and it creates the viewing
subject as passive voyeur, as a member of an audience, not an ambu-
latory participant. In fact, Los Angeles is the production capital of
spectacular culture – the consumerist fantasies and simulations of the
mass media.

Social control

In Disneyland social control is refined to an art, the art of moving crowds by their own motivation instead of coercion. D-land represents the ideal in this regard. It is the perfection of subordination: people digging their own fantasy graves. Los Angeles, in contrast, is the site of the coercive mechanisms of wage labor, ideology, and state power. This space also controls by the separation and isolation of people. As Debord states, "Urbanism is the modern accomplishment of the uninterrupted task which safeguards class power: the preservation of the atomization of workers whom urban conditions of production had dangerously brought together. The constant struggle whichhad to be fought against all aspects of the possibility of encounter finds its privileged field in urbanism."[14]

Economics

Disneyland presents the illusion of cornucopia. After paying a lump sum at the entrance to the park, participants enjoy an abundance of opportunity for amusement. Prior to the 1980s rides were portioned out by varied individual prices, some of which were relatively expensive. Since July 1981 the lump sum payment, which is over $20 a person, now allows visitors to unlimited access to all rides – a true cornucopia, if you can afford the entrance fee.

In the theme park space, class distinctions are minimized and ignored, because the poor have been screened out of the park by the price of admission. In this world, corporate control is benevolent and even paternal. A ride is "brought to you by," "with the compliments of," and "presented by." These epithets are unobtrusive and subliminal. They are extended in the manner of a gift, therefore they invoke the traditional economy of a tribal society. The insidious implication here is that such courtesies are reciprocal.[15] In Los Angeles, by contrast, we have late capitalism with its increasing class divisions, uneven development, production for profit, and periodic crises of accumulation. We also have "symbolic exchange" and an image-driven culture where the gift is only subliminal or the "dead sign" of signification.[16]

Everything in the Los Angeles milieu has a price, and due to stagflation the price keeps rising. There are no bargains outside the park, only the tryanny of the budget. Here corporate control is predatory, not paternal.

Architecture

In Disneyland, the built environment is entertaining. Every edifice has symbolic value (see the paradigmatic analysis below), much as was the case for ancient and medieval cities. Disneyland, as the most successful theme park, helped inaugurate the entertainment culture of postmodernism.[17] It is the ludic town *par excellence*. By contrast, the built environment in Los Angeles possesses limited meaning. It is what Françoise Choay[18] calls "hyposignifiant" – that is, atrophied in meaning and restricted for the most part to the signifying of instrumental function. Los Angeles housing is a sign vehicle for equity or social status, and is built for a profit. Housing design is conformist and regulated through zoning and building codes. Business and commercial establishments are located in functionally designed centers that have only one semiotic value (i.e., monosemic): namely, the signification of the mundane activities of production and consumption themselves.

Politics

Disneyland is also an exercise in group decision making. The goal of social control is ambulation. With crowds moving all the time, it matters little that individuals are allowed to make their own choices about what to do there. In addition, people are ushered out of amusements so fast that they never get to consider whether they should change the ride or make it more to their liking. This participation without social change is like an audience with a powerful religious or political leader, such as the president, and it invokes the child's version of the adult "treat." You are given the honor of a special occasion; whether or not it is satisfying is irrelevant, because the treat is its own reward. Fittingly, Disneyland even includes a special visit to the "greatest" American president of them all, Abraham Lincoln, cloned into action by the hydraulic, plastic technique of audio animatronics to look real.

Finally, Disneyland inverts the structure of family authority. While most families, regardless of class, are adult-directed even if they are child-centered,[19] a visit to D-land is ostensibly for children (or tourist visitors who then are ascribed the status of children). Here the child gets to direct the adults. Invariably they choose the rides, the food, and the schedule. Parents become chaperones or vicarious thrill seekers through the eyes of their own offspring. Once outside the park and back in the quotidian world of Los Angeles, the father returns to his role as "the master,"[20] with both parents reassuming their familial division of labor in "bringing up" the children.

In sum, the urban environment of Disneyland offers a world free from the crisis of the quotidian; free of pathological urban experiences produced by an inequitable and class society such as slums, ghettos, and crime. It is a safe place in all its dimensions, in contrast to the security precautions taken by average citizens even in the privacy of their own homes. Disneyland embraces people in the bosom of a paternal corporate order. It entertains them and stimulates the externalization of their private fantasy lives. Visitors assume the status of a pedestrian wanderer and participate in a festival of self-directed entertainment. This is especially true for children, who get to taste this freedom perhaps for the first time. In contrast to Los Angeles, Disneyland is a ludic, utopian built environment, despite the negative features of its own instrumental purposes and control of the population for profit. It possesses the "illuminating potentiality" of a space occupied by the symbolic and the imaginary,[21] in which something fantastic can and usually is always happening.

Paradigmatic Analysis

As indicated above, the space of Disneyland is subdivided into four separate realms. Each is organized around some distinct, unique theme which derives from the global motif of the park itself, much like the shopping mall. Within these realms elements of the built environment are associated with each other in support of the subdivision's theme. Thus we pass from the theme park as a whole, which is a sign itself, to the subdivided realms, which are also overarching signs, but which derive from the park theme, to the separate elements of the realms, which constitute additional concordant signs. The entire ensemble from theme park to subdivision elements is structured by the associative relationship. Hence, in addition to the operation of metonymy and syntagmatic relations, meaning in the park is also created by metaphorical or paradigmatic relations and intertextuality. The latter associations are many-leveled and also work through the phenomenon of difference.

According to a Disney brochure, "Disneyland was the first to use visually compatible elements working as a coordinating theme avoiding the contradictory 'hodge-podge' of World's Fairs and amusement parks."

This observation about other parks holds as well for the modern city, which also possesses the same anarchy of architectural styles because buildings last longer than the historical change in design fashions. Each of the subspaces of Disneyland, in contrast, is unified by the concordance of associative themes drawing upon the overarching code of the Disney semantic field. For example, Adventureland is designed as a trip to the Third World and recalls the Disney Studio's films about exotic locales. It contains the popular rides "Jungle Safari," which seems located in Africa complete with automated Black "natives" (perhaps the highest minority population in the park), and "Swiss Family Robinson," representing colonialist adventure at its most rustic. Frontierland, in contrast, contains "Tom Sawyer's Island," a Mississippi paddle boat ride to America's past, especially the "Wild West." Fantasyland is the centerpiece of the magic realms and is crowned by the fairy-tale castle of Sleeping Beauty. Tomorrowland presents the world of science and technology at its most spectacular. It includes a trip below the polar ice cap in one of Disney's fleet of "atomic" submarines, and an "outer space" roller coaster ride.

The town areas also contain amusements and are unified around a single theme. New Orleans Square is an open air festival of sidewalk cafes. It is host to the very popular ride "Pirates of the Caribbean", a visit to a treasure trove. On Main Street you can ride in a horse-drawn carriage alongside small shops and pass under the window of Walt Disney's private apartment, where he used to sit in the afternoons and watch the crowds of visitors to his land. Finally, Toontown is a recreation of the land of cartoon characters similar to the world depicted in the film *Roger Rabbit*. It is a space explicitly directed by media fantasies and cartoon images.

Given this appearance, our paradigmatic reading of Disneyland requires us to ask the following question: Is there any underlying semantic field that the associative themes organizing the separate realms tap into and which serves to unify structurally the separate messages? Using socio-semiotic terminology, this question becomes the need to identify the "form of the content," or the codified ideology which articulates with the "substance of the expression" that is the built environment of the park itself.

One way of addressing this question, proceeding socio-semiotically, is by linking the construction of Disneyland – i.e., the production of its space – to the larger society that contains it. Given that we dwell within an American, late capitalist social formation, the separate realms can be viewed as corresponding to the various states of capital or, rather, as linked with the different "faces" of capital throughout the latter's historical development in the United States. This associative link exists at the connotative level necessary for signification; i.e., these places connote such meanings not by their function, but by their appearance and, thus, they become metaphors. They are, in sum, aspects of codified ideology, or the "the form of the content" which inspires the associative realms of Disneyland.

The signifiers "Frontierland," "Adventureland," "Tomorrowland," "New Orleans Square," and "Main Street" can be linked to the signifiers of "the faces of capitalism" as follows:

- Frontierland – predatory capitalism
- Adventureland – colonialism/imperialism
- Tomorrowland – state capitalism
- New Orleans – venture capital
- Main Street – family and competitive capitalism

While "Bear Country" (now defunct) seems a signifier for "the country" or "the idiocy of rural life," Fantasyland signifies bourgeois ideology in mythical form.

In the above associative reading, Disneyland becomes the fantasy world of bourgeois ideology, a kind of capitalist family album documenting the development of its different personality manifestations in the United States and providing the themes for the fantasies of the Disney Corporation. The space of Disneyland has thus been produced by the formal representation of this ideology articulating with the processes of urban construction and real estate development.

Such an analysis, however, leaves us with a puzzle. Disneyland was at one time the most popular attraction in the United States (surpassed now by Disneyworld in Florida, which is ten times its size and the most popular attraction in the world), receiving more visitors each year than even the monuments of the nation's capital.[22] There are, however, many other presentations of bourgeois ideology as entertainment, and there are even other amusement parks offering "fantastic" rides on the same scale. In fact, two of the largest in the United States – Knotts Berry Farm and Magic Mountain, which both surpass Disneyland in size – are located nearby in the Los Angeles area.

We must, therefore, ask the question why Disneyland, in particular, is so much more popular than all these other public amusement places, which might also be analyzed as representations of bourgeois ideology. It is my contention that Disneyland is more than just a showplace of capitalist images. Taking a socio-semiotic perspective in the particular sense, we need to tie this space to the personal context (i.e., the background and intentions) of its creator, Walt Disney. As a corporation brochure states,

> Disneyland, the dream, was born long before 1955, in the creative mind of Walt Disney. As a pioneer in the motion picture industry, Walt developed an intuitive ability to know what was universally entertaining. When his daughters were very young, Walt would take them on what he later called "very unsatisfying visits" to the local amusement parks. He felt there should be something built where parents and children could have fun together. He wanted Disneyland to be a place where "people can experience some of the wonders of life, of adventure and feel better because of it".

The above sentiments are obviously promotional statements, but they constitute a part of the discourse surrounding the codification of a personalized valorization of the park's signifiers. This discursive study, which might begin with the promotional literature on the context of Disney's life and the production of this space from his perspective, can continue with an examination of more detailed accounts of Disney's ideas. In this way we avoid the highly personalized and, often, thoroughly impressionistic "reading" of the park by independent analysts.

Familiarity with Disney's personal background[23] supports a second interpretation of the underlying code from which the signifiers of the park were derived, in addition to capitalist ideology. The literature on Disney's personal experience suggests that Disneyland can also be "read" as a fantastic representation of Walt Disney's lost youth. This connection to a simplified and nurturing small town environment conceived of by Disney may partly explain the popularity of the park. D-land, therefore, stands at the intersection of two overlapping and somewhat contradictory semantic fields, one of which is the ideological representation of the faces of capitalism, as seen above, and the other, the personalized self-expression of its creator. The park is a creation of a corporation that is linked to other corporations, but it is also the artistic production of an exceptional talent that seems capable of entertaining millions of people on an ongoing basis because of the ability to strike some chord or desire within the audience by playing on personalized themes.

Considering the map of Disneyland above (figure 5.1), it is my contention that each of its areas corresponds to compartmentalized aspects of the world of a young boy growing up in a midwestern town. These metaphors are as follows:

- Adventureland – childhood games, comic-strip superheroes, backyard play
- Frontierland – summer vacation, Boy Scouts
- Tomorrowland – spectacular careers in science and technology
- Fantasyland – dreams/fables, bedtime stories

In this schema, which contrasts with the previous interpretation following the codes of capitalism, Adventureland signifies the backyard games or empty-lot world of everyday play among children. This is the staging ground for group games such as "cowboys and Indians" and "Tarzan" or other jungle adventures. Frontierland, in contrast, connotes escape to the rustic regions, such as a camping trip or a summer vacation, especially those family excursions to historical sites and American monuments to the colonial past. Fantasyland connotes the world of dreams and nursery fairy tales, such as the traditional fables brought to the screen by Disney – *Snow White*, *The Three Little Pigs*, and *Cinderella* – which constitute the oral tradition of young people in our society. These are the bedtime stories that Disney knew so well and which enabled him to make his fortune through animation. Little wonder that Sleeping Beauty's castle in Fantasyland has become the centerpiece of the park. Finally, Tomorrowland signifies the world of work and industry as it is presented to children, and not as it is experienced in actuality by adults, such as in the annual "science fairs" of small towns. It is industrial society glamorized with a 1950s sheen so that even the military looks appealing with spectacular, technologically oriented careers in atomic power and outer space.

Disneyland also presents three visits to small towns. Main Street serves as the opening area for people entering the park. It is an icon and is a self-referencing recreation of the small town fetishized by Disney complete with "ma and pa" shops, horse-drawn carriages, and "tin-horn" cops. It is a replicated midwestern settlement space that provides the material foundation for the utopian fantasies in the rest of the area, because it recreates the urban place of Disney's youth. Main Street, in short, may well be the simulated real foundation for the simulated fantasy of the other realms or sections of the park. Main Street is the small-town simulation within which the midwestern boy as adult dreamed the dreamscape of Disneyland.

In contrast, New Orleans Square signifies this same town glamorized in festival form. It is the small town as population center, liberated from the cyclical time of holiday, a perennial celebration with sidewalk cafes and ambulating Dixieland bands. Finally, Bear Country (now defunct), which studies have shown to be the least popular part of the park,[24] signified a visit to rural relatives or the "country bump-kins" who never quite made it to the petit bourgeois life of their small town relatives back on Main Street. These final significations can be illustrated as follows:

- Main Street – small town as icon (as the real foundation for which the other realms represent fantasy worlds)
- New Orleans Square – small town as festival
- Bear Country – lumpen proletarian relatives

Conclusion

Disneyland has been called variously as illusionary, ideological, capi-talist, fantastic, and even utopian by cultural analysts. In some of the more trenchant discussions much has been made of its invocation of the middle-class virtues of small-town, mid-American life, and of the morals and value system of Walt Disney himself.[25] In what ways then, have we improved upon these observations by subjecting Disneyland (and the reader) to an arcane semiotic analysis? It seems that further insight has been derived by demonstrating that this produced space is the juncture of two separate semantic fields, one personal and the other specific to the social formation of late capitalism, which play themselves out in the constructed space of the park. This articulation is a *mythical* construct[26] or hypostatization (see chapter 1) because space defined by capitalism is articulated by space as interpreted from the personalized referent of an idealized youth. The associational axis is many-layered. That is, Disneyland is overdetermined with meaning and mythical in form. No single interpretation can capture the sym-bolic experience of the park.

Disneyland is the myth of small-town America if advanced indus-trial society would have articulated with this settlement space without changing it, except by leveling its class and racial distinctions. It is not only a spatial representation of capitalist ideology, as believed by previous observers, but also the fantasy of a Walt Disney who yearned as much for an idealized youth as he did fetishize the benevolence of the system itself. That is, there is both a social and a personal context to this space. In the larger society, especially Los Angeles, the massive regional suburban environment has evolved from the small town. But there, aerospace industries, mass media, multinational global involvement, and technology have obliterated this form and its social order. Los Angeles is the real future that has unfolded for small-town America. Confronted by this vista, we must pause and wonder why Disneyland has drawn criticism when the area around it represents this acknowledged failure of urban planning.

Disneyland is the wish of its creator and it is as much a reflection of his personalized code as it is of corporate signifiers. In this sense, therefore, it is a consummate, three-dimensional work of populist art entertainment for the masses. It invokes the structure of small-town life, where the only price for participating in the benevolent, moral order of America was the loss of individuality and the adherence to strict social conformity. It is the "happiest place on earth," because many of its visitors, especially those from California, subscribe to the very same values as Disney and come from similar backgrounds. These attitudes have been ignored more by advanced capitalism and its specific urban growth patterns than they have been appropriated by the system for its ideological productions. The park indicates as much about the victimization of small-town life just as it also extols the same system that perpetuated that victimization. This is the contradiction shared by Disney and the larger society in which he lived.

Notes

1 Jean Baudrillard, *America*, translated by C. Turner (New York: Verso, 1988); Sharon Zukin, "Postmodern Urban Landscapes," in *Modernity and Identity*, edited by S. Lash and J. Friedman (Oxford: Blackwell Publishers, 1992), pp. 221–47; see also, Miriam Hansen, "Of Mice and Ducks: Benjamin and Adorno on Disney," *The South Atlantic Quarterly*, 92, 1 (Winter, 1993): 27–61.
2 Jean Baudrillard, *Simulations* (New York: Semiotext(e), 1983), p. 23.
3 See, especially, Sharon Zukin, *Landscapes of Power* (Berkeley: University of California Press, 1991), and "Postmodern Urban Landscapes."
4 In 1993 it was announced by the Disney Corporation that the French theme park was losing so much money that they were considering its closing.
5 M. Real, *Mass Mediated Culture* (Englewood Cliffs, N.J.: Prentice-Hall, 1977).
6 Louis Marin, *Utopics: The Semiological Play of Textual Spaces* (Atlantic Highlands, N.J.: Humanities Press, 1984), pp. 239–59.
7 Alexandros Lagopoulos, "Semiotic Urban Models and Modes of Production," in *The City and the Sign: Introduction to Urban Semiotics*, edited by M. Gottdiener and A. Lagopoulos (New York: Columbia University Press, 1986), pp. 176–201.

8   Walt Disney Productions, n.d., p. 12.
9   Guy DeBord, *Society of the Spectacle* (Detroit: Black and Red, 1970).
10 Robert Kling, Spencer Olin and Mark Poster, *Postsuburban California* (Berkeley: University of California Press, 1991); see also M. Gottdiener, *The New Urban Sociology* (New York: McGraw-Hill, 1994).
11 Lauren Langman, "Neon Cages: Shopping for Subjectivity," in *Lifestyle Shopping: The Subject of Consumption*, edited by R. Shields (New York: Routledge, 1992), pp. 40–82.
12 Henri Lefebvre, *The Production of Space* (Oxford: Blackwell Publishers, 1991).
13 Henri Lefebvre, *Everyday Life in the Modern World*, translated by Sacha Rabinovitch (New York: Harper and Row, 1971); see also DeBord, *Society of the Spectacle*.
14 DeBord, *Society of the Spectacle*, p. 172.
15 Marcel Mauss, *The Gift* (New York: Norton Publishers, 1967); see also Jean Baudrillard, *Symbolic Exchange and Death* (London: Sage, 1993).
16 Baudrillard, *Symbolic Exchange and Death*; Arthur Kroker and David Cook, *The Postmodern Scene* (New York: St Martins Press, 1986).
17 Langman, "Neon Cages."
18 Françoise Choay, "Urbanism and Semiology," in *The City and the Sign*, edited by M. Gottdiener and A. Lagopoulos, pp. 160–175.
19 Herbert J. Gans, *The Levittowners* (New York: Vintage Books).
20 Wilhelm Reich, *The Sexual Revolution* (New York: Farrar, Strauss and Giroux, 1974).
21 Lefebvre, *Everyday Life*.
22 Real, *Mass Mediated Culture*.
23 L. Gartley and E. Lebron, *Walt Disney: A Guide to References and Resources* (Boston: G. K. Hall Publishers, 1979); R. Shickel, *The Disney Version* (New York: Simon and Schuster, 1968); B. Thomas, *The Walt Disney Biography* (New York: Simon and Schuster, 1977).
24 Real, *Mass Mediated Culture*.
25 Ibid.
26 Roland Barthes, *Mythologies*, translated by A. Lavers (New York: Hill and Wang, 1972).

6

Postmodern Architecture and
the City

All those familiar with the founding papers on postmodernism as a
form of cultural studies are also familiar with the central role that
architecture plays in that discussion. The term itself, although used
many years before,[1] was popularized by the architectural critic Charles
Jencks in a speaking tour during the 1970s culminating in his book,
The Language of Post-modern Architecture.[2] Some observers even fix
the advent of the postmodern architectural age at 3:32 PM on July 15,
1972, when that symbol of modernist ideals, the Pruitt-Igoe low-
income housing project, was demolished by the city of St Louis.[3]

Without question the operation of postmodern ideas and their effects on culture is clearest in the case of architecture. On the one
hand, there was and still is an existing ideology of architectural design
that is self-identified as modernism or, more specifically, "high modern." On the other hand, there was and still is an equally clear revolt
against high modernism by a select group of architects, such as Michael
Graves and Robert Stern, whose commissioned buildings are considered "postmodern," and who have also influenced famous "modernist" architects, such as Philip Johnson, to become "postmodern." An
architectural practice, therefore, has resulted in the production of material objects – namely, buildings – that are recognized as exemplifying the "postmodern" style. Above all other cultural manifestations
then, postmodern architecture has tangibly changed the face of our
material environment.

The importance of a postmodern architectural practice can be contrasted, for instance, with the claims of certain writers who *read in* an
interpretation of some city or some built form as exemplifying
"postmodernism" without documenting the nature of the productionist
ideology and its material and symbolic practices. This gesture can
transform just about anything one wishes into some vaguely defined

aspect of cultural change called "postmodernism." Certainly there has
yet to be consensus regarding what this concept means in general.

To be sure, it is always possible to argue for the conception of a
"postmodern" experience on the part of the users or readers of space.
However, this distinction between production, on the one hand, and
conception at the level of consumption, on the other, has been ignored. Instead, critics offering readings of the postmodern simply
provide personal interpretations that lack a grounding in social or,
more specifically, architectural practice[4] and the "dirty" world of
production. The problem with all such personal interpretations of
cultural forms is that they privilege the point of view of the interpreter and neo-Kantian aesthetic criteria which ultimately require
foundations.

The socio-semiotic approach is opposed to this type of interpretive
spatial and material analysis. Yet, the importance of postmodern architecture to cultural change cannot be denied. Through the efforts
of critics like Jencks we, perhaps, have the clearest understanding of
what is meant by the postmodern when it comes to architecture. This
chapter will consider the kind of change it has engendered within the
fabric of the city from a socio-semiotic perspective.

The Language of Postmodern Architecture

Postmodern architecture is articulated as both an ideology and a
material practice. As such it is manifested as both the "form of the
content" and the "form of the expression" of a new architectural sign
which articulates with capitalist production practices to create a
postmodern "substance of the expression" or "sign vehicle" for
postmodern architecture. According to the socio-semiotic perspective, this mode of signification represents codified ideology articulating with materialist practice in the production of space. At the level
of production, meaning is constrained by the norms of architectural
practice. Thus, if there is a "free play" of signifiers, then this
phenomeon, which is usually privileged by postmodern critics, is
specific to the level of consumption and to a "reading of space" alone,
not the production of space. The production of buildings always
involves an articulation between the instrumentality of power and/or
profit taking and aesthetic design practices that expresses the sign
function of the producers. Implicit in this practice may also be designs composed with a particular consumer market in mind, such as
chain restaurants (Denny's, Bob's Big Boy), theme restaurants (oldies
diners, California hamburger shops), theme malls, theme parks, and

the like. Thus, production and consumption ideologies articulate in the construction of buildings.

As an ideology postmodern architecture involves a rejection of the uniform practices of the International School founded in the 1920s and '30s by Walter Gropius, C.-E. Jeanneret (Le Corbusier), and others which was both a generalized ideology of modern life, or the "substance of the content" known as the social ideology of modernism, and a specific ideology of architectural practice, or the "form of the content" known as modernist design principles. Disjunctures between the substance and the form, between the general ideology of the socius and particular architectural practice, produced variations in the designs of modernist architects (and artists) over time.

Postmodern architecture, in contrast, possesses a well-articulated desire to change the appearance of built forms in contradistinction to modernism, just as modernism rejected the eclecticism of the Victorian era, but it possesses only a weakly articulated ideological alternative to the modernist vision of society. I shall return to this important distinction between the two styles in the last section of this chapter. Consequently, postmodern architecture is described almost exclusively as a change in, or *negation* of, the conception of space envisioned by high modernist architects. Its sign possesses an attenuated and limited signified that privileges the "form of the content." The particularized design ideas are formulated in opposition to high modernism, but they lack the kind of generalized articulation of the "ought" that characterized modernism's social theory.

The break with the International School involves a rejection of development on a large, technically rational scale emphasizing the abstract and functionally efficient elements of building, especially a rejection of modernism's privileging of the straight line and the rectangle as forms, and steel and glass as materials. In its place, postmodernism seeks a link with social context and local history (in opposition to abstraction), with a more human scale of design that reasserts a place for intimacy, with an eclectic pastiche of styles that are more self-expressive of locale or the significance of corporate clients, and, at times, with an apotheosis of the vernacular that breaks down the distinction between mass and high cultural forms (see below for examples).

Because postmodernism is a concrete practice of architects, it is possible to show how, on the one hand, this ideology is central to many of the main ideas of the currently emerging "theory of postmodernism," and, on the other, how the performative disjunctures and immanent critiques of postmodern architectural practice limit the significance or relevance of postmodern cultural change despite the globalized claims of its high priests. In what follows I shall address each of these issues. I shall then apply the socio-semiotic method to a concrete examination of postmodern material forms by way of both appreciation and critique for what has been accomplished, and, in a final section, I shall discuss how the advent of postmodern architecture relates to changes in the city and especially why the concept of a "postmodern city" is fallacious.

The Centrality of Postmodern Architecture in Postmodern Theory

Two-thirds of the way through Fredrick Jameson's[5] monumental statement on the postmodern as a cultural dominant, he states: "It is in the realm of architecture, however, that modifications in aesthetic production are most dramatically visible, and that their theoretical problems have been most centrally raised and articulated; it was indeed from architectural debates that my own conception of postmodernism . . . initially began to emerge."[6]

According to Jameson, the revolt against high modernism or the International School drove a new aesthetic consciousness which objected to the work of architecture as a free-standing sculpture divorced from the historical and environmental context.[7] Borrowing from the ideas of Robert Venturi, postmodernists also sought to break with the formative disjuncture between high and mass forms of culture practiced by modernists by preaching an "aesthetic populism." For Jameson, "The new postmodern buildings no longer attempt, as did the masterworks and monuments of high modernism, to insert a different and elevated, new utopian language into the city fabric, but rather to seek a vernacular lexicon that reflects the mass tastes."[8]

Jameson, however, makes a curious choice to illustrate these ideas in practice. He uses the Western Bonaventure Hotel in downtown Los Angeles as his example. There are some very interesting aspects of this constructed space designed by John Portman, but Jameson's choice contradicts his claims about the specificity of the postmodern. Simply put, it would be hard to find better examples of buildings that exist as radical disjunctures from their historical and social contexts as the creations of Portman, especially the Bonaventure Hotel. As Mike Davis has observed, a few short blocks from this hotel exists the "other" of Los Angeles, the original pueblo site both recolonized by United States capitalism and unevenly developed into slums: the space of homelessness, low-rent ethnicity, racial exclusion and despair.

From a socio-semiotic perspective the Bonaventure Hotel is an example of postmodernism only because Jameson has said so.[9] Portman's design clearly rejects the canon of modernism. But his creations are more unique and stand independently aside from the many consciously produced postmodern buildings that have appeared recently. I would call Portman an anti-modernist architect, but, unless the term postmodernism lacks any specificity, I would not consider his designs postmodern (and wonder if any ever bothered to ask him about the label). The Bonaventure, however, does provide examples of a new use of space, and Jameson is quite accurate in his assessment of this experience. At the level of the readings of space, some new and interesting relations have been introduced by Portman's design. Thus, in this and other examples of postmodern cultural criticism, it is the consumption of material culture, or a reading by a specially situated and elitist user, which is privileged. Confining observations to the phenomenological experience of the new cultural changes is not, however, without its insights.

The Bonaventure, Portman's Hyatts, and his other creations – Peachtree Plaza in Atlanta and The Renaissance Center in Detroit – are very much like the fully enclosed shopping mall (see chapter 4). They are self-contained worlds which, when entered, unfold into a massive interior space that contains a quasi-public environment, much like the introversion of a large Mayan temple, in the case of the Hyatts, or a cylindrical, glass-enclosed Oz, as in the case of the Bonaventure. As Jameson notes, the hotel has three entrances but none are on the main floor and they only afford access that is a distance away from the main desk: "the entryways of the Bonaventura [sic] are, as it were, lateral and rather back door affairs." This contrasts with the monumental marquees of older hotels that announce their entrance at the street level with doormen, red carpets and valets.

Once inside, "you are immersed without any of that distance that formerly enabled the perception of perspective or volume. You are in this hyperspace up to your eyes and your body" . . . and, in the lobby, "milling confusion, something like the vengeance this space takes on those who still seek to walk through it. Given the absolute symmetry of the four towers, it is quite impossible to get your bearings in this lobby."[10] This observation, which is quite accurate, is very much like the experience of the fully enclosed mall.

For Jameson, this "postmodern hyperspace," or the collapse of perspective in the immense, disorienting spaces of the new buildings, has finally succeeded in transcending the capacities of the individual human body to locate itself, to organize its immediate surroundings

perceptually, and cognitively to map its position in a mappable exter-
nal world."[11] Hyperspace, and the disorientation, the supra-individual
experience of space that it engenders, is very important to Jameson's
argument that postmodernism is a periodized stage of capitalism. As
he suggests,

> this alarming disjunction point between the body and its built
> environment . . . can itself stand as the symbol and analogue of
> that even sharper dilemma which is the incapacity of our minds,
> at least at present, to map the great global multinational and
> decentered communicational network in which we find ourselves
> caught as individual subjects.[12]

At this point in Jameson's commentary he switches from a
phenomenological reading of the interior space to pure nominalist
discourse. Dependent as he is on creating metaphors for the principal
architectural change – namely, the closure of the space itself – as
"postmodernism" and as the "symbol and analogue" of late capitalism, his interpretation ignores specification according to the system
of signification of the architectural signifiers and leads the way, instead, to contradiction. The introverted construction of the hotel, like
the fully enclosed mall, which is separate from its social context and
from the city – indeed, functioning, as Jameson states, as an alternative to the city – contradicts what others say are the core elements of
postmodern architectural practice. In the end, then, Jameson leaves us
only with his metaphors for global capitalism as an independent reading of the phenomenology of space, despite its important insights.

Yet, we cannot deny that the new architectural practice has produced cultural change. In particular, the appearance of buildings with
self-contained, immense interior spaces for hotels, shopping centers
and mixed-use residential/shopping complexes constitutes a design
logic that supercedes high modernism. In some of the better examples
of this type of construction, such as the immense scale of the Mall of
America in Minnesota, or of Disneyworld in Florida, the inside/out-
side and building-to-building relations of the old urban fabric have
been rejected in favor of a new, introverted, and self-contained model
of space.

Change, therefore, has occurred, but we need to look elsewhere to
obtain a clearer understanding of postmodern architectural practice,
since these hyperspaces may simply represent another mode of construction without a postmodernist ideology and may, in fact, be better

described as anti-International style, which is neither postmodern nor even anti-modern.

Anti-Modernism and Postmodernism

There is ample evidence that a full revolt against modernism exemplifies much architectural practice today. This anti-modernism has attacked not only the design ideology of modernism, but also its emancipatory and utopian ideology which has given birth, through its own immanent contradictions, to concentration camps and the tedium of Stalinist city planning. According to Leon Krier, once described as the "Le Corbusier of the New Right,"[13] "Modernism has fathered a meaningless uniformity and uniform meaningless. Mies and Aalto are fine brothers in arms. Stark puritanism and bizarre expressionism . . . are symptoms of the same derangement . . . Auschwitz, Birkenau and Milton Keynes [a new town in England] are children of the same parents."

Harris and Lipman[14] suggest that one strain of anti-modernism represents a patrician return to conservative, classical roots of western civilization. This is meant to anchor social life at a time when it is experiencing rapid change, much in the way conservative critics such as Bell, Bloom, and Lasch argue for a reassertion of traditional social values. Scott Lash[15] calls attention to the same strain of thought and identifies the return to the classics as a motif of postmodern architecture. He quotes the architect Charles Moore, who says,

> The psychic spaces and shapes of buildings should assist the human memory in restructuring connections through time and space . . . so that those of us who lead lives complicatedly divorced from a single place in which we can find roots, can have through the channels of our memories, through the agency of building, something like these roots restored.[16]

The classical variant of the new anti-modernist ideology can also be exemplified by remarks made in a famous speech by Prince Charles: "architects have consistently ignored the feelings and wishes of the mass of ordinary people in this country . . . Why can't we have those curves and arches that express feeling in design? What is wrong with them? Why has everything got to be vertical, straight, unbending, only at right angles – and functional?"[17]

A second strain of anti-modernism that is identified with an emergent postmodern architectural ideology has been called "anthropometrism."[18] Revolting against the massive scale of the modernist design ethos (presumably a second way to see the contradiction in Jameson's use of Portman), postmodernists seek a human scale to design. Some examples of anthropometrism as postmodernism are Robert Krier's use of the human body as a column, thereby figuring the body itself once again as the "measure of all things" (and taken to a level of postmodern parody in the Disney headquarters at Burbank; see below); the deconstruction of the modernist rectangle by Eisenman or Gehry which explodes the box and makes its parts more accessible; or the scaling down of public space through the use of pedestrian streets and house porches by town planner Duany.

A third and final characteristic of anti-modernism that has been associated with an emergent postmodernism counters the patrician search for classical grounding with a celebration of the vernacular or populist forms of building. This strain of thinking was most coherently stated by Robert Venturi and associates in 1980 with the book *Learning from Las Vegas*. This return to populism, however, was based less on postmodernist ideology and more on an anti-modernism, as Venturi states: "The forms of Modern architecture have been created . . . at the expense of their symbolic meanings derived from association . . . Early Modern architects scorned recollection (symbolism) . . . rejected eclecticism and style . . . in their almost exclusively technology-based architecture."[19]

The populist strain of postmodernism is well represented by architects and critics who celebrate the vernacular forms of building, such as fast-food stands, trompe l'oeil murals, streamlined coffee shops (Ships in Los Angeles), car washes, motels, Morris Lapidus' hotels in 1930s Miami, neon signs, and so on. The apotheosis of the vernacular also involves the breakdown between high and mass culture. Theme parks are now considered postmodern (but see chapter 5), especially Disneyland and Disneyworld. Exemplary are the hotels designed by Michael Graves at Disneyworld: "Graves chose friendly animal-and-water motifs that mediate the natural environment of South Florida and the artifice that created Mickey and Minnie as cultural icons. But the hotels are also monumental in scale and lavish in their treatment of space."[20]

The postmodern architect Robert A. M. Stern argues that populist architecture can also assume classical proportions by connecting with history and social context, even if these referents are relatively recent creations themselves. The Disney headquarters in Burbank, California, which Stern designed, sports a peaked roof held up by human-sized columns (see Krier, above) in the shapes of the seven dwarfs.

With this gesture Stern pays homage to the corporate sponsor of the building. He also allows for a ludic dimension in postmodern architecture that has been praised but not frequently emulated.

In sum, while there is a general consensus that "The Modern Movement in architecture is dead,"[21] the present represents a disconnected melange of different anti-modern styles. Clearly, it is the sheer nature of the present eclecticism that perhaps can be pointed to as the singular characteristic of postmodernism, rather than some articulated transcendent ideology. In fact, the latter does not exist in a positive sense, only as a negation, as a critique of modernism. In place of some unified ideology we have, instead, a series of anti-modernist ideologies and anti-modernist design practices that celebrate eclecticism and the synthesis of styles. As such, modernist ideology remains the referent creating the *difference* in the postmodernist architectural sign. That is, despite the furor over the failings of modernism, the latter still operates in the minds of architects and in their practice. In its negativity, modernism still exists. The view that postmodernism expresses negation will be explored more fully below.

The transformation of the built environment by postmodernist/anti-modernist practice

The above assessment of the ideologies of postmodernist architecture and cultural criticism represent only one way of coming to terms with cultural change. Anti-modernist and postmodernist architectural practices have also transformed the built environment. Genuine material changes have occurred in contemporary spatial environments. Consequently, this cultural transformation is amenable to socio-semiotic analysis. Furthermore, the accomplishments of the new modes of architectural practice can be assessed and their contradictions isolated for future use as referents and sources of difference. That is, by analyzing the performative successes and failures of postmodern architecture, it is also possible to point towards some new directions in the desire to escape from modernism which may also supercede what is called "postmodernism."

I prefer to begin a socio-semiotic analysis of the contemporary urban environment not with the buildings themselves but with change as confronted by city dwellers – that is, the users of space, who are often ignored in architectural criticism. Thus, I start at the same place as Jameson: namely, a reading at the level of the consumption of space.

Greimas[22] observes that the urban inhabitant relates to city space according to the axiological distinction of "euphoria/dysphoria." In this sense, the individual's response to the city corresponds to the contrast between the aspirations of architects, planners, and politicians promoting some academic notion of utopia, and the dystopia revealed by the everyday statistics on crime, traffic congestion, housing, and pollution, or by the grisly future projections of city life found in recent Hollywood films. We locate the urban experience somewhere between paradise and hell, between ecstacy and terror.

Yet the hedonistic orientation of the urban dweller is simply a device to enable negotiation through settlement space. Thus, the user of the city navigates among various uncomfortable conditions produced by the dynamics of dense population concentration, massive regional growth, and uneven socio-spatial development in late capitalism. Pleasure is not connected to some larger vision of a liberated city that has been effectively realized by architects and planners. It is solely a function of the *ex post* realization that everyday chores and tasks have been somehow performed without an encounter with urban disaster – i.e., pleasure as the avoidance of pain. This increasingly problematic everyday life and the large pleasures that are now obtained when the simplest daily tasks are performed without tragedy is exemplified by the film *Grand Canyon*.

As Ledrut[23] observes, however, the reduction of city living to the hedonistic oppositions noted by Greimas is a direct outcome of the powerlessness and marginality of the typical city dweller. As he states, "the 'ordinary inhabitant,' entirely powerless in regard to urban development and totally marginalized, cannot but withdraw into purely affective relations with the city which tend to become more and more infantile and phantasmal." Were inhabitants also producers of the built environment and able to articulate their needs directly, this disjuncture between pleasure and pain would not be the basis for the urban experience.

Thus, more often than not, the city inhabitant encounters architecture, even in its magnificent postmodernist variant, without inspiration, as only the backdrop to the daily schedule's regimen of commuting, work, and consumption. Buildings stand principally as "sign functions," as indexes for work, shopping, and elite social institutions. This contrasts with the kind of signification characteristic of cities in the past that endowed buildings with richly textured symbolism and monumental scope. The modern (or postmodern) experience of the built environment lapses into passivity and distraction, as Walter Benjamin[24] observed – a perception of the material world only in passing while on the way to the next stop in the daily routine.

According to one variant of postmodern architecture, designs intentionally connect to some aspect of the historical social context in an effort to supercede the monumental, self-referential architecture of high modernism. The purposive links to the larger society of postmodernism, however, are manifested only at the level of the "form of the expression," as the morphological elements that comprise the new architectural practice. They do not invoke new signifieds of use or habitation among city dwellers, but only connect with signifiers dredged up from the past by architectural practice. Lash[25] is correct to term this movement one of "historicity" rather than "historicism" because it is selective, eclectic, and lacks the coherence of a true historic revival.

On the one hand, meaning in the built environment is revived after years of minimalist and functionally defined signification by the International style because of the introduction of new design elements in architectural practice. On the other hand, the re-establishment of the architectural sign is a limited gesture that does not complete the semiotic circle to transform the role of the inhabitants. All efforts at innovation and at articulating the postmodern sign retain their focus on reproducing the status of the user as consumer. As Harris and Lipman[26] note, whether we consider the patrician or the populist strains of postmodernism, its architectural practice remains elitist and in the service of corporate capitalism.

According to Françoise Choay,[27] the modernist city was all function and form, leaving it "hyposignifiant" – i.e., without deep-level or second-order signifieds. This minimalist signification contrasts with the rich, symbolic texture of classical and pre-industrial settlement space.[28] Hyposignification is represented by the twin towers of the World Trade Center in New York, which may also represent the apogee of modernist architecture. As Baudrillard[29] suggests, the two virtually identical towers constitute a binary opposition in which the tension of difference or signification has been eradicated. Meaning is replaced by cloning, by reproduction according to the modernist model (also exemplified by Tom Wolfe's "rue of regret" – i.e., Avenue of Americas above 42nd Street in New York City) with buildings merely referencing or reflecting their own image.

Postmodern architecture, in contrast, revives meaning in the urban fabric. By re-introducing new architectural facades at the level of the "substance of the expression," through the deployment of a new design ideology at the level of the "form of the content" and matching morphological design elements at the level of the "form of the expression," postmodern construction creates new sources of contextual

difference within the city. Signification is revived, but only metonymically, at the level of appearance as the texture of contiguous relations between building and building is changed. The new meaning of
the city is not produced by architecture, despite the revival of architectural semiosis, but by the changed nature of social relationships
within the city that are functions of a rapidly restructured society
under conditions of late capitalism.

Postmodern design practice creates difference in a variety of ways.
At times new buildings possess environmental referents and may involve the judicious placement of structures with facades indented and
turned toward the axis of the sun in order to maximize reflections at
sunrise and sunset. Elsewhere, the pyramiding or peaking of formerly
flat office building roofs becomes a means both of escaping from the
constraints of the International style and of bringing back environmental sense to rooftops that must deal with the elements – snow,
rain, and the like.

In other cases, the architectural signifier recirculates symbols of the
past in stylized forms. This more contemporary version of "le retro,"
whether it is expressed as pastiche, raw postmodern eclecticism, or
more systematic gestures, serves to infuse symbolism in the urban
milieu after years of barren modernist minimalism. The new postmodern language revives the architectural sign both at the level of the
"form of the content," through syntagmatic difference with the modernist style, and at the level of the "form of the expression," through
development of paradigmatic design choices that have become the
repertoire of postmodern practice.

Intentional changes have now been systematized by a meta-
ideology of postmodern criticism and architectural discourse. Postmodern practice is no longer perceived as idiosyncratic or isolated
examples of momentary design lapses. It supplies new meanings
through both paradigmatic and syntagmatic contrasts or differences.
Yet, for the inhabitants of the built environment, the city remains
very much as it has in the past. Architecture stands, as it always has,
as the representation of real estate interests, growth networks promoting boosterism, corporations promoting signature building or
profit making theme environments, and elite city interests in competition with elites located in other cities.

In sum, postmodernist architecture provides a more robust language for the urban fabric, but it remains a language of exchange
value with much the same message as in the past. Inhabitants remain
consumers and, as users, they key into constructed space according to
the same first-order denotative signs of the functionalist, modernist

city. The bank or telephone company office building remains for the city dweller – despite being redesigned, as the AT&T building by Philip Johnson in New York was, along postmodern lines – a bank or large, impersonal and profit-making bureaucracy.

What remains different in the urban context is the growing gap between the renewed vitality of city life represented by the restructured, postmodern center and the contrasting surrounding area that is afflicted with the pathological effects of uneven capitalist development. Over the past several decades that gap between affluence and poverty, or the paradox of the contiguous relation between wealth and impoverishment, has increased and become more pathological in the city. The everyday life of inhabitants has deteriorated at the same time that the accomplishments of the revolt against modernism represented by the postmodern signify a new, more robust architectural practice. This is both the immanent critique of postmodernism and the fallacy of its ambitions towards difference.

Why There Is No Postmodern City

I shall conclude this chapter with a review of some recent writing that argues for the perception of the contemporary city as a manifestation of postmodernism. Socio-semiotically speaking, this claim is fallacious because it implies the universal semanticization of the contemporary built environment by the ideology of postmodernism. Almost all cities are polysemic agglomerations of historically variant design practices. Only some ancient cities (see chapter 3) and specific current examples, such as Brasilia or Soviet town planning, exemplify universal semanticization.

According to Zukin,[30] postmodernism is a social process of dissolution and redifferentiation: "The social process of constructing a postmodern landscape depends on an economic fragmentation of older urban solidarities and a reintegration that is heavily shaded by new modes of cultural appropriation."

This is the kind of writing that says nothing. It is so general that it can apply equally to modernism, or any other global change in architectural practice. It ignores the issues of agency, periodization, contingency, and a theorization of social change. In short, it is quite representative of most writing by academics on "postmodernism." What we are really being offered is an impressionistic, personalized reading of space (see above). As in the case of Jameson, buildings are singled out, not just as examples of change, but as exemplars of postmodernism. This kind of interpretation seeks to turn a tendency

into a universal semanticization of the built environment. It also ignores the articulation of ideology and material culture at the level of
the production of space. That is, it proceeds without an examination
of productionist ideology, of the interests of designers and corporate
sponsors, and of the instrumental, functional purpose for the production of space in the global system of capitalism.

Writers have felt free to proclaim the advent of a postmodern city,[31]
postmodern planning,[32] or more evasively, a postmodern urban condition.[33] What they really all point to are examples at the level of an
independent reading of the signifiers (i.e., of the material forms) and
the changed nature of the urban fabric due to new construction which
are nominally and metaphorically claimed to stand in for or represent
something more than the material environment – namely, the idealist
personification of a productionist ideology "postmodernism." As
discussed in the last section, this is a very limited way to analyze
social change.

The privileging of changes in appearance by those commenting on
the advent of a postmodern city can be exemplified by what is noticed
most. According to Zukin,

> Pressed for examples they all point to the same illustrations.
> They understand a postmodern urban landscape in terms of tall,
> sleek towers that turn away from the street using technology to
> create self-contained worlds . . . On the other hand, a postmodern
> urban landscape refers to the restoration and redevelopment of
> older locales, their abstraction from a logic of mercantile or
> industrial capitalism, and their renewal as up-to-date consump-
> tion spaces behind red-brick or cast-iron facades of the past.[34]

Not only do these changes owe more to a generalized ideology of
anti-modernism than postmodernism, but very little can be understood about social change if analysis never fails to pierce behind the
level of appearance to deeper exploration of changes in design practices. In the above discussion, a socio-semiotic analysis revealed that
postmodern architecture can be best specified as a negation of modernism's design ideology. This negation makes for a new source of
difference in the city fabric and, consequently, a new source of architectural meanings at the level of sign vehicles – i.e., the "substance of
the expression" – alone. Despite the claims of academic interpreters,
these changes produced by a negative moment in response to
modernism do not constitute a "new" city fabric or in any sense a

specifically postmodern city. The limitations of postmodern changes can be highlighted by comparison with modernism.

Recall that the modernist ethos, as exemplified by the ideas of Gropius, Le Corbusier, and their followers, represented a consciously subversive gesture. Modernism sought a total rupture with the fabric of bourgeois society and its neo-classical forms that dripped with patrician symbolism, not the re-introduction of difference through contiguous contrast with its urban fabric, as in the case of post-modernism.[35] Modernism sought equality of space, uniformity of design, and simplicity through the unadulterated celebration of the straight line, the rectangle, and the circle. Modern technology, such as the automobile and the telephone, were to be harnessed to provide people with a new city, a radiant city, that would flow efficiently from the uniformly designed working-class highrises to the new matching factories connected by wide boulevards exclusively for use by automobiles. The design of home, work, and recreation, the shape of the inside and the outside, would all follow the same principles and forms of design. In sum, modernism was not only the negation of premodernist design ideology, its "form of the content," but a further negation of that negation which was expressed as a mode of totality, an ideology of social life, a totalizing "substance of the content" that was meant to replace entirely bourgeois society.

Modernist architecture and the modernist city, in short, were intimately linked by the conceptions of space of the founding members of the International School, Gropius and Le Corbusier, in particular. As is well known, this urban ideology articulated with the ideology of socialism.[36] Modernism at the Bauhaus, for example, became a design practice pertinent to the production of workers' houses, of retirement homes, of mass home furnishings, of the perfection of industrialism, advanced technology of transport, and the use of modern architectural materials.

By the 1960s in the United States, the limitations of the modernist movement were already apparent. The social project of anti-bourgeois sentiments and the pursuit of equality and democratic city living, which embodied the general ideology of modernism, were already abandoned. All that remained was the particular design ideology of the International School which produced the physical, material examples of the modern style sponsored by the emerging multinational corporations. Architects such as Mies van der Rohe labored in the service of corporate America and its elite institutions, feeding the voracious need of global capitalism to consolidate a material hold on the center of the city for the coordination of its activities. In city after city, quaint and picturesque downtowns were replaced by rectangular highrises with flat roofs that celebrated the hegemony of corporate capital in sterile steel and glass. The physical form of modernism made all large cities look the same by the 1970s, but the utopian and socially transformative vision of the modernist project had been long abandoned.

The result was both a new, gigantic scale in the relationship between people and their buildings, and an attenuation of the building-to-building relationship within the urban fabric, since all structures took on the appearance of the International style clone. Due to the former, the city assumed a new sense of alienation and dehumanization – a result that constituted the fundamental legacy of the modernist project, its immanent critique, its failure – the death of urban life. Jean Baudrillard is correct in his assessment of the twin Trade Towers as the apogee of modernism. They are the eradication of all meaning by the self-referencing process of cloning characteristic of modernist architecture.

The social ideology of modernism was not ignored or abandoned everywhere. In England and even the USSR it informed ideas of city planning. Here too modernism failed to make the clean break from the previous society because, as a mode of architecture, it could never divorce itself from service to the elites of society. Architecture's bane is that it is an elitist practice because it is part of the productionist effort of stratified society. The generalized social ideology of modernism led to the production of the only modernist city, which is also its most monumental failure: namely, Brasilia. As brilliantly analyzed by James Hoston,[37] because Brasilia was designed from scratch as a new city and as the capital of Brazil, it provided the occasion for the totalizing design practices of the general social ideology of modernism – that is, its universal semanticization. As an environment within which people have now lived for several decades, it provides evidence for the contradictions of this same totalizing discourse.

In Brasilia, the death of the street in the design of movement which privileged the automobile became the death of urban culture. The large superblocs destroyed the quest for community, much in the same way that this need was thwarted by material design in the low-income housing projects inspired by Le Corbusier and built in the United States. The class segregation between professional bureaucrats and their office workers, for whom the city was intended, and the lower-paid service workers that were marginalized by Brazilian society resulted in the creation of two cities, one privileged, the other peripheralized in favellas. The open space and superhuman-scaled throughways, plazas, and flat concrete vistas became the ideal hunting grounds for muggers and other criminals. Transparent windows facilitated the panoptic gaze and gave precedence to the social rather than the personal scale of daily life. They also fostered new heights of individual alienation. In short, immanent critique compounded immanent critique, contradiction compounded contradiction as the lived experience of Brasilia as *the* modern city negated the well-articulated social ideology of modernism. In effect, by the 1970s modernism had already died as a source of inspiration through its own contradictions. The postmodern change only faced inertia, not active ideological belief or vision. Hence, it needed no social vision of its own.

The more things change . . .

Postmodernism has not produced a "substance of the expression" that could be called a postmodern city, in contrast to modernism. In keeping with the elitism of architecture in the United States, it exemplifies practice without social vision. As we have seen, however, it has produced, through negation, new signifiers and new expressions of architectural practice that reject the totalizing and austere conventions of modernist architecture. The main effect of postmodernism has been the re-introduction of architectural semiosis through the creation of difference within the city fabric. To claim, however, that some postmodern city has been produced through this practice goes too far and also reveals the idealist nature of much writing about "postmodern" change.

The study of change in the city must look elsewhere for substance. What is new and different, and even disconcerting, is the changed nature of social relations within the city (as indicated above). Violent and random crime, new immigrant groups and a changing social order, housing crises and homelessness, graphic contrasts between poverty and affluence, hyper-ghettoization of blacks, new forms of amusement and "pleasure places," a veritable cornucopia of eating experiences, new stages for the voyeur, flaneur, poseur.[38] In short, a new, heightened and, perhaps, "postmodern" calculus of pleasure and pain which simultaneously attracts and repels, which affirms the best but demonstrates the worst, of what we now call everyday life.

Notes

1   Ihab Hassan, "The Culture of Postmodernism," *Theory Culture and Society*, 2 (1985): 119–131; see also *The Postmodern Turn* (Columbus: Ohio State University Press).

2 Charles Jencks, *The Language of Post-Modern Architecture* (New York: Rizzoli, 1977). For a summary discussion of modern architecture and examples, see Leonardo Benevolo, *History of Modern Architecture*, translated by H. Laudry (London: Routledge and Kegan Paul, 1971); Kenneth Frampton, *Modern Architecture, 1851–1945* (New York: Rizzoli, 1983); Manfredo Tafuri and Francesco Dal Co, *Modern Architecture*, translated by Robert Wolf (New York: H. N. Abrams, 1979).

3 David Harvey, *The Postmodern Condition* (Oxford: Blackwell Publishers, 1989).

4 See, especially, Ed Soja, *Postmodern Geography* (London: Verso, 1988) and Sharon Zukin, *Landscapes of Power* (Berkeley: University of California Press, 1991), for personalized, impressionistic accounts of sociospatial change.

5 Fredrick Jameson, "Postmodernism, or the Cultural Logic of Late Capitalism," *New Left Review*, 146 (1984): 53–92; see also the extended, book-length discussion of these ideas in *Postmodernism, or the Cultural Logic of Late Capitalism* (London: Verso, 1992).

6 Jameson, "Postmodernism," p. 54.

7 Most of these issues had already been raised, albeit in a hackneyed way, by Tom Wolfe, *From Bauhaus to Our House* (New York: Farrar Straus & Giroux, 1981).

8 Jameson, "Postmodernism," p. 81.

9 For some unknown reason Jameson spells the name of this hotel "Bonaventura," which is incorrect.

10 Jameson, "Postmodernism," p. 82.

11 Ibid.

12 Ibid.

13 Howard Harris and Alan Lipman, "Viewpoint: A Culture of Despair: Reflections on 'Post-Modern' Architecture," *The Sociological Review* 34, 4 (1986): 837–54, p. 838.

14 Ibid.

15 Scott Lash, "Postmodernism as Humanism?: Urban Space and Social Theory," unpublished manuscript (University of Lancaster, 1989).

16 Ibid., p. 5.

17 The Prince of Wales, "Give Us Design with Feeling," *The Times*, May 31, 1984, p. 16, as quoted in Harris and Lipman, "Viewpoint," p. 387.

18 Lash, "Postmodernism as Humanism?", p. 5.

19 Robert Venturi, Denise S. Brown, and Steven Izenour, *Learning from Las Vegas: The Forgotten Symbolism of Architectural Form* (Cambridge, Mass.: MIT Press, 1980), as quoted in Harris and Lipman, "Viewpoint," p. 843.

20 Sharon Zukin, "Postmodern Urban Landscapes," in Scott Lash and Jonathan Friedman, *Modernity and Identity* (Oxford: Blackwell Publishers, 1992), p. 235.

21 Harris and Lipman, "Viewpoint," p. 837.

22 Algirdas Greimas, "For a Topological Semiotics," in *The City and the*

Sign: An Introduction to Urban Semiotics, edited by M. Gottdiener and A. Lagopoulos (New York: Columbia University Press, 1986), pp. 25–54.

23 Raymond Ledrut, "The Images of the City", in *The City and Sign*, edited by M. Gottdiener and A. Lagopoulos, pp. 219–40.

24 Walter Benjamin, *Illuminations* (New York: Schocken Books, 1969).

25 Lash, "Postmodernism as Humanism?", p. 19.

26 Harris and Lipman, "Viewpoint."

27 Françoise Choay, "Urbanism and Semiology," in *The City and the Sign*, edited by M. Gottdiener and A. Lagopoulos, pp. 160–75.

28 Alexandros Lagopoulos, "Semiotic Urban Models and Modes of Production," in *The City and the Sign*, edited by M. Gottdiener and A. Lagopoulos, pp. 176–201.

29 Jean Baudrillard, *Simulations* (New York: Sociotext(e), 1983).

30 Zukin, "Postmodern Urban Landscapes," p. 221.

31 Philip Cooke, "The Postmodern Condition and the City," *Comparative Urban and Community Research*, 1 (1988): 62–81.

32 Michael Dear, "Postmodernism and Planning," *Environment and Planning D: Society and Space*, 4 (1986): 367–84; Mike Davis, "Urban Renaissance and the Spirit of Postmodernism," *New Left Review*, 151 (1985): 106–13; Soja, *Postmodern Geography*.

33 Harvey, *Postmodern Condition*; Mike Davis, *City of Quartz* (London: Verso, 1990).

34 Zukin, "Postmodern Urban Landscapes," p. 227.

35 For a discussion of the contradictions of modernism, see James Hoston, *The Modernist City* (Chicago: University of Chicago Press, 1989). For other statements on the social aspects of the modernist movement in architecture see: Manfredo Tafuri, *Architecture and Utopia* (Cambridge, Mass.: MIT Press, 1976); Walter Gropius, *The Scope of Total Architecture* (New York: Collier, 1966); Elizabeth Wilson, *The Sphinx in the City: Urban Life, the Control of Disorder and Women* (Berkeley: University of California Press, 1991); Brent Brolin, *The Failure of Modern Architecture* (New York: Van Nostrand Reinhold, 1976); Alberto Perez Gomez, *Architecture and the Crisis of Modern Science* (Cambridge, Mass.: MIT Press, 1983); Tom Wolfe, *From Bauhaus to Our House* (New York: Farrar Straus & Giroux, 1981).

36 Hoston, *Modernist City*; Tafuri, *Architecture and Utopia*.

37 See note 35, above.

38 Benjamin, *Illuminations*; see also Iain Chambers, *Popular Culture: The Metropolitan Experience* (New York: Methuen, 1986); for a review of current changes in cities due to restructuring see *Urban Life in Transition*, edited by M. Gottdiener and C. G. Pickvance (Newbury Park, Calif.: Sage, 1991).

7

The Political Economy of Postmodernism: The Signs of Growth

Architectural semiotics takes for its object of analysis individual buildings and/or spaces. When dealing with forms of settlement space as a whole, however, such as cities and regions, it is necessary to pass from architectural to spatial semiotics. This is so because of the failure of the former to extend itself successfully from the analysis of spatial units to the agglomeration of those units. Early optimism that textual analysis and Lacanian insights regarding behavior could support an urban semiotics based on discourse with the city considered as a text[1] has given way to a more sober inquiry, grounded as much on the limits of an urban semiotics as on its possibilities.[2] In particular, as Ledrut has shown, any contemporary city is but a hodgepodge of different historical styles of building whose intertextuality involves, at the level of production, a number of separate intentional constructions spanning many decades. Multivocity also exists at the level of the consumption of space, because the city means many things to different people. Hence the city is only a "pseudo-text."

At least two distinct trains of thought attempt to capture the articulation of polysemic modes of meaning and the built environment. On the one hand, exploration into the semiotics of objects in general as applied to the question of meaning in space has moved urban semiotics away from the universal semantization of usage[3] and towards the work of Prieto,[4] culminating in the synthesis of semiotics with psychology, as in the approach of Krampen.[5] On the other hand, the limitation of approaches to urban semiotics of all kinds which does not account for its social nature and the role of groups or classes in sustaining spatial meanings has inspired a synthesis of spatial semiotics with sociology – namely, socio-semiotics, the approach of this volume. In both cases the process of semiosis no longer accounts for the whole of social behavior but is downgraded as only one of several social practices including as well the exo-semiotic or materialist processes involving the production of space (see chapters 4 and 5).[6]

The socio-semiotic approach, in contrast, views meaning as the set of codified ideologies which articulate with the exo-semiotic processes of economic and politico-juridical relations. These codes derive from socially sustained conceptions rather than individual perception alone; i.e., they are interactive products. Both the production of meaning in space and its consumption by users rely on connotative ideological practices that precede denotation. Thus, denotative sign functions which tag aspects of the built environment according to their practical purpose articulate with codified ideologies that connote social status and become sign vehicles for social distinctions.

To study material culture socio-semiotically means locating the processes of sign production and consumption within the context of exo-semiotic processes and social practices that provide an interdependent, mutually reinforcing matrix of social relations and activities for the relatively autonomous operation of ideological interpretive codes. This approach can be contrasted with most postmodern cultural criticism, which privileges individual readings of material culture, often proposed by independent analysts that are idealistic, elitist, and divorced from social context or group practices.[7]

Some of the most important discussions of postmodernism relate culture to exo-semiotic economic processes. This type of analysis "socializes" the question of postmodernism[8] by linking its dynamic to changes in the structure of capitalism. According to Jameson,[9] postmodernism is periodized concretely because it is the cultural correlate of the late capitalist stage of capitalism.[10] In contrast, Harvey[11] considers postmodernism as only a loosely coupled phenomenon of culture and the economy explaining it as a response by capital to its crisis of overaccumulation. He suggests that in the past the crisis of overaccumulation was countered by the extension of capitalism into new markets around the world, especially in third world countries. As these opportunities have declined in the present, capital reworks the home markets by accelerating the turnover in use of commodities with the aid of advertising and by switching to new, more customized production techniques, such as flexible organization. The outcome, at present, is the articulation of commodity production with fashion and a rapid, speeded-up process of consumption that is based on the consumption of image alone – all of which are characteristics of postmodernism.

While those analysts who have socialized the discussion of postmodernism have some interesting insights, I do not think they go far enough in specifying the relationship between culture and the structure of capitalism as a social system. Furthermore, while an image-driven culture is undoubtedly a defining characteristic of post-modernism, the use of images and expressive symbols in order to sell material goods has been quite prevalent for some time and predates postmodernism to such an extensive and well-established extent that we are dealing with conditions only in matters of degree. Specifying the role of postmodern cultural elements in the economy requires a more specific analysis that captures the pertinency of expressive symbols to the process of capital accumulation.

The following illustrates the socio-semiotic approach to space in an empirical study of the role of signs in the sale of new residential homes. I will discuss the study site and its objects of analysis; describe the relation between codified ideology, in this case, and its exo-semiotic links; and, finally, provide a semiotic analysis of the signs themselves. The preliminary steps taken before the latter is carried out are, in fact, the distinguishing features of the socio-semiotic method itself. Before proceeding with this case study, however, let us consider the need for a more detailed analysis of the relationship between expressive symbols, postmodernism, and the economy.

The Role of Culture in the Accumulation of Capital

If we consider the circuit of capital accumulation, there are several ways in which ideology operates as mediation. First, the production process is considered by Marx as the valorization of capital and it consists of industrial production where labor is controlled so as to extract surplus value. As is known, ideology operates throughout this process, from creating a work atmosphere conducive to capital's needs[12] within the factory itself, to the hegemonic management of class conflict and relations of production, including hegemony of the democratic political process.[13]

In the earlier, pre-1970 phase of capitalist development, ideological interventions functional for capital are summed up best by what Aglietta,[14] following Gramsci, calls "Fordism": the acculturation of immigrant labor to the norm of consumption and the norm of monetary success. Massive restructuring following the Great Depression also helped produce a culture of consumption among the working class which stressed, in particular, home ownership, automobiles, and the relatively frequent replacement of other consumer durables – that is, the "norm of consumption."[15]

More recently, because a mass culture of consumption and financing arrangements, such as extensive and easy credit, have been so successful, generalized or normative appeals for workers to consume are no longer as necessary as they were in the 1930s. Instead, the new needs of capital require a labor force acculturated to leading a highly mobile existence, perpetual job insecurity, and work in split labor markets. Ideological mechanisms such as fatalism, racism, and individualism seem more relevant in managing the new demands of a flexible society. These new attitudes are the personal ideological correlates for the new culture of "post-Fordism",[16] and although they can be related to the concept of a postmodern culture, productionist ideologies have been largely ignored.

At a different location in the circuit of capital accumulation, after the valorization process of production, ideological mediation again becomes important. Once commodities are delivered to the market and put up for sale, capital enters a new phase, the realization and circulation of surplus value through markets and conduits for investment. The importance of sign value, according to the work of Baudrillard,[17] and of the ideology of consumerism play major roles at this juncture. In fact, it is at the level of the circulation of capital that postmodern cultural analyses are concentrated, because they privilege the study of consumer culture.

Commodity purchasing according to desires manufactured by the logotechniques of mass cultural fashions, the production of new cultural forms and needs, and the orchestration of use by the advertising industry are all aspects of the realization of capital. As long as surplus value remains embodied in the unsold object, capital accumulation cannot be realized. The sale of the commodity depends on its exchange value, just as the realization of surplus value depends on its exchange value. If the price of sale does not meet the costs of production, no profit is made.

Capital, therefore, not only has a problem with production, one that is personified by the class struggle, but also a problem with the realization of surplus value which depends on the market. While Marx focused on the former, and marxist studies concentrates on the historical, capital crisis and ideological aspects of the class struggle, Baudrillard[18] has shown how critical the realization process is for an understanding of capitalism. It is for this reason that sign value and the connotations of consumerism become important in capitalist society, as Baudrillard has shown in his analysis of the role of modernist ideology in the system of home furnishings (see chapter 2). In fact, for Baudrillard, the realization (market) rather than the valorization (factory) process of capital currently dominates society, which prompted him to criticize Marxian political economy (*The Mirror of Production*).

As commodification of daily life proceeds, sign values dominate the culture, and, through the hegemony of consumer culture, everyday life becomes commodified. This is a multi-leveled process that is as characteristic of modernity as it is of postmodernity.

This socio-semiotic approach to material culture has some implications for postmodern theory. The suggestion by Jameson,[19] for example, that postmodernity is a particular hegemonic mode of late capitalism does not periodize the process of commodification, hence it lacks historical grounding. Jameson's analysis of the appearances or forms of our contemporary culture is quite fascinating, but it fails to specify, at the deep structural level, an adequate periodization of changes in the logic of consumer culture. The latter has privileged the connotative level of the sign, or the image and its symbolic rather than functional value, since the origin of mass advertising techniques during the turn of the century. The cultural dominant of commodification that is hyposignifiant, which replaces the importance of use values in daily life, already existed during modernity, as Baudrillard shows in home furnishings.

The image-driven culture of late capitalism, then, is probably less a new hegemonic mode of society than a recent trend of contemporary life – a "late modernism," rather than postmodernism, which correlates with "late capitalism." Electronic media techniques and the general speed-up of information processing and assimilation, which Harvey[20] points to as providing the relative uniqueness of postmodern culture in his own version of periodization, have simply amplified tendencies which already existed during modernity. What is perhaps different today, according to Harvey, is the extent to which the realization processes of capital are so dependent on the rapid turnover of consumption through fashion and the relevance of images to the activity of consumption.

In the following case study, I shall argue against this view. Although it is prevalent as one tendency of consumer culture, there exist other logics to consumption that constrain both the relevance of images and the pressure of fashion for quick turnarounds in use. Thus, in both Jameson's and Harvey's periodization of postmodernism, totalizing and reductionist statements obscure a more loosely coupled and polysemic basis for the link between capital realization and ideologies of consumption. My contention will be discussed in the conclusion of this chapter. Futhermore, as indicated in chapter 2, none of the recent analysts of postmodernism can match the pertinent and specified precision of the role of consumerist ideology in cultural change as the early models provided by both Baudrillard (*System of Objects*) and Barthes (*The Fashion System*; see chapter 9).

The Case Study: The Housing Market and the Real Estate Sign

The object of my analysis is the real estate sign (see figure 7.1). It is utilized to advertise housing that is for sale in the United States. My case study focused exclusively on the sale of new residential construction and the use of real estate signs to entice prospective buyers shopping around for a new home. Thus, research centered on the role of the real estate sign as a mediation of the transition between production and consumption in the case of housing. The sign becomes a tool for the realization of capital, as is the case for other types of advertising and the expressive symbols they deploy.

The study site was the corridor corresponding to an axis of east–west housing development within the Los Angeles basin area. This

Figure 7.1

corridor followed old route number 66 from the boundary of Los Angeles County eastward across San Bernardino county, ending up at the easternmost border of home construction in what is now undeveloped farm land (see figure 7.2). Differences in housing value within the study site are a function of distance from Los Angeles and as measured by the median value of housing from the US census.[21] That is, *in general* and with several definite local deviations, the closer towards Los Angeles one moves (moving westward) from the interior (i.e., the closer one moves to the Pacific Ocean from the desert), the more expensive are both new and resold housing.

In this case study, I documented the ideological codes that governed the images found in a sample of real estate signs which were used to mediate the sale of new housing. Second, I studied whether or not differences in the images were related to differences in housing price. The latter does not qualify as a class analysis because I did not collect any information on the backgrounds of buyers, but it is reasonable to suggest, for the case of the United States and possibly elsewhere, that some correlation would exist between class membership and the differential ability to purchase housing. In any event, the difference in the price of housing is the principal means of income and racial segregation in the United States. Consequently, the real estate sign is not only a tool that mediates the transition from production to consumption, from the valorization to the realization of capital, but also the spatial segregation of the population according to class and race.

Figure 7.2

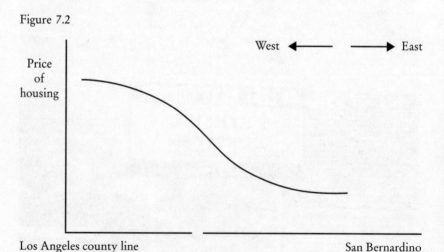

The social context

The socio-semiotic approach does not view the operation of semiosis in a cultural vacuum. It seeks to establish the links between sign production and consumption, on the one hand, and exo-semiotic social processes of economics and politics, on the other. The key to these links is the specification of social context. This is meant as both a specification of synchronic intertextuality at a particular point in time and a diachronic placement within historical periodization. The purpose of socio-semiotic analysis is to abstract the processes of signification and communication from other deep-level societal processes within this social context, such as the material production of surplus value or the operation of power relations (see chapter 3), keeping in mind that these distinctions are not Cartesian dichotomies which exist in reality, because in practice all behavior, even capital accumulation, is meaningful and cannot make sense otherwise.

With regard to exo-semiotic processes in this case study, for example, it is necessary to connect the mediation of production and consumption in the housing industry to aspects of new home purchasing in the United States since the post-war years (i.e., 1945). Over 60 percent of all Americans have become owners of single family homes, the highest ratio in the world, and an average of 30 percent of all home sales involve new homes,[22] although the latter figure varies with economic cycles. Housing and property development represents an industry four times the size of domestic auto production in total value. Due to its low organic composition of capital, its high volume and price produced by competition within separate real estate markets, and the formidable presence of active state subsidies, real estate constitutes a second circuit of capital alongside the primary circuit of industrial production.[23]

The second circuit of capital is comprised of the following conjuncture of political and economic elements which sustains the large volume of real estate activity in the United States and makes home purchasing possible for most Americans.

1 The state: subsidization of home purchasing through tax breaks to buyers and through various government programs offering loan guarantees.
2 A money market for real estate: highly fragmented and reaching many levels of the population, it draws investment into the second circuit from a variety of sources. These financing arrangements

make capital available for real estate despite fluctuations in the business cycle.

3   An extensive real estate market: fragmented and localized, the real estate market exploits to the limit the ability of land to assume a variety of urban uses and transmutes space under the influence of profit-taking and buying.

Typically for the case of new home construction, houses are built in large quantities as developments on fringe area land. Most commonly in agricultural use, land elected for development is bought up by speculators. After lying unused as vacant land for a period, a developer assumes control of the property and builds houses in volume.

Once a housing development is executed, the individual houses must be sold as rapidly as possible, especially because the aggregate level of financing is quite high. It is at this point that the real estate sign advertising the seller's commodities is mobilized. However, the ideological appeals of the signs are not the only reasons why people purchase a house. Several elements take precedent over the mechanism of the sign itself, so that the behavior of home purchasing is not driven completely by images of residential life. The appearance of residential space is not only a product of architectural practice, but is also dictated by the developer who acts in conformity with a particular industrial practice that maximizes profit in both the construction of housing and the layout of the arrangements among houses in a mass development. The appearance of the house within certain constraints is relatively unimportant.

The primary factors in the sale of housing are price, floor space (in a functional rather than aesthetic sense), location vis-à-vis other urban areas and services, incidence of crime at the location, relative age of neighboring families, and other basic family use values. The style of house itself does not have to appear on the real estate sign, but this other information, or some of it not signified by location per se, must. Thus, although image-driven culture is mobilized in the realization of capital and may even assume the proportions of hyperreality and simulation argued for by Baudrillard, the image is but one of several equally important factors in the process of consumption.

In short, residential homes are material objects that are also meaningful objects. As in the case of other aspects of material culture, meaning can be analyzed at both the denotative and connotative levels. Socio-semiotics argues that the latter dimension not only overshadows the former, but also precedes it. Thus, a home as object denotes the sign function of "shelter." At the connotative level, however, the meaning of that same object is many-layered and highly articulated with the social context. The latter dimension includes the specific codes of daily life which regulate such things as financial arrangements, normative expectations for shelter, expectations for family and neighborhood living, status connotations which are often dominant and equity considerations. For the case of domestic homes, the social context constitutes a highly structured connotative realm that is over-burdened by functional as opposed to aesthetic con-siderations. This state of affairs contrasts greatly with the more import-ant place of appearance and architectural design in the production of office buildings, shopping malls, and hotels.

Regarding the real estate sign, then, within the social context of home purchasing, it must be acknowledged that homes are not sold through the appeal of these signs alone. Yet, ideology does have a place in the conversion from production to consumption of housing – i.e, in the process of capital realization. Hence, it is necessary to move to an analysis of the real estate sign as a mediation device in the circulation of capital. I proceed socio-semiotically by specifying the codes representing the "form of the content" and deriving from generalized non-codified ideology, or the "substance of the content," which then articulate with the "form" and "substance of the expression" that is the material artifact or the sign itself.

A Socio-Semiotic Analysis of the Real Estate Sign

The object of analysis, the real estate sign, exists quite literally as a sign that is intended, and used, to attract customers to new housing developments (see figure 7.1). As a "substance of the expression" it literally hangs in space, usually alongside a road or highway, and mediates the transition between valorization and realization of capital in the production of urban housing by advertising homes for sale. Several aspects of this sign are important.

1 The system of real estate signs is deployed in space and, therefore, possesses location. This type of sign is specific to housing developments that vary greatly in the price of the home. Consequently, they mediate a socio-spatial process of residential housing segregation in the single family home market that is restrictive in both class and racial distinctions.

2 Real estate signs are structured syntagmatically as well as paradigmatically, hence they comprise a system of signification organized

according to certain generic categories of sign images drawing upon well-defined ideological codes.

3 Although the set of real estate signs constitutes a system of signification, we cannot talk about a syntax of sign elements overarching every real estate sign or some coherence among signs at the level of the "form of the expression." Rather, the system of real estate signs constitutes a pseudo-text comprised of several ideological codes that, in some cases, actually overlap and penetrate the same real estate sign.

Because there is no uniform real estate sign for all types of housing, it is possible to correlate ideological codes used in signs with the prices of housing in the developments within which they are located. This enables us to connect the semiotic aspects of the sign to its correlate processes operating through the capitalist housing market, including the importance of class and racial segregation to that market. The system of real estate signs operates both socio-semiotically through differences in the meaning of images as well as exo-semiotically in a differential system of socio-spatial residential location. The remainder of this discussion reports research on the correlation between the codes found in signs and the relative price of housing.

Results of sign analysis

There are two axes of variation found in real estate signs according to differences in the "form of the expression" and the "form of the content." First, variation in the "form of the expression" can be linked directly to differences in the ideological codes structuring sign elements.[24] I found four separate codes which I have termed: a naturalist anti-urban code, a topographic/geographic code, an English gentrification code, and a neo-Fordist code. Most signs were polysemic; i.e., they contained a mixture of several codes. One sign (see figure 7.3), in fact, avoided any semblance of syntax by depicting elements from at least three separate codes in a melange of symbols. The use of a woodpecker to signify naturalism in the purchase of housing, for example, is at the least peculiarly ironic.

Second, signs varied according to the "form of the content." Some signs operated principally at the denotative level. That is, they provided a text that communicated information of a non-ideological nature in addition to codified ideology at the level of connotation. Information conveyed by signs included: the price of housing, loan arrangements, square feet, interest rates, and actual community features such

Figure 7.3

as "country club" or "golf course" living (see figure 7.4). One sign (figure 7.5) was so explicit that it depicted an iconic reproduction of the interior of the homes for sale. The active presence of so much denotative information in signs calls into question some basic ideas promoted by postmodernists.

According to Baudrillard,[25] consumerism is so highly developed at present that all signs have been reduced or overcome by pure ideological representation and simulation. Signifieds and deep-level or practical meanings which support sign functions no longer exist. Signification is simply a process of the free play of signifiers in an image-driven culture. In this case study real estate signs with an attenuated or absent denotative content would qualify as an example of the dominating logic of sign value, in the Baudrillard or postmodern sense. However, as indicated, I did not find this to be true of all signs. For a select group of signs, in contrast, the "form of the content" stressed specific and concrete information. The active use of denotative information which has significant meaning in the sale of housing contradicts the postmodern conception of a culture dominated by pure images or free-floating signifiers alone. I shall return to this observation in the conclusion of this chapter.

Figure 7.4

Figure 7.5

The majority of the signs in my sample, however, were ideological representations devoid of denotative content. The connotative level can be described in terms of one or more of the following codes which helped to structure the image/elements – i.e., the "form of the expression" – of the signs.

Naturalist anti-urban code

These are signs that signify scenes of nature – the escape from the city. This code operates as free-floating signifiers because the natural environment has itself been destroyed to make way for urban and suburban development.

Examples: Stone Creek (figure 7.6), California Dawn (figure 7.7), Glenbrook, Atrium Valley, Mountain Meadows (figure 7.8). The amorphous aspect of these appeals and their failure to denote actually existing objects makes these signs the clearest examples of free-floating signifiers and postmodern simulation. There are no "mountain meadows" in the Mountain Meadow development – i.e., this reality does not exist.

Figure 7.6

Figure 7.7

Figure 7.8

Topographic/geographic code

These signify status/class because in practice the affluent groups usually command the residential heights or best scenic views. However, these appeals are used where housing itself does not denote an upper-class commodity and for housing that is only moderately priced. In this sense, such signs are another example of connotatively codified ideology or simulation.

Examples: San Antonio Heights (figure 7.3), East Haven, Southridge, California Hills (figure 7.9).

English gentrification code

Signifies status/class using signifiers from the Golden Age of the Bourgeoisie. This is another code which signifies relatively expensive housing that is not, however, upper class nor denotes location in the English countryside. Hence, it is another example of image-driven simulation.

Examples: Hillsborough (figure 7.10), Victoria Estates, Chelsea Park (figure 7.11).

Figure 7.9

Figure 7.10

Figure 7.11

Neo-Fordist code

This code represents acculturation to the needs of restructured late capitalism. It stresses images of leisure, opulence, high personal consumption, home ownership as fulfillment of success, affluence as the goal of lifestyle.

   Example: American Dream (figure 7.8), the Country Club (figure 7.4).

Correlation with price of housing

Real estate signs not only vary according to their semiotic elements but also with regard to the price of housing they advertise. The principal axis of differentiation involves the mix of denotative and connotative elements at the level of the "form of the content." The highest priced housing was linked to signs with the most denotative content. The iconographic sign in figure 7.5 advertised a high-priced development, as did the one depicting country club living (see figure 7.4). In contrast, the lower the value of homes in a development, the more connotatively robust and image driven at the expense of denotation was the real estate sign. The least expensive housing belonged to the "California Dawn" development (see figure 7.7), a sign without any apparent connection to signifieds of any kind, least of all housing. Additional examples of purely image-driven, free-floating signifiers were "Atrium Valley" and "Stone Creek" (see figure 7.6).

   According to these results the domination of sign value and the prevalence of free-floating signifiers in the process of semiosis is a quality of signs appealing to the relatively *less* affluent. Wealthy home buyers are appealed to by signs that offer more concrete information and which possess robust denotative signification in addition to the presence of codified ideology. That is, advertising for the wealthy contains signifiers that mean something specific. Both the neo-Fordist code and the naturalist anti-urban code were most characteristic of the least expensive housing, although the former articulates with signs of high-priced housing as well. Lying in the middle and correlated to homes of intermediate value were the topographic/geographic code and the English gentrification code, with the latter more commonly associated with higher priced homes. Within this middle group was found the San Antonio Heights sign (figure 7.3) that mixes elements from the codes of naturalism, topography and English gentrification. The free-floating signifiers without denotative qualities most prevalent in real estate signs of this group were "Estates," "Park" and "Heights." Finally, an interesting aspect of the development with the highest priced homes, absent for other classes, was its signs with direct appeals to security (as in figure 7.5), or luxury amenities (as in figure 7.11) such as golf courses, that were part of the actual physical plan of development. These denotative, and in some cases iconic, elements constituted the "form of the content" for the most affluent class real esate sign which mixed the real object with ideological representations (the later drawing mainly upon the neo-Fordist code).

I have observed this same phenomenon of varying denotative specificity in other cases of advertising, where the claims of postmodernists regarding the hegemony of an image-driven culture privileging free-floating signifiers alone are contradicted by the class differences of consumption. Automobile ads, for example, are highly differentiated with regard to price. More affordable, least expensive cars have advertising appeals that are invariably image driven. Free-floating signifiers, such as happiness, attractiveness to women, youth, fun, security, stylishness, and fashion, are the most common ideological appeals that articulate with suggestion to purchase the car. Only a direct denotative framing of the car's actual price serves as the one concrete mode of information in this kind of advertising.

In direct contrast, expensive cars often are advertised with concrete information on safety specifications, engineering attributes, motor specifications, suspension or acceleration characteristics, and the like. Thus, the group of affordable cars are sold through hyperreality and sign value, while expensive cars are sold using denotative information on use and exchange value, as well as such sign values as status considerations. Magazine ads for the same cars are even more illustrative of this difference. In the latter case, ads for expensive cars such as Mercedes often employ engineering diagrams, and lists of concrete specifications about performance or safety. Thus, when it comes to expensive purchases, reality does play a role in culture. If there is a domination of postmodern cultural forms, it afflicts the middle class more than other classes (see chapter 11).

Regarding aspects of the observed set of real estate signs at the level of the "form of the expression," more can be said about the social context of the codes producing these elements. This provides some understanding for the relative effectiveness of the signs themselves – i.e., the contextual mechanisms that trigger off appropriate conceptions in the minds of buyers as they shop around by visiting real estate developments. Two of the codes, naturalism and topographism, contrast distinctively with the area within which the developments are placed: namely, suburban Southern California.

As indicated above, suburbanization in the Los Angeles region has virtually erased the signs of nature and replaced the natural environment with a massive split-level region of single family homes and privatized backyards stretching for over one hundred miles from the ocean to the desert. Signs of nature are recirculated within this milieu as free-floating signifiers and simulations in the mass consumption practices within the built environment. They appear as animals on the labels of shirts, as the quality of organicism in the preparation of foods, in the names of automobiles, as two-dimensional posters hung on the interior walls of homes whose mocking quality is all but lost on the local residents, and in the labels of housing developments portrayed by real estate signs.

The signs themselves may, therefore, be effective precisely because they link up to this conjuncture between lost and desired communion with nature and the refuge of homeownership as the minimal opportunity to control a piece of land. The connotative ideologies represented in real estate signs are used predominantly to appeal to the relatively least affluent home buyers, perhaps, because other distinctions that rely on the content of the purchase itself, such as potential equity, security, amenities, and affluent status, cannot be acquired for this social group. Like the organic breakfast cereal promising escape to the vitality of a more active, pristine lifestyle through the act of consumption, the naturalist code of the real estate sign appeals in the same way to the self-alienation of the suburbanized and post-industrialized working class.

The topographical code is more ironic and, therefore, postmodern (i.e., hyperreal) but probably operates through a similar contrast. Because the environment of the Los Angeles basin is overwhelmingly flat, areas with some elevation become the privileged domains of the more affluent. The signifiers "Heights" or "Mountain" do not denote a difference in elevation, because all of the homes are in the flatlands, but can make this connection to affluent areas, thereby expropriating prestige associations. Thus, they too operate at the connotative level because they are used to front developments that have no visible topographical difference with others around them.

The neo-Fordist code does not function through metonymical contrasts to the surrounding area, but it does operate in a manner not very different from the code of naturalism. Comprised exclusively of free-floating signifiers deriving from the broad-based, deeply structured culture of contemporary capitalism, this code also functions because of its conjuncture with institutionalized elements in the larger society. The latter would include mass culture itself which is programmed at its most fundamental level to validate at the same time both the *consumption norm*,[26] which through a high level of consumption facilitates the realization of capital, and the norm of monetary success, which comprises difference structure of social distinctions.

Neo-Fordist signifiers penetrated the signs of *every* level of housing price, sometimes appearing as a single word such as "luxury" (see figure 7.5). As with the code of naturalism, neo-Fordist signifiers can work alone to front the least expensive housing when appealing to consumers without much choice in the market.

In order to sell homes to people with greater choices available to them due to their higher income, appeals need to be more concrete as well as symbolic. The real, materialist foundations of home purchasing and owning enter into consideration in these circumstances. Thus, consumers with some choice making an expensive purchase have some concern about the prospective value of the home over time. This enters into the purchase consideration through valuations of the type of people that will also buy housing in the development and by assessing the comparative location of the neighborhood vis-à-vis others of either higher or lower housing prices. The topographical code, therefore, may help producers of housing signal buyers about relative location. However, it is up to the purchaser to discern whether topographical or locational appeals denote differences or merely connote status without a real basis. This ambiguity at the level of the "form of the content" is a fundamental mechanism enabling all signs to function successfully.

A similar observation can be made about the last code, English gentrification. On one level none of the signifiers denote real differences according to the Victorian practices of gentrification and town planning. Hence the signs represent free-floating signifiers and a hyperreal image. Yet, because they are used almost exclusively to advertise developments with homes of a higher than average price, they function to signal prospective buyers that their neighbor will belong to the same upwardly mobile group. Signifiers such as "Chelsea Park" (see figure 7.11) may connote this connection. Usually, such symbolic appeals cannot work alone. A more typical sign of this group of development is "Hillsborough" in figure 7.10. Here concrete information on square feet, a very important indicator of future home value, is conveyed directly by the sign. This kind of concreteness is absent in the free-floating signifiers of the less expensive housing.

Conclusion

The socio-semiotic analysis of the real estate sign for new residential developments reveals the following.

1 The sign mediates the sale of housing only in conjunction with other exo-semiotic processes that include the production of needs and the stimulation of real estate circuit activity by elements of capital and the state.
2 The sign mediates the process of residential housing segregation as well as home purchasing. It is part of social as well as semiotic effects.
3 The system of real estate signs constitutes a pseudo-text comprised of several intersecting codes. Intertextuality and polysemy are most extreme at the intermediate level of housing price (e.g. figure 7.3). At the lowest price level are found signs that are pure representations of single ideological codes, as in "American Dream" (figure 7.8), or "Stone Creek" (figure 7.6). At the highest level of price, ideological representations are mixed with concrete denotative aspects of housing features, such as security (figure 7.5) or the denotation of square feet.
4 Signs show variation according to two axes – the "form of the expression" and the "form of the content." It was not the case that all signs expressed the "logic of sign value",[27] reducing other elements of consumption, such as exchange value and use value, to the free play of signifiers and image-driven culture (the hyperreality of simulation). The higher the price of housing, the more concrete were the appeals of the signs and the more specific or denotative was the information they conveyed. This phenomenon of differentiation in level of hyperreality according to class differences in society is a counterexample to the totalizing claims of postmodernists that argue for the domination of image-driven culture in the present conjuncture.
5 Ideological codes varied between those without any apparent objective referent to those possessed of a real base in societal practices. Naturalism and topographism are examples of the former, while neo-Fordism and English gentrification exemplified the latter.

Finally, this chapter has helped demonstrate the role of semiosis in political economy. Several observations can be made along these lines. First, previous efforts at socializing the postmodern question have connected culture with aspects of capitalism. These efforts, while important, are quite limited because in all cases they take both capitalism and culture as totalities. The work of both Jameson and Harvey, in particular, effects a synthesis between culture and political economy but fails to transcend marxism because of the failure to jettison totality. Jameson, for example, points out some interesting features of postmodernism but effects a correlation with late capitalism only through metaphor (see chapter 6). Harvey attempts greater specificity. However, he too links culture and political economy only in the broadest terms. In his case, capitalism seeks to solve its overaccumulation crisis through the modulation of culture and consumption. This is simply a functional explanation which, in its own way, is also metaphorical. It asks us to believe in a global logic of "capital in general" which guides the development of culture and endows postmodern features with specific powers that modify consumer behavior in ways that are functional for capital.

The socio-semiotic approach has the advantage of being able to specify in rich detail the articulation between culture and political economy. In particular, we have seen how the realization of capital is structured through the use of markets and ideologies. Cultural appeals are polysemic and derive from ideological codes that cover a variety of consumer outlooks and behaviors. Rather than some totalizing view of culture, I have argued for a conception that specifies the operation of polysemic and differentiated ideologies which articulate with the act of consumption. While some ideologies are characteristically postmodern, others are not. What dominates is not some version of culture, as Jameson would have it, but the way class considerations and the market modulate the effect of images. Signs matter in the current economy, but not in the way either Jameson or Harvey suggest. In fact, of all the writers associated with postmodernism, only Baudrillard avoids the traps of marxist thinking through a specification of the role of cultural processes in political economy. In the next chapter I shall show how this version also fails to escape totalizing discourse but how we can use Baudrillard to effect a viable approach to culture.

Notes

1   Roland Barthes, "Semiologie et urbanisme," *L'Architecture d'aujourd'hui*, 153 (1970–71): 11–13.
2   See, for example, Raymond Ledrut, *Les images de la ville* (Paris: Editions Anthropos), also excerpted in *The City and the Sign: An Introduction*

to *Urban Semiotics*, edited by M. Gottdiener and A. Lagopoulos (New York: Columbia University Press, 1986), pp. 219–40.

3 Umberto Eco, *A Theory of Semiotics* (Bloomington: Indiana University Press, 1976).

4 Luis Prieto, *Etudes de linguistique et de semiologie generales* (Geneva: Librarie Droz, 1975). Prieto's approach to semiotics is important to the perspective of this book; see chapter 8.

5 Martin Krampen, *Meaning in the Urban Environment* (London: Pion, 1979).

6 Henri Lefebvre, *The Production of Space* (Oxford: Blackwell Publishers, 1991); M. Gottdiener, *The Social Production of Urban Space* (Austin: University of Texas Press, 1985 and 1994).

7 David Harvey, *The Condition of Postmodernity* (Oxford: Blackwell Publishers, 1989); Sharon Zukin, *Landscapes of Power* (Berkeley: University of California Press, 1992); Ed Soja, *Postmodern Geography* (London: Verso, 1988).

8 Stephan Cook, Jan Pakulski and Malcolm Waters, *Postmodernization: Change in Advanced Society* (London: Sage, 1990).

9 Fredrick Jameson, "Postmodernism, or the Cultural Logic of Late Capitalism," *New Left Review*, 146 (1984): pp. 53–92.

10 Ernest Mandel, *Late Capitalism* (London: Verso, 1975).

11 Harvey, *Condition of Postmodernity*.

12 Michael Buroway, "Thirty Years of Making Out," in *On Work*, edited by R. E. Pahl (Blackwell Publishers, 1988), pp. 190–211.

13 Antonio Gramsci, *Selections from the Prison Notebooks* (New York: International Publishers, 1971).

14 Michel Aglietta, *A Theory of Capitalist Regulation* (London: New Left Books, 1979).

15 Mike Davis, *Prisoners of the American Dream* (London: New Left Books, 1986).

16 R. Boyer and J. Mistral, "La Crise: pensateur et potentialite des annees quatre-vingt," *Annals: Economies, Societes, Civilisations*, 4 (1983); M. Gottdiener and Nikos Komninos, *Capitalist Development and Crisis Theory* (London: Macmillan, 1989); Harvey, *Condition of Postmodernity*.

17 Jean Baudrillard, *For a Critique of the Political Economy of the Sign*, translated with an introduction by Charles Levin (St Louis, Mo.: Telos Press, 1981).

18 Ibid.

19 Jameson, "Postmodernism."

20 Harvey, *Condition of Postmodernity*.

21 United States Government Printing Office, *United States Census of Population* (Washington, DC: 1980).

22 John Agnew, "Home Ownership and the Capitalist Social Order," in *Urbanization and Urban Planning in Capitalist Society*, edited by Michael Dear and Alan Scott (New York: Methuen, 1981), pp. 457–80.

23 Gottdiener, *Social Production of Urban Space*; Joe R. Feagin, *Houston:*

The Free Enterprise City (New Brunswick, N.J.: Rutgers University Press, 1988); Lefebvre, *Production of Space.*

24	About 15 percent of the signs observed in the study site contained signifiers drawing on codes that were different from the ones analyzed here. Because not enough of these signs could be found, no attempt was made to include them in this analysis. Some seemed to draw on signifiers that connote status (e.g., signs prominently displaying the name of the builder). With a larger study area, perhaps more could be said about them.

25	Baudrillard, *Critique of the Political Economy of the Sign.*

26	Aglietta, *Theory of Capitalist Regulation.*

27	Baudrillard, *Critique of the Political Economy of the Sign.*

Part III

Cultural Studies and Socio-Semiotics

8

Hegemony and Mass Culture:
A Socio-Semiotic Approach

In Jameson's[1] classic account of the relationship between postmodern culture and political economy, he suggests that the former represents the cultural dominant during the present phase of late capitalism. His argument is based on Gramscian notions of hegemony which allow for the possibility of several cultural systems existing at the same time within an historical conjuncture. This way of framing the problem of specifying domination avoids totalizing a type of global culture for society as a whole and allows for differences among various cultural forms rather than the reduction of all culture to the logic of a particular form.

Jameson's argument, however, does not go far enough in specifying the composition of mass culture. Postmodernism is treated as an abstraction which exists in domination within a cultural complex composed of other abstractions. Thus, totalizing discourse is not really avoided, it is only abstracted to another plane. Jameson's discussion never specifies the dynamic of cultural production and consumption as a set of social relations. Both the structure and agency of culture remain for him abstractions. Let us re-examine the issues of hegemony, mass culture, and postmodernism through the optic of socio-semiotics, because this will enable us to specify cultural differences and the production and consumption of culture in great detail.

Cultural Studies

The analysis of mass culture involves a three-way relationship among (1) cultural objects that are produced by an industrial process, (2) a set of institutions that produce and distribute such objects on a relatively large scale, and (3) a collectivity(ies) or social group(s) of those who use such objects in contexts that can include use within a creative or connotatively polysemic setting. A mass cultural "object" can include everything from perceptual products (a television program) to highly substantial experiences (Disneyland). The distinguishing characteristics of mass cultural forms are found in the means by which these objects are produced and distributed – that is, by mass marketing industries[2] – and in the nature of their use primarily, though not exclusively, for entertainment.[3] Finally, the contents of mass cultural production involves people or events in society as well as the objects themselves.

Over the years the threefold relation of mass culture – producers/objects/users – has been kept in the background of analysis while three main organizing traditions have dominated the field. Initially, analysts of mass culture were concerned with whether it was good or bad. This debate, often passionately engaged, has been covered in an extensive literature.[4] The second tradition, coexistent with the first, has centered on the Lazarsfeldian school's study of media effects or influences and utilizes market research techniques.[5] Recently, a third tradition, termed the "production of culture" perspective, has emerged.[6] According to this view, the best way to analyze mass cultural processes is to focus on how media industries function as complex organizations. It asserts that corporate/bureaucratic decision-making processes, along with marketing and distribution arrangements, so interpose themselves between the creators and the consumers of mass culture that organizational logic has come progressively to characterize the very nature of mass culture itself.[7]

Each of the three mass culture traditions has amplified the tripartite relationship among producers, objects, and users in some way. The first approach, for example, has helped clarify the nature of the mass cultural object by distinguishing it from objects with a more developed aesthetic. This cleavage in culture is homologous to the stratified structure of classes in modern society.[8]

The primary focus of the second tradition eschews the question of relative merit in favor of empirically measuring the social and psychological effects of mass cultural objects and events. This research has expanded our understanding of the relationship between human subjectivity and the sociocultural milieu. The sum total of work in this tradition has uncovered little evidence that mass media produce substantive, direct effects on individual behavior.[9] Instead, mass cultural events are mediated for the individual by others who are situated within their own respective group contexts, an insight developed most fruitfully by symbolic interactionists, especially with regard to postmodernism.[10]

Finally, the third tradition has extended our knowledge of mass media industries themselves as being composed of complex organizations involved in the everyday necessity of producing and marketing mass cultural products. Mass culture can be analyzed, from this perspective, according to the dynamics of the particular milieu within which production takes place, the specific commonalities that affect all cultural industries, and the contingencies that are most often encountered in production.[11] Most important, analysts have discovered that marketing and distribution may have a more significant effect on certain styles of mass culture than the nature of the product itself.[12]

Taken as a whole, however, some 40 years of mass culture research has left knowledge of the three-way relationship in a rather undeveloped state. Advocates interested in the intervening role of producers, for example, tend to lump users into a passive, undifferentiated mass.[13] Even where the composition of the audience is discussed,[14] the relationship between users and producers is relatively unexplored by production of culture advocates. In contrast, those researchers focusing on the effects of mass culture view cultural production as occurring within an institutional black box, if they consider it at all. In short, although American mass culture analysis has contributed to our understanding of the producer/object/user relationship, it has done so in a piecemeal fashion. Furthermore, there is only a limited understanding of how these three aspects are related. For the most part, interrelatedness has been considered, but only as a derivative interest in the more central discussion of mass culture's effects.

Despite the assessment above, there is an additional extant perspective that does cut across these three approaches and that articulates a synthetic view of the role of the three-way relationship in modern society. This integrated approach analyzes mass cultural industries within the functional context of capitalist domination and is associated with Gramsci's notion of hegemony.[15] Hegemony theory is the dominant approach of American Marxian critics of mass culture. Its most recent application has been in Jameson's discussion of postmodernism as the cultural dominant of late capitalism. In its most common formulations, hegemony theory synthesizes the aspects of media study by viewing mass culture as a fundamental ruling-class instrument used to maintain political and social control through the production of ideological "false consciousness"[16] or "contradictory consciousness" in the minds of the working class. According to hegemony theory, the media industries are only one of several institutions that dominate class-specific perceptions of reality.[17]

There are, however, serious limitations to the Marxian critique of mass culture, not the least of which is its functional reductionism. The underlying theoretical assumption of this approach, whose untenability I discuss below, implies that structural or institutional practices are automatically transformed into deep-level psychological ones through the agency of media control. According to hegemonists, consciousness is either "false" (i.e., the masses perceive illusion and not reality) or "contradictory" (the masses are confused and their judgment is fragmented). Basically, this is a very simplistic view of humanity and the nature of cultural expression in everyday life.

In the following I explore the producer/object/user relation in its full intertextual complexity. I propose an alternative means of capturing interdependency, using the approach of socio-semiotics that highlights the important reciprocal linkages between producers and users as mediated through mass cultural objects. This perspective is important because it focuses explicitly on symbols and their exchange by specifying precisely the places within social interaction where meaning is created, communicated, and received. The socio-semiotic approach that I propose is inspired by recent European work that derives from the internal criticism of the Marxian structuralist approach to ideology and that defines itself clearly as being opposed to "false consciousness" theory. Before discussing this cultural interaction model, however, I will review this more contemporary Marxian approach to cultural control in order to show its differences from the prevailing American one. This review should be helpful to the understanding of the socio-semiotic alternative.

The Critique of Mass Culture as Cultural Domination

By "hegemony," Gramsci means the way in which the entire ideological complex of beliefs, values, and perceptually based attitudes that function for the reproduction and sustenance of ruling-class domination comes to saturate every aspect, and particularly the social institutions, of society.[18] According to hegemony theory, the corporate domination of mass culture in a class-stratified society has as its ultimate consequence an industrial control of consciousness.[19] The capitalist class not only controls the production of mass culture in order to accumulate wealth, it also, by dominating the belief system(s) of the working class, reproduces its rule. In particular, according to hegemony theory, the abilities of the working class to think reflexively and to analyze the social and individual conditions of everyday life have been short-circuited by this consciousness industry.[20]

Consequently, cultural hegemony is one of the reasons that the working class does not revolt against the conditions of its own oppression.

Hegemony theory is reductionist because of its primitive understanding of human subjectivity. By asserting that class consciousness is controlled in the interests of the bourgeoisie through the mediation of mass culture, hegemonists assume the unity of all thought and beg the more essential theoretical question concerning the constitutive nature of the human subject. Consciousness itself can never be controlled in the manner suggested by this theory because it implies the existence of a homogeneous human subject who has been produced by modernity and whose mental state has a reflexive thought capacity that is indistinguishable from consciousness, or even subconsciousness. At its core, therefore, the assertion of consciousness control commits the fallacy of idealism, attributed to Lukacs,[21] which implies that the mental activity of individuals can be separated so easily from the material conditions of their existence that consciousness can be "false."

The criticism of this hegemonic tradition has been carried out with great sophistication by European marxists, beginning with the anti-humanist arguments of Althusser.[22] More recently the Marxian approach to ideology and ideological control has been critically refined by European debates among structuralists, post-structuralists, and "scientific humanists".[23] In some cases, attempts have been made to integrate Althusser's work with that of Gramsci to revive and utilize the latter's humanist premises.[24] I shall return later to the possibility of using this within a socio-semiotic context.

In Althusser's original formulation, he strove for a more complex view of the human subject as a somewhat contradictory amalgam of mental states that included post-Freudian-like, subconscious influences. Althusser makes the distinction between consciousness and a second feature of thought that is a mental capacity organized around the "imaginary," a capacity that is qualitatively separate from the ordinary consciousness of everyday life. The concept of the imaginary is close to Berger and Luckmann's[25] notion of reality construction, because it represents the individual's interpretation of reality, constructed through reflexive thought contemplating the experience of societal interaction. According to Althusser's original formulation, people cannot understand the real forces in the social formation that produce social events, because these function in ways that are not readily apparent. Their interpretation of the events perceived by consciousness, therefore, is an imaginary one, and it is the representation of this realm that Althusser terms "ideological." As Hirst indicates,

> Mens [*sic*] conditions of existence cannot be manifest to them
> and in consequence they live their relation to these (absent) con-
> ditions in an imaginary mode. They live them in an imaginary
> presence "as if" they were given. Ideology is a representation of
> this "imaginary" modality by which men live their relation to
> the (absent) totality of their existence. Ideology is not "con-
> sciousness," it is a representation of the "imaginary." This "im-
> aginary" relation is not the experience or consciousness of an
> already constituted subject – it is in the imaginary that the sub-
> ject is formed as subject.[26]

This more contemporary Marxian theory of ideology is opposed
directly to the hegemonists' notion of false consciousness because it
sees consciousness and ideology as two separate things. The study of
consciousness requires a theory of the subject; hegemonists presume
they possess this, but, in reality, they do not. Once the study of
ideology is separated from that of human individuality, however,
analysis is free to examine the social processes associated with the
imaginary relation itself and its interconnection to socially produced
forms of representation on the one hand and individual subjectivity
on the other. A wide range of different post-structural perspectives
have recently appeared that address this problematic by overcoming
Althusserian limitations. These theories include those proposed by
Hirst,[27] McConnell and Robins,[28] Rossi-Landi,[29] and Seve.[30] This recent, collective effort has retained Althusser's essential critique of
"false consciousness" theory despite the transformation of its original
structuralist premises. Thus, there is reasonable consensus among
European marxists that (1) although there certainly are ideological
institutional apparatuses that control social relations (schools, churches,
the state, mass media) and (2) although these are not all reducible to
separate manifestations of the state itself as Althusser once supposed,
there can never be a consciousness "industry." Consequently, the control of ideology in society is a much more volatile and contingent
process than hegemonists suggest.
  Recently, hegemonists have expressed more awareness that their
treatment of ideology has been comparatively deterministic and functionalist and have strained for a more dialectical, processual approach to
mass culture. They now recognize that the relationship between mass
culture industries and the mass audience is more complex than was
previously thought. In particular, analysts have highlighted the existence of cultural resistance[31] and of the creation of alternative forms of
culture defined in opposition to aspects of domination.[32] Yet the need

for a general theory that captures such a dialectic remains.[33] By following the post-structuralist approach, however, it is possible to discard all assumptions in the analysis of mass culture that concern the effect of ideology on consciousness. As Rose[34] has argued, there are many social forms, such as the law, that control individual values but do not rely on dominating subjectivity. By dispensing entirely with a theory of ideology that links psychological states with societal ones, the contingent relation between mass culture and hegemonic control can be captured. An analysis of this type involves studying the relative success of ideological production and reproduction at the level of social relations themselves. In fact, a purely sociostructural approach to ideology has been articulated in Europe, using the analytical paradigm of semiotics. This perspective is most often associated with Barthes' work on culture, especially *Mythologies*.[35] Other researchers, however, have successfully applied it to a wide variety of cultural forms that are not necessarily within an ideological context such as the cinema;[36] art;[37] fashion;[38] the novel;[39] poetry;[40] modern culture, principally its aesthetically developed forms;[41] and even settlement space.[42]

The essential difference between the semiotic approach to culture and those better known in the United States (such as ethnomethodology and symbolic interaction, which also focus on symbols and social interaction) is the emphasis in semiotics on objective systems of signification and the intersubjective basis of meaning. That is, following Saussure, the production of meaning takes place only by virtue of a social relation, because language is a sui generis social construction. Although other approaches focusing on interacting subjects use a situational conception of social interaction, the object of analysis in semiotics is the socially sustained system of signification, including its material objects and their interdependencies, that produces and sustains meaning through sociostructural interaction. See chapter 3 for a more extensive discussion concerning the differences between the socio-semiotic approach and such sociological traditions in the analysis of culture as symbolic interaction. In what follows I propose a socio-semiotic model of the producer/object/user relation which is able to specify the operation of hegemony in great detail.

The Socio-Semiotic Approach to Mass Culture

The question raised by a semiotics of objects is: In what sense can I say that meaning resides in the material world? The answer: In *no* sense, as long as I do not take human subjects into account. More specifically, people are the bearers of all meaning, either in the isolation of personal use or as the product of complex social processes of group interaction. In the first case, semiotic analysis merges with psychological inquiry and there has even been a proposal for a psycho-semiotics.[43] In the second, social groups of all kinds, including status and political collectivities as well as classes, are understood to be the bearers of meaning. Here, semiotics merges with sociological inquiry. As we have seen in the following chapters, socio-semiotics avoids the sheer eclecticism of this merger.

In what sense, then, can signification among objects be said to exist, given the social and psychological basis of meaning? There are two traditions in semiotics that attempt to answer this question but do so following different assumptions about the epistemological nature of semiotic inquiry. The first follows Barthes' "translinguistics" and the second involves recent work, inspired more by Peirce than Saussure, on the semiotics of objects. According to Barthes,[44] every object becomes a sign of its own function. Thus, an automobile functions not only as a mode of transportation but also as a commonly (almost universally) recognized sign of that function. In the early work of Barthes, this "universal semantization of usage" was extended to every system of objects that could be structured as a system of signification – that is, possessed of paradigmatic and syntagmatic axes.[45] By so doing, he was able to analyze such systems of objects as dress, food, professional wrestling, and photographs, using linguistic analysis.

According to Krampen, the logical extension of Barthes' early work would be an assertion that all of culture is accessible through linguistic analysis, and this statement is a fallacy. The "linguistic fallacy" implies that "since all languages are made up of words and all words are signs, all things made up of signs are languages."[46] This "translinguistic"[47] approach to culture has unfortunately come to characterize "pop-semiotic" analysis, just as fashion, nonverbal gestures, architecture, and so on have all been endowed analogically with the fallacious status of language.

The linguistic fallacy has been criticized by some of the best semioticians, including Eco, Ledrut, and even Barthes himself.[48] While working with the *Tel Quel* group, Barthes repudiated his translinguistic approach to culture. His shift to the study of written language resulted in a position that no longer stressed an analysis of cultural objects themselves but focused instead on discourse about objects.[49] Such discourse is clearly a linguistic phenomenon, and, in the special cases of prose and poetry, the object of analysis becomes written

This line intentionally blank

language, or the text. For Barthes (and Julia Kristeva and Jacques
Derrida, among others), semiotics after 1969 became the study of the
text or discourse, most especially in written form (such an inquiry is
sometimes known as "second generation" or "philological" semiotics). For example, although Barthes showed that the objects of Dress
constituted a system of signification and that Dress was therefore
amenable to semiotic analysis, he observed that the dress sign existed
only in Fashion – that is, in the discursive world of writing and
speaking about clothes – rather than as something intrinsic to the
object itself or to its function (see chapter 10). Thus, the discourse of
Fashion becomes the code by which the clothing industry "clouds the
calculating consciousness of the purchaser" and achieves momentary
domination of the market.[50] Barthes' theory, therefore, separates the
object itself from the ideological web surrounding it in which the
hapless consumer is entrapped. It is this web that frames the semiotic
object of analysis in the study of ideology – a mode of representation
that Barthes calls the "simulacrum": the mass cultural object literally
intertwined with ideologically woven connotations, as distinct from
the material object itself.

Baudrillard, in particular, has followed Barthes' approach by
analyzing mass culture as ideology and simulacrum, using a semiotic
analysis of advertising discourse. To him, the material world of commodities has been transformed into a symbolic world of ideological
meanings attached to commodities.[51] This ideology of consumerism
has reduced all material objects to their "sign value" – that is, a meaning constructed through advertising and consumer manipulation by
the logotechniques of capitalist corporations. It is the sign value of the
object that superimposes itself upon the sign function of the object,
transforming the meaning of objects that comes from their everyday
use into the ideology of consumerism. This process is for Baudrillard
the specific characteristic of postmodernism, and the concept of an
image-driven culture dominated by sign value is also the defining
feature of postmodernism in the work of others, such as Jameson.

I shall return below to Baudrillard's notion of sign value and the
transformation involved in converting use values to ideology and the
material object to its simulacrum. At this stage it is sufficient to point
out that the effect of ideological control asserted by Baudrillard operates at the level of the sign and not through intrasubjective domination. My critique of Baudrillard, then, will also serve as a critique
of Jameson, Harvey, and others who fail to specify the semiotic basis
of image-driven culture themselves, but rely on the specification of
Baudrillard.

The second tradition in the semiotics of objects starts from the early criticism of Barthes' translinguistics and never really looks back (unlike the work of Baudrillard and the later work of Barthes). As Krampen has indicated, it reverses the Barthesian tradition that reduces objects to signs by asserting that signs can be reduced to objects.[52] Such a reduction attempts to ground semiotic analysis firmly within a materialist context in order to carry out an analysis of objects that avoids the radical idealism of the first tradition, as exemplified by Baudrillard's analysis of mass culture.[53]

This second approach to semiotics, which is opposed to the Barthesian tradition, is exemplified by the work of Eco[54] and Prieto[55] and follows the tradition of Peirce (see chapter 1). It deals with the full range of relationships between individuals and objects, including use, status as indexes as well as signs (following Peirce), and roles in systems of signification that are not systems of communication (that is, that do not possess the property of signaling). According to Krampen, the essential conceptual device of this approach for identifying the process and, in fact, the social basis of semiosis is the phenomenon of "transfunctionalization,"[56] or what I prefer to refer to as the *transformation of connotative meanings*. According to this perspective, a distinction is made between the use of objects to fill their immediate function and a socially sustained use of the object, which produces a second-order meaning for that object. The first-order imputation of meaning, at the level of denotation, produces the sign function of the object – i.e., its meaning according to its immediate function. The second-order imputation of meaning, or the connotative meaning, signifies its social context. It is this level that transfunctionalizes the object to socially prescribed meanings. Furthermore, when the second-order use of objects is explicitly designed to signal a message, communication (intentionality) as well as signification is said to be present.

For example, this approach distinguishes between an automobile used for transportation and that same object used to represent a particular social status. In the second sense, signification is present and the connotative meanings of the object, or the object as a sign vehicle, has been "transformed." Furthermore, if an individual purposely purchased a particular car in order to signal its social status, this connotative transformation of the auto as meaningful object is a form of communication in which the receiver is the society as a whole or the "generalized other." Finally, and most important to the model presented below, through the study of this behavior, psychological reductionism is avoided by the isolation of those specific cultural codes that help structure individual response to the auto and that, therefore, govern the behaviors constituting semiosis. A socio-semiotics of mass culture, then, must trace the ways in which objects produced by industry have their connotative meanings transformed by social processes. However, because this can take place through the actions of producers as well as those of consumers, the connotative transformation process characterizes the entire producer/object/user relation. Finally, the study of mass culture as signification involves the identification of those codes that, in structuring the behavior of producers and consumers, thereby explain the meaningful relation of human subjects to objects and, in turn, to each other. Basically, the socio-semiotic approach often involves a historical sociological study of codes that have been discovered and identified by the analyst. This perspective offers a new type of cultural criticism which avoids the idealism of current postmodern interpretation (see last section).

These two semiotic traditions work from separate premises. Still, both possess implications for an analysis of mass culture. The first tradition (i.e., Baudrillard) emphasizes the symbolic life of objects in society and the way in which mass culture can be viewed as a mode of discourse about objects produced by industry. The second (i.e., Prieto) acknowledges that all of mass culture cannot be reduced to merely the status of a sign. Objects possess a material existence, and it is only when they are used to signify second-order functions that they can be said to communicate meanings. Here the sign becomes an object in the communicative act and is manipulated by the intention-ality of the sender. Hence the sign has been reduced to an object, a tool of communication. In short, it seems that both perspectives con-cern themselves with separate aspects of the signifying process and are germane to a theory of mass culture that stresses the transforma-tion of connotative meanings and the archaeological study of the codes that govern that process. But can these two traditions be reconciled by some synthesis? I shall now attempt to do so by appreciating the many ways in which the semiotic status of the commodity can be conceptualized, according to the variety of codes that can be de-ployed in signification.

Before I proceed with a semiotic model of the producer/object/user relation for mass culture, two preliminary remarks are necessary. First, other approaches to cultural hegemony, such as Jameson's and Baudrillard's, slight the volatile and sometimes contentious nature of the mass culture marketplace. As Gans has observed, there is a pol-itics of culture in society, "ranging from governmental conflicts over censorship to adverse comments people make about the cultural tastes of their neighbors. The most interesting phenomenon, in America, however, is the political struggle between taste cultures over whose culture will provide society with its symbols, values and world view."[57]

So long as they equate the production of false consciousness with ideological control, marxist critics are unable to grasp the potentially contentious nature of cultural politics. In fact, many marxists would no doubt dismiss Gans's conceptualization above as politically naive, because they believe that ruling-class ideology would function to hem in and attenuate challenges to cultural orthodoxy. Yet it has long been observed that even singular examples of media events, such as a news report or a television show, can mean different things to different people. Control of the parameters involved in the possible interpretations of events may lead to the reproduction of ruling class ideology in mass culture, but it is not guaranteed to produce false consciousness. Therefore, ideological domination of the mass culture industries is also not guaranteed to control or even affect an audience's behavior. It is necessary to specify in concrete detail the mechanisms which generate multiple meanings for any cultural object and how cultural politics provides the background for the play of ideological conflict. This ideological clash takes the form of a contentious struggle between separate and often oppositional codes. An inquiry into this struggle becomes a rich area of research on mass cultural phenomena.[58]

Second, mass culture analysts tend to view the audience as a consumer market. If "taste publics" are discovered to vary, this merely signifies that producers must supply a variety of products to satisfy a stratified market structure. Such a view of the mass culture public as an aggregate of consumer groups is reductionist in that it fails to recognize the broadly based nature of group life in modern society. The market segments of the mass culture audience are not made up only of consumers; they include individuals involved in social networks with complex, highly variegated linkages to the larger society. In short, the users of mass culture constitute heterogeneous aggregations or "subcultures." I use the term "subculture," despite its shortcomings,[59] to flesh out the reductionist picture of the mass culture audience, because I wish to draw upon an extensive body of work in mass culture research carried out primarily in the United Kingdom.[60] According to Clarke et al.,[61] for example, the study of subcultures can only be grasped as a "double articulation": first, with regard to a contrast with some parent culture, a contrast blending class, ethnicity, and the like; and, second, with regard to a contrast with the dominant culture of the larger society. Thus, a socially stratified society is composed of numerous social groups and networks, each pursuing a particular subcultural life-style. These groups interact with their parent cultures, as well as with the dominant ideology in society.

In addition, there is considerable variation in the extent to which any one network is integrated into either its parent culture or the dominant one. Thus, some subcultures are unique, but others possess more amorphous boundaries, and any given individual can participate potentially in more than one subcultural circle. In short, by conceptualizing the users of mass culture in subcultural terms, I obtain considerably greater analytical clarity about both the relevance of social context in media effects and role of users in the creation of cultural styles than either the Lazarsfeldian or the "production of culture" perspectives can provide.

Recognition of these two aspects of mass culture – its inherently polysemous nature and its audience of relatively heterogeneous subcultures – also leads to the establishment of two long-recognized principles in the semiotic analysis of culture. First, I acknowledge the multicoded nature of social life and the multiplicity of sign systems that coexist in any given society.[62] The concept of polysemy as characteristic of cultural perception has been an established tenet of semiotic analysis since Barthes' pioneering work.[63] Second, by grounding analysis of the threefold mass cultural relation in the group life of individuals, I recognize the primacy of meaning in all other typifications of social behavior. This means that, before there is "mass" culture, there must be "culture" – that is, the conceptual forms and accumulated knowledge by which social groups organize everyday experience within social and material contexts.[64] Sahlins, in particular, has insisted productively that human behavior is always meaningful and that, consequently, social life is organized first and foremost around systemic, symbolic modes of interpretation. Thus, group life possesses its own "relative autonomy" from economic and political processes. The impact of mass culture must always be understood within the social context of this ongoing, localized process of meaning creation and group interpretation.

A Model of Mass Culture

The proposed model attempts to specify the production and exchange of meanings in the producer/object/user relation in great detail. According to Eco, any object (e.g., an automobile) can be considered in any of five separate ways: (*a*) physically, as a material object; (*b*) mechanically, as an instrument or tool that performs a function (that is, possesses use value); (*c*) economically, as possessing exchange value; (*d*) socially, as a sign of some status; and (*e*) semantically, as a cultural unit that can enter into relationships with other cultural units in a discourse about automobiles and transportation.[65] These five ways of analyzing any object specify its variegated ontological statuses in the group life of social relations. That is, the significance of Eco's approach, as is true of socio-semiotics in general, is that it enables us to think clearly about the separate ways in which social groups can assign meaning to objects.

For example, status *e* specifies the usual domain of semiotic analysis itself. Both denotative signification (the object automobile means "automobile") and connotative signification (the object automobile means "transportation") are included here. Status *d* represents a separate level of connotation also amenable to semiotic analysis that ascribes a second-order level of meaning to objects, as in the object automobile means "wealth" or "social status." It is safe to contend that both *d* and *e*, while not the same, are representative of what Baudrillard calls "sign value" or the object signified by a socially sustained sign, which for Baudrillard *dominates* the relation between individuals and material objects.

In Eco's schema, however, *d* and *e* are not the only possible semiotic categories. Both of the statuses, "use value," or *b* and "exchange value," or *c*, can be converted through social interaction into signs of that function and enter into the type of relationship described by *e*. As indicated above, there are two approaches to signification with regard to function. If I follow Barthes or Baudrillard (essentially the French semioticians and French-inspired postmodern cultural criticism), any object can also be considered as possessing sign value (this is the source of Baudrillard's radical reductionism). If, however, I follow Eco Prieto, Krampen,[66] and the Peircian approach detailed in chapter 1, I must distinguish between an object as an indicator of function and an object that signifies. Socio-semiotics considers the meaning of material objects as a product of social context, which involves the imputation, through social interaction and use, of a secondary function for an object in addition to its primary purpose. This means that, although any non-semiotic status of an object can be converted to what Baudrillard calls "sign value," this process is specified by insertion within a social context and is not inherent in the object itself. Consequently, of the five separate statuses of the object, *d* and *e* are semiotic objects of analysis, whereas functions *b* and *c* can be transformed into semiotic objects of analysis through social interaction.

Furthermore, any existing sign value can also be reconverted to other meanings through the transformation of its social function into third, fourth, and other sign vehicles. From the perspective of this framework, status a, the object itself, is considered the material foundation for the social relations of use, exchange, and sign values that characterize the role of objects in social organization, but it does not itself possess meaning until it enters social interaction. Finally, the entire process is governed by the codes that structure meaningful behavior, as Eco[67] has shown, and these must be identified by analysis in order to explain the precise nature of transformations in sign functions.

The distinctions above accomplish more than the identification of separate semiotic objects of analysis. They imply that any material commodity can assume a multiplicity of meanings through social interaction. This is so because the latter is structured by the intersection of separate codes, often involving contentious oppositions (Gans's "cultural politics" specified more precisely). This property of polysemy or multivocity, as indicated in chapter 1, wreaks havoc with Saussurrean semiotics. According to the socio-semiotic approach, however, the sources of codes can derive from only three modes of social interaction: the ascription of social status that is in part a historical process (sign value per se); use value transformed to sign value, through the variety of separate cultural activities; and exchange value transformed to sign value, especially under capitalist relations of production. In short, the sources of polysemy for mass cultural objects and events are specified by the socio-semiotic approach as deriving from three separate fields of social interaction, making the control of meaning in mass culture, or hegemonic domination, a highly problematic task. This explains both perceptual polysemy and the contingent nature of the hegemonic process.

Before proceeding further, I must emphasize one additional point. The possibility that any object can be transformed by social interaction into meanings that are socio-semiotic objects of analysis does not negate its ability to possess a non-semiotic status. Statuses a, b, and c exist initially as sources of sign functions but are not direct conveyors of signification. In effect, I reject the radical reductionism of Baudrillard, which views all objects in society as possessing sign values. For socio-semiotics, there can never be a pure semiotic analysis of culture at the level of the text itself, because all cultural objects are produced by non-semiotic processes of economics and politics in addition to culture, and because the social context produces second-order and other connotative statuses of sign value. For example, the wearing of a raincoat for protection from rain, and for no other purpose, may "mean" that the use of that raincoat is an index of climate. In this case, mass culture interposes itself only when the raincoat, through fashion, is worn for second-order effects as well.[68] Mass culture, therefore, cannot dominate all aspects of signification. This socio-semiotic view allows for forms of resistance as a signifying process (see below).

The producer/object/user relation at the core of mass culture can now be specified, using the above distinction. Because it has been established that the meaning of an object is a function of the use of that object in social interaction, the symbolic transformations that constitute mass cultural control can be specified by locating people, objects, and events within the social relationships of production, distribution, and reproduction. All that is needed is to focus on the separate social locations. The key aspect of mass cultural production and control is the transformation process located within the social context – that is, the production and control of ideological meanings through group interaction. I visualize this process as operating in three separate stages.

First stage of semiosis: Producer/User

In the first stage, capitalist commodity manufacturers produce objects for their exchange value, whereas purchasers of those objects desire them for their use value. This use value is embedded in a cultural life whose meaning systems preexist the first stage of semiosis associated with mass culture – that is, they exist as society's ideological substratum, or the "substance of the content." The intention of the producer, therefore, draws on a different social practice from that of the user. Exchange value is linked with use value through the discourse of sign value that is so superimposed on this discordant relation by the "logotechniques" of advertising and market control as to "cloud the calculating consciousness of the purchaser."[69]

Thus, domination of consumer behavior is not automatic, as advocates of "false consciousness" theory believe. It is a relation between producer and user that must be superimposed on consumer behavior. The success of its control varies, as any advertising person can testify. The link between exchange value and use value, which is characteristic of the producer/user relation, is designated as the first stage of semiosis for mass culture and involves the transformation of commodities from exchange value to an arbitrary sign value status in order for them to be sold. The success of this relationship cannot always be predicted. This relation is illustrated in figure 8.1. The study of hegemony in this first stage becomes the analysis of the logotechniques of marketing and distribution that are used to seek and secure relatively stable consumer markets.

Figure 8.1   The first stage of semiosis

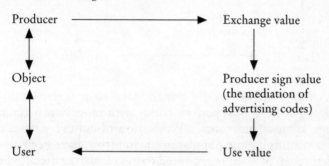

Second stage of semiosis: User/Object

Objects involved in the everyday life of social groups are used because they perform some practical function. As I have indicated, however, these use values can also be transformed by users into sign vehicles that signify a second-order function. This activity constitutes the second stage of semiosis for mass culture: the user/object relation. This second stage involves the creation of culture by the users of objects, a stage that is almost always neglected by critics of mass culture, even postmodern academic interpreters. One example of this aspect of meaning production is illustrated by the process of personalization,[70] in which users modify objects of mass consumption in order to express certain socially meaningful cultural symbols, or in connection with specific group practices, or for use in subcultural activities. Members of the Chicano subcultures of the Southwest, for example, modify automobiles to produce a distinctive "low rider" form. This modification transforms the primary use value of the automobile, transportation, and encodes the object as a sign of belonging to a subculture. In fact, their substitution of hydraulic for normal suspension, their extra small tires, and their small chain-link steering wheels – all distinctive elements in the low rider look – make such vehicles impractical as modes of daily transport.[71] In effect, the commodity has become so personalized by subcultural practice that it has had its primary function attenuated. This second stage of semiosis is illustrated in figure 8.2.

Figure 8.2   The second stage of semiosis

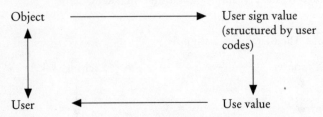

Mass culture analysts in the United States have neglected this stage of semiosis, as have postmodern critics with reductionist claims that this stage is now hegemonic. Production-of-culture advocates, for example, in studying the popular music industry, have been careful to show that much of what is produced derives from the dictates of complex organizational imperatives[72] and/or market structure[73] in industries driven by the profit motive. In contrast, prolific research has been carried out in the United Kingdom on the subcultures that use popular music as expressive symbols.[74] This work includes studies of teddy boys,[75] skinheads,[76] Rastafarians,[77] mods,[78] and the relationship between rock music and youth subcultures.[79] In fact, for over a decade, analysts of the British scene have all observed that youth subcultures organize their activities partly by using aspects of popular music, regardless of whether these are the aspects favored by the industry and often in opposition to what industry leaders intended (see next chapter for a case study in the United States). In this way, youth subcultures have had a profound and lasting effect on the kind of music that has eventually become popular in any given historical period.

The semiotic transformation of objects by users in this second stage is a major source of material for mass cultural sign values. Creators in the culture industries pay careful attention to the codes that govern such subcultural activity. The more deliberate the transformation process at this stage, the more distinctive the cultural elements of the counterculture produced by group practice will be, in comparison with the mainstream. For example, punk rockers in the early stage of their formation (1976–7 in the United Kingdom) consciously sought cultural forms offensive to mainstream sensibilities and incorporated them into the ensemble of punk subcultural appearance. In this way, punk rockers transformed the sign vehicles of all aspects of the youth subculture, including fashion, music, dance, and graphic design. This cultural production, which took place outside and in opposition to the mass culture industry, was highly influential as a source of mass cultural change, even if the radical signifiers of punk were stripped away by that industry from its objects, as I shall discuss below.

Finally, the phenomenon of punk was not understood until the oppositional codes structuring this subcultural behavior were discovered, a process that cultural analysts like Hebdige[80] were only partially successful in studying because of limitations in case study efforts (a subject to be discussed in the next chapter). In sum, therefore, the second stage of semiosis requires study in its own right with careful attention to the subcultures of society that exist outside the mainstream and that create meanings for their own expressive purposes, despite the formidable presence of ideological domination in culture industries (see chapter 9).

Third stage of semiosis: Producer/Object

There is yet a third stage of mass cultural semiosis, one that involves the creation of meanings by producers themselves. The socio-semiotically transformed objects produced by social groups and the needs that are generated by everyday life eventually become the raw material for cultural production by the mass culture industries. This activity, representative of the user/producer relation, can also be viewed as a form of sign value creation. That is, if subcultures can take the objects of mass culture and provide them with second- and other-order meanings, mass culture producers can do the same to the personalized objects of subcultures (see figure 8.3). In general, the transformation of meanings at this stage takes the form of symbolic leveling or trivialization. This constitutes a second, distinct aspect of ideological control in addition to that discussed in the first stage.

Subcultural signifiers are divorced from their everyday codes and transformed by culture industries into more marketable, less radical meanings. For example, the signifier "punk rock" was sanitized by the Top 40 radio industry and changed to "New Wave." Whereas the former connotes a revolutionary counterculture, the latter is a marketing statement utilizing the powerful stimulus "new" to indicate a change in product. Consequently, this third stage is extremely important to the process of hegemonic control associated with the study of ideology. In fact, most marxist studies of cultural hegemony focus on this stage.[81] Figure 8.3 illustrates the complete, three-stage model of the producer/object/user relation and indicates the process of value

Figure 8.3 The three stages of semiosis

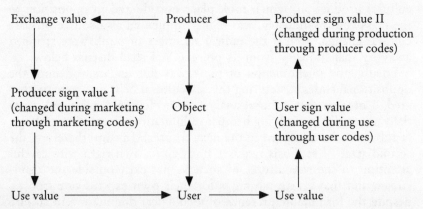

circulation from exchange to use to sign, as well as the points at which the transformation of socially sustained meanings takes place.

My focus on the production of meaning indicates how the creation of sign values by producers is linked directly to cultural creation arising from the daily practices of subcultures. Undoubtedly, however, mass culture industries have the ability to manipulate, if not dominate, the process of cultural production. This observation raises the question of the status of ideological control in the preceding model. In other words, in what sense is the American Marxian critique of mass culture represented by the socio-semiotic processes described above? For most Americans, exposure to the group life of the "other" takes place through the agency of mass culture. Studies of the internal workings of these industries help document the first and third stages of semiosis in figure 8.3 and provide evidence for the ways in which subcultural meanings are first altered by an industry and then fed back to the mainstream audience. In this sense, the semiotic approach is highly complementary to Gramscian and Althusserian analyses of institutional ideological hegemony.

The socio-semiotic perspective offered here is useful because it focuses explicitly on meaning production and the social transformation process of sign vehicles. As indicated, industry producers of commodities change the meanings of objects in two ways. First, they graft advertising sign values to the apparent use value of commodities in order to sell them on the competitive market. This activity is the first aspect of ideological control by "big business." Second, the group use of objects and their transformed meanings are again altered by the culture industries when such objects become candidates for mass cultural production. This activity is a second component of ideological control. Together the two stages of ideological production constitute a powerful social practice by which the user/object relation is controlled for the purpose of reproducing the social relations necessary to capitalist production. Finally, the study of these two stages centers on the codes used to structure the creation of meanings. Clearly, these will change over time, as the history of advertising shows, even if the intent behind such activities remains the same. In short, hegemonists, by focusing on the intent, miss the richness of the contentious conflict between codes as they alter over time.

The model above, however, indicates that hegemony may not be attained in any particular historical conjuncture, a view close to Gramsci's own conception of the nature of ideological control. At each stage of semiosis, values counter to the status quo can seep in because cultural creation is a process and not a schematically controlled product. Furthermore, approaches that advocate ideological domination fail to appreciate the importance of the relative autonomy of subcultural life (see chapter 9). In one sense, the consumption habits of individuals are so manipulated by the mass culture industries as to transform the production of meaning by subcultures into a managed market purchase. But this does not always happen, because consciousness itself can never be controlled. The group life of individuals produces cultural artifacts ranging from those subtle, distinctive touches of style found in individuals' appearances that are often envied by fashion designers to active, total assaults on mainstream sensibilities by countercultures, such as that of punk rock. Even though aspects of semiosis are controlled by the "consciousness industry," to use an obsolete term from critical theory,[82] important degrees of freedom remain for the production of meanings that are independent of either the logic of exchange value or the dominant cultural sensibility, despite what has been said of postmodernism as being the current cultural dominant.[83] In fact, because subcultural signs have lives of their own and are meaning concepts at a deep level, they become sources of raw material for producers of mass culture. The two realms of cultural production are dependent on each other.

Conclusion

The producer/object/user relation at the core of mass culture involves three distinct processes of meaning production and the transformation of connotative sign vehicles. The task of mass culture analysis becomes one of linking textual analysis of the media object with these stages of semiosis. At present, the relation between the mass media and the subcultures of users is less appreciated in the United States than in the United Kingdom. Recent sociology in the US has privileged the production of culture at the industrial level, making cultural studies a branch of the sociology of organizations. Postmodern cultural studies in other fields, such as literary criticism, improves on sociology by carrying out an analysis of the material object and its powers of signification, but postmodernism privileges the independent interpretation of sign value by the analyst and often neglects social context.

The model presented here integrates three separate levels of analysis by emphasizing the transformation of connotative meanings that are derived from three distinct sources. Case studies following this conceptualization should trace the production, circulation, and transformation of expressive symbols among industrial producers, distributors, and the heterogeneous aggregations of subcultures throughout the different stages of semiosis (see next chapter).

The semiotic approach modifies the concept of hegemony as it is conceptualized by many marxist critics of mass culture. Ideological control in modern society can never attain closure and there is a struggle over meanings for cultural objects and events that both the dominant and subordinate groups in society must face. Furthermore, the volatile nature of meaning production and sustenance is characteristic of all stratified societies. All modern states, communist as well as capitalist, confront similar problems in legitimating their rules, even if their social bases for state control differ historically and ideologically. Consequently, the process of hegemony specified by the three stages of semiosis has a generalized applicability to all societies that must legitimate stratified patterns of class, status, and power.

Finally, the socio-semiotic approach calls for a new form of textual criticism that varies from the current practice of both mass culture critics and postmodernists. It rejects the common form of critical review that is based on the individual critic's own interpretations of objects and events. Instead, understanding mass culture from this perspective requires a reading of social practices of cultural use, exchange, and communication in which the history of production and the stages of meaning creation and change can be laid bare. This involves disassembling the creative cycle into its production, distribution, and subcultural consumption or usage components which correspond to the three stages of semiosis outlined above. Most important, this *decompositional* mode of criticism, as opposed to deconstruction, is necessary for isolation of the various influences, from both subcultural and industrial sources, and their interaction in the complete cycles of mass culture production.

The purpose of cultural criticism, from our decompositional perspective, is to recover the lost codes that possess deep, complex cultural intentions which are often altered ideologically in the process of hegemonic control (see chapter 11). Through this process we can also recover the intentionality and deep-level meanings produced by the subcultural and marginal groups which provide the dominant mass culture with many of its most innovative changes.

Notes

1 Fredrick Jameson, "Postmodernism, or the Cultural Logic of Late Capitalism," *New Left Review*, 146 (1984): 53–92; see also the extended, book length discussion of these ideas: *Postmodernism, or the Cultural Logic of Late Capitalism* (London: Verso, 1992).

2 Herbert J. Gans, "The Famine in American Mass-Communication Research: Comments on Hirsch, Tuchman and Gecas," *American Journal of Sociology*, 77, 4 (1972a): 697–705, p. 701.

3 Charles Wright, *Mass Communication* (New York: Random House, 1975).

4 For example, Herbert J. Gans, *Popular Culture and High Culture* (New York: Basic Books, 1975).

5 Paul Lazarsfeld, Bernard Berelson and Hazel Gaudet, *The People's Choice* (New York: Columbia University Press, 1948).

6 R. Peterson, *The Production of Culture* (Beverly Hills, Calif.: Sage, 1976); *Social Research*, Special Issue, edited by Louis Coser, 45, 2 (1978).

7 Peterson, *Production of Culture*.

8 Gans, "Famine in Mass-Communication Research."

9 Todd Gitlin, "Media Sociology: The Dominant Paradigm," *Theory and Society*, 6 (1978): 205–53.

10 Norman Denzin, *Images of Postmodernism* (London: Sage, 1991).

11 Coser, *Social Research*.

12 Paul DiMaggio, "Market Structure, the Creative Process, and Popular Culture: Toward an Organizational Reinterpretation of Mass Culture Theory," *Journal of Popular Culture*, 11, 2 (1977): 436–52; R. Peterson and D. Berger, "Cycles in Symbol Production: The Case of Popular Music," *American Sociological Review* 40 (1975): 158–73.

13 Paul Hirsch, "Production and Distribution Roles among Cultural Organizations," *Social Research*, 45, 2 (1978): 315–30.

14 R. Peterson, "The Production of Cultural Change: The Case of Country Music," *Sociological Research*, 45 (1978): 292–314.

188   *Cultural Studies and Socio-Semiotics*

15   Antonio Gramsci, *Selections from the Prison Notebooks* (New York: International Publishers, 1971); Joseph Femia, "Hegemony and Consciousness in the Thought of Antonio Gramsci," *Political Studies*, 23, 1 (1975): 29–48; Walter Adamson, *Hegemony and Revolution: Antonio Gramsci's Political and Cultural Theory* (Berkeley: University of California Press, 1980); Carl Boggs, *Gramsci's Marxism* (London: Pluto Press, 1976); David Sallach, "Class Domination and Ideological Hegemony," *Sociological Quarterly*, 15, 1 (1974), 38–50.
16   Georg Lukacs, *History and Class Consciousness* (Cambridge, Mass.: MIT Press, 1971).
17   Gramsci, *Prison Notebooks*.
18   David Livingstone, "On Hegemony in Corporate Capitalist States: Material Structures, Ideological Forms, Class Consciousness and Hegemonic Acts," *Sociological Quarterly*, 36 (1976): 235–50; David Cheal, "Hegemony, Ideology and Contradictory Consciousness," *Sociological Quarterly*, 20, 1 (1979): 109–18.
19   Stuart Ewen, *Captains of Consciousness* (New York: McGraw-Hill, 1976); Gaye Tuchman, *The TV Establishment* (Englewood Cliffs, N.J.: Prentice-Hall, 1974); Hans Enzensberger, *The Consciousness Industry* (New York: Seabury, 1974); Robert Goldman, "Hegemony and Managed Critique in Prime-Time Television," *Theory and Society*, 11, 3 (1982): 363–77.
20   Tuchman, *TV Establishment*, p. 38; Todd Gitlin, "Prime Time Ideology," *Social Problems*, 26, 3 (1979): 251–66, p. 253.
21   Lukacs, *History and Class Consciousness*.
22   Louis Althusser, "Ideology and the Ideological State Apparatuses," in *Lenin and Philosophy* (New York: Monthly Review Press, 1971), pp. 127–88.
23   For example, see Paul Hirst, "Althusser and the Theory of Ideology," *Economy and Society* 5, 4 (1976): 355–412, *On Law and Ideology* (New York: Humanities Press, 1981); Simon Clarke, Terry Lovell, Kevin McDonnell, Kevin Robins and Victor Seidler, eds, *One Dimensional Marxism* (London: Allison and Busby, 1980); Rosalind Coward and John Ellis, *Language and Materialism* (Boston: Routledge and Kegan Paul, 1977); Diana Adlam, A. Salfield and N. Rose, "Psychology, Ideology and the Human Subject," *Ideology and Consciousness*, 1 (1977): 5–56; Lucien Seve, *Man in Marxist Theory and the Psychology of Personality* (London: Harvester Press, 1978).
24   C. Hibben, ed., *Politics, Ideology and the State* (London: Lawrence and Wishart, 1978); Ferruccio Rossi-Landi, *Semiotica e ideologia* (Milan: Bompiani, 1972), *L'Ideologia* (Milan: Isedi, 1978a).
25   Peter Berger and Thomas Luckmann, *The Social Construction of Reality* (Garden City, N.Y.: Doubleday, 1966).
26   Althusser, "Ideological State Apparatuses."
27   Hirst, "Althusser," p. 386.
28   Kevin McDonnell and Kevin Robins, "Marxist Cultural Theory," in *One Dimensional Marxism*, edited by Clarke et al., pp. 157–231.

29 Ferruccio Rossi-Landi, "Sign Systems and Social Reproduction," *Ideology and Consciousness*, 3 (1978b): 49–65.

30 Seve, *Man in Marxist Theory*.

31 Working Papers in Cultural Studies (University of Birmingham, 1975), *Resistance through Rituals* 7/8 (Summer).

32 Raymond Williams, *Marxism and Literature* (Oxford: Oxford University Press, 1977); Dick Hebdige, "The Meaning of Mod," Working Papers, 87–98.

33 Gitlin, "Media Sociology."

34 Niklos Rose, "Fetishism and Ideology," *Ideology and Consciousness*, 2 (1977): 27–54.

35 Roland Barthes, *Mythologies*, translated by A. Lavers (New York: Hill and Wang, 1972).

36 Christian Metz, *Language et cinema* (Paris: Larousse, 1971); Jurij Lotman, *The Semiotics of the Cinema* (Ann Arbor: University of Michigan Press, 1976).

37 Jurij Lotman, *The Structure of the Artistic Text* (Ann Arbor: University of Michigan Press, 1977); Jack Burnham, *The Structure of Art* (New York: Braziller, 1971).

38 Roland Barthes, *Système de la mode* (Paris: Seuil, 1967).

39 Roland Barthes, *S/Z*, translated by Richard Miller (New York: Hill and Wang, 1974); Umberto Eco, *A Theory of Semiotics* (Bloomington: Indiana University Press, 1976).

40 Michael Riffaterre, *Semiotics of Poety* (Bloomington: Indiana University Press, 1978).

41 Jean Baudrillard, *Symbolic Exchange and Death* (London: Sage, 1993); Jean-Joseph Goux, *Symbolic Economies: After Marx and Freud*, translated by Jennifer C. Gage (Ithaca, N.Y.: Cornell University Press, 1990); Arthur Kroker and David Cook, *The Postmodern Scene* (New York: St Martins Press, 1986).

42 M. Gottdiener and Alexandros Lagopoulos, *The City and the Sign: Introduction to Urban Semiotics* (New York: Columbia University Press, 1986).

43 Charles Morris, *Foundations of the Theory of Signs* (Chicago: University of Chicago Press, 1938); Martin Krampen, *Meaning in the Urban Environment* (London: Pion, 1979).

44 Roland Barthes, *Elements of Semiology*, translated by A. Lavers and Colin Smith (New York: Hill and Wang, 1969).

45 Ibid., p. 106.

46 Krampen, *Meaning in the Urban Environment*, p. 34.

47 Eco, *Theory of Semiotics*.

48 Eco, *Theory of Semiotics*, p. 30; Raymond Ledrut, *Les Images de la ville* (Paris: Editions Anthropos, 1973); Barthes, *S/Z*.

49 See Diana Adlam and Angie Salfield, "A Matter of Language," *Ideology and Consciousness*, 3 (1978): 95–111.

50 Coward and Ellis, *Language and Materialism*, p. 31.

51 Jean Baudrillard, *Le Systeme des objets* (Paris, Gallimard, 1968), *For a Critique of the Political Economy of the Sign*, translated by Charles Levin (St Louis, Mo.: Telos Press, 1981).
52 See Krampen, *Meaning in the Urban Environment*, p. 6.
53 Ibid., p. 12.
54 Eco, *Theory of Semiotics*.
55 Luis Prieto, *Etudes de linguistique et de semiologie generales* (Geneva: Librarie Droz, 1975), *Pertinence et Pratique* (Paris: Editions de Minuit, 1977).
56 Krampen, *Meaning in the Urban Environment*, p. 36.
57 Herbert J. Gans, "The Politics of Culture in America," in *Sociology of Mass Culture*, edited by D. McQuail (Baltimore: Penguin, 1972b): 372–85, p. 378.
58 See, e.g., Todd Gitlin, *The Whole World Is Watching* (Berkeley: University of California Press, 1981); Dick Hebdige, *Subcultures* (New York: Methuen, 1979).
59 R. Peterson, "Revitalizing the Culture Concept," *Annual Review of Sociology*, 5 (1979): 137–66.
60 Working Papers.
61 Clarke et al., *One Dimensional Marxism*.
62 Jurij Lotman and B. Uspensky, "On the Semiotic Mechanism Culture," *New Literary History*, 9, 2 (1978): 211–32.
63 Barthes, *Système de la mode*; see chapter 1, above.
64 Clarke, et al., *One Dimensional Marxism*; Lotman and Uspensky, "Semiotic Mechanism Culture"; Marshall Sahlins, *Culture and Practical Reason* (Chicago: University of Chicago Press, 1976).
65 Eco, *Theory of Semiotics*, p. 27.
66 See discussion above.
67 Eco, *Theory of Semiotics*, p. 27.
68 Yves Delaporte, "Communication et signification dans les costumes populaires," *Semiotica* 26, 1/2 (1979): 65–79; see also chapter 1, above.
69 Barthes, *Système de la mode*, p. 9.
70 Alfred Willener, *The Action Image of Society* (New York: Pantheon, 1970).
71 Luis Plascencia, "Low Riding in the Southwest: Cultural Symbols in the Mexican Community," in *History, Culture and Society: Chicano Studies in the 1980s*, edited by G. Keller and M. Garcia (Ypsilanti, Mich.: Bilingual Press, 1983).
72 Peterson, "Production of Cultural Change"; Hirsch, "Production and Distribution Roles."
73 DiMaggio, "Market Structure."
74 Hebdige, *Subcultures*.
75 Tony Jefferson, "Cultural Responses of the Teds: The Defense of Space and Status," Working Papers, 1975: 81–6; S. Cohen and P. Rock, "The Teddy Boy," in *The Age of Affluence*, edited by V. Bogdanor and R. Skidelsky (London: Macmillan, 1970).

76 J. Clarke, Stuart Hall, Tony Jefferson, and Brian Roberts, "Subcultures, Cultures and Class: A Theoretical Overview," Working Papers, 1975: 9–74.
77 Hebdige, "Meaning of Mod"; S. Davis and P. Simon, *Reggae Bloodlines* (London: Anchor, 1977).
78 S. Cohen, *Folk Devils and Moral Panics* (London: MacGibbon and Kee, 1972).
79 N. Cohn, *Awopbop a Loobop* (London: Paladin, 1970); G. Melly, *Revolt into Style* (London: Penguin, 1972).
80 Hebdige, *Subcultures*.
81 Gitlin, *Whole World Is Watching*.
82 Enzensberger, *Consciousness Industry*.
83 Jameson, "Postmodernism."

9

Group Differentiation in a Metropolitan High School: The Influence of Race, Class, Gender, and Culture

The concept of "subculture" has always been a sturdy tool of the field researcher's kit. Yet, it has not been used without problems. For example, overuse and lack of specificity have led some analysts to reconsider its value.[1] In addition, Fine and Kleinman[2] list no less than four serious limitations of the term. These include: confusion between the concepts of subculture and subsociety; the lack of a meaningful referent for subculture; the homogeneity and stasis associated with the concept; and an undue emphasis on defining subcultures in terms of values and central themes.[3]

Despite such limitations, researchers of adolescent and/or student behavior have relied repeatedly on the notion of subculture in organizing their analyses over the years. This has occurred in notable studies of the past,[4] as well as in more recent work.[5]

Dick Hebdige's[6] work on British working class subcultures provides a seminal basis for the analysis of the relation between adolescent subcultures and the mass culture industries – specifically, the rock music industry. He has shown how subcultures with articulated ideologies use objects as symbols that express deep-level connotations. By infusing material culture with meanings, subcultures also create a richly detailed and meaningful group life, including the use of fashion, music, drugs, food, and interactive behaviors to signify group membership.

In the previous chapter I introduced a decompositional model of the relation between subcultures and the mass culture industry using socio-semiotics. I argued that both subcultures and dominant cultures are linked together through an exchange of symbolic values and the use of material objects as sign vehicles. I also suggested that cultural creation can be specified socio-semiotically in one of two ways. Either the use of objects is transformed by new cultural practices to new uses which then become new sign vehicles, or new objects are created as expressive symbols of some cultural practice.

Two particular subcultures can be used to illustrate the semiotic process of cultural creation. Through use, the punk subculture transformed common objects, such as safety pins, into graphic indicators of their oppositional ideology. Punks also created new objects of signification, such as the "pogo" style of dancing, which were used as sign vehicles of the subculture (see chapter 11). In another example, Rastafarians created a host of new sign vehicles that had never been seen before, such as dreadlocks, "skanking" dance styles, and "dub" music. They also connotatively transformed previously existing modes of cultural expression, such as reggae music and organic foods, into sign vehicles of the Rastafarian ideology.

Both kinds of cultural creation, new symbolic contexts for old objects and new objects with new signifiers, are highly innovative, and they both rely on the general process of the transformation of connotative meanings along with the transformation of material culture into new sign vehicles that express subcultural ideology.

The socio-semiotic approach to mass culture also studies the relations among cultural levels, as indicated above. Mass culture industries draw upon the cultural creations produced by the lived experience of users for new inspirations and products. In turn, subcultures respond to mass culture through oppositional or accommodational ideologies. The cycle of use value, exchange value and sign value is intertwined with the relation between the mass culture industries and subcultures, some of which may exist in other societies around the globe. Thus, subcultural signifiers may be imported, exported, and refined by global processes of mass cultural production.

According to postmodern cultural analysts, the present moment is characterized by:

1 domination of all cultural forms by the logic of fashion, so that signifiers rapidly move in and out of favor with the consuming public while fast product turnover promotes the circulation of capital as well as signs themselves;[7]
2 pastiche, liminality, and the implosion of cultural styles in an overarching eclecticism that ignores ideological differences;[8]
3 the domination of difference expressed as the free play of signifiers

which typifies cultural creation. Deep-level meanings or signifieds no longer exist, because all culture is only simulation and hyperreal reproduction through cloning.[9]

Case studies reveal that the claims of postmodern observers are limited. They neglect the three-way relation of use, exchange, and sign value and the relatively autonomous relationship between sub-cultures and the dominant mass culture. In short, postmodern critics, in a self-contradictory stance, advocate a totalizing and generalized conception of culture (or subcultural life) which cannot capture the contentious and multi-vocal basis for the creation of difference. As the decompositional model suggests, in contrast, meaning creation and the use of objects as expressive symbols are loosely controlled affairs filled with often conflicting sources for polysemic differences, on the one hand, and attempts by industry to reign in meaning through mass market symbols, on the other. It is wrong to believe that deep-level signifieds have all disappeared, or that a rapidly changing logic of fashion pushes all individuals through a series of never-ending stylish hoops only to alter the basis of consumer choice at every jump. Studies of adolescent subcultures, in particular, reveal historical and trans geographical continuities in subcultural practices, richly textured and deep-level signifieds belonging to codified ideologies, fundamental disjunctive beliefs that shield subcultural consumption from the demands of mass culture, and highly innovative, creative forms of self-expression using material cultural objects that have not all been appropriated by mass culture industries.

The following case study of group interaction in a metropolitan high school illustrates these characteristics and examines adolescent subcultures as a means of qualifying generalizing and totalizing statements by postmodern critics. It seeks to document the real subcultural differences, using empirical data, among a group of high school students. It also shows the relative dependency of adolescent subcultures on mass cultural forms which leads not only to passive consumption in some cases, but to oppositional cultural creation and real, non-simulated, non-hyperreal difference, which is the basis of semiosis and cultural innovation.

This case study explores the extent to which high school students organized themselves into distinct subcultural groupings during informal periods of socializing in the school day. Field observations of student interaction were carried out with permission of school authorities for three months in a high school located in a medium-sized city (population 160,000) in Southern California. Central High School (pseudonym), one of four high schools in the city, is the largest (student population 1900); 73 percent of the students are white, 11.7 percent are black, and 10.4 percent are Chicano (i.e., Mexican-American). Observations in the school were limited to three days a week during lunch hours (11:00–1:00). During these hours almost all of the students could be observed. More specifically, the "lunch court" area of the cafeteria was observed where several hundred students ate and socialized five days per week.

Observations were made of appearance, behavior, and the use of space. No formal interviews or surveys were conducted among the students; however, several students who befriended the observer became informants and drew their friends into this role as well. On occasion, students were asked informally to name activities and objects or to explain events. Through the informal interviews a conception of subcultural ideologies was obtained. After two months of observations, two well-informed full-time high school counselors were interviewed formally to explore certain working hypotheses developed by the observer regarding the use of material culture in group practices and the articulation of group differences through ideologies.

Adolescents in this city high school differentiated themselves into at least ten separate groups. Thus, there were significant cultural differences. Although only the lunch court was observed, we infer that the students carry these group identifications with them in their everyday lives. In many cases, difference was manifested through material objects but was based on deep-level ideological codes. The following discussion defines and explains this diversity of groups. Because this study was limited to observations, the research did not uncover the social mechanisms which structured intra-group interaction. Nor did we learn about other criteria which could be at play, such as, if students grouped themselves into couples (i.e., heterosexual pairs) versus singles, whether the non-couple boys and girls differentiated amongst themselves according to gay or straight orientation, or whether they clustered by grade level (i.e., 9th, 10th, and so on). The focus was on collecting easily observable information about their appearance, their use of language, their tastes in music, whether they fought or not, and where they located themselves in the space of the lunch court. Finally, we cannot explain the genesis of subgroup identification – i.e., why a particular student adopts the behavior of a particular subgroup within the boundaries of race and class. Observations were recorded in field notes under the main headings of appearance, race/ethnicity, and the use of space.

Action at the Lunch Court

The lunch court is an architectural feature of many California high schools.[10] It is a large cement patio fronting the lunchroom where students can dine *al fresco*. The lunch court at Central High accommodates 30 small tables, each seating six students. Other students eat on several concrete steps around the area. The court and steps offer a certain freedom and openness absent indoors. By sitting in any section of the lunch court it is possible to observe the entire area. Students use this open space to eat lunch, socialize with friends, and differentiate themselves from other students.

In the lunch court, blacks, whites, and Chicanos clustered in separate groups. This pattern of informal group clustering by race and ethnicity exists within an integrated school in a city with no observable militancy against racial integration. However, such clustering within the informal space of the lunch court mirrors the spatial segregation in the community at large. At least one researcher has suggested that within school environments minorities and whites participate in this voluntary clustering by race and ethnicity.[11] Yet, we do not know if students who cluster when they are in the lunch court also socialize in these same groups outside of school. Therefore, we do not know if they maintain this same voluntary form of segregation after school hours. Quite possibly there are other groups present in the community that may draw these clusters together, but such integrating mechanisms were absent at the lunch court, if they exist at all.

Racial differences among lunch court students do not end the process of subcultural differentiation. Distinct divisions also exist within each of these racial and ethnic groups with regard to appearance, manifestations of class, and the use of space. These differences were more important than gender. Within each subgroup, males and females tended to dress alike and to hang out together (i.e., share space). In short, the students at the lunch court clustered in distinct ways. First, whites, blacks, and Chicanos sat separately. Second, within each of these larger groups, smaller clusters were observed which were also different in appearance, behavior, and spatial distance from other subgroups.

The Student Groups of Central High School

White students

White students separated themselves into five groups: Frats, Stoners, Surfers, Punks (elsewhere called Hessians), and Goody-Goodies (elsewhere called Nerds). The most numerous group was the Frats. These students adopted a "preppy" look which is a fad advocated in popular fashion magazines for teenagers and which is a dominant mass cultural orchestration of appearance.[12] Frat fashions for boys includes designer clothing, such as Calvin Klein jeans, La Coste shirts, and penny loafer shoes. Frat girls wear skirts and blouses, in contrast to the more casual attire (e.g., jeans or pants) of non-Frat girls. Frat boys often wear dress shirts and an occasional jacket. According to Frat informants, high status clothing for this group consists of famous designer labels rather than impersonal brand names, except in the case of Levi's which is high status (especially the expensive 501 jeans). In general, Frat females tend to wear designer clothing more than males, with the latter characterized instead by high status, non-designer brand name use.

Frats or preppies follow the mass styles of the culture industry. They are slaves to designer labels and other marketing devices. They willingly conform because their clothing and its labels are sign vehicles for high social status, signifying wealth and prestige among the middle class. Non-Frat students view this group as "stuck-up" or "snobbish." This group is not perceived as more successful academically in school than other whites even though they appear to "dress for success." According to informants among the Frats, this group's taste in music is "Top 40" (i.e., the general category of popular culture for music), although they are familiar with other forms such as New Wave and reggae. This is another strong indicator that their tastes are orchestrated by the mass culture industry. Finally, there are more girls than boys among the Frats.

White males were split between the Frat group and other, anti-Frat, subgroups: Punks or Skinheads, Goody-Goodies (Nerds), Stoners, and Surfers. According to informants, Stoners are vaguely identified with the counter culture of the 1960s. Their recreational interests are smoking pot and using other drugs, such as psychedelics, and following rock music, especially heavy metal bands, or, more lately, the Seattle "grunge" sound. The popularity of the latter has sparked a kind of 1960s revival among some students. Stoners wear old pants, torn or faded jeans, colored T-shirts that are either tie-dyed or printed with the logos of heavy metal rock groups, sweatshirts, and/or Levi jean jackets (501 style).

Surfers wear designer clothing but only California brands specializing in leisure or beach wear, such as Hang-Ten, OP, or Lightening Bolt. According to informants, most of the Surfers at Central High do not actually surf (although some do) because Central is located a good 50 miles from the beach. Instead, they identify with the subculture and surf on occasion, whenever they manage to get to the Pacific Ocean. A distinctive Surfer look includes wearing thongs or sandals. If tennis shoes are worn (called "Vans," a manufacturer's name), socks are not. Surfers do not borrow Stoner styles, such as rock group logos, but often cross over into Frat fashions, such as wearing La Coste shirts. According to informants, Surfers are like the Frats in their musical tastes (i.e., preferring Top 40 popular music), although some also like the same music as the Stoners, especially grunge. That is, subcultural preferences are not as focused as in the case of the Stoners.

In addition to the Frats, two other groups involve women as well as men: the Punks or Skinheads and the Goody-Goodies. Punks are distinctive because of their extremely short hair which is often dyed unusual colors, such as electric blue, pink, or bleached white. The males wear military clothing, ripped and faded jeans, and T-shirts that may be dirty and torn or ones similar to those of the Stoners, and absolutely *de rigueur* Doc Marten shoes similar to the boots worn by the skinheads of the UK.[13] Some Punks have a distinct preference for black clothing. Females often wear the same tops as males but with short skirts. Hard core Punks follow "maximum rock and roll" or "Oi!" music, but non-hard core punkers listen to grunge and may cross over into Stoner subcultural behavior. Most of the members of this group are males.

The last group among whites are the Goody-Goodies. Their distinctive characteristics are limited to school behavior. That is, while they tend to dress like Frats, they cluster with each other in separate groups and engage in intellectual activity oriented towards doing well in school. Thus, they are rather inconspicuous and, in fact, few congregate in the lunch court. The successful academic reputation of Goody-Goodies in school is spoken of condescendingly by other students. Most of what was learned about this group came from statements by informants from other groups because the Goody-Goodies were not readily observable at lunch court.

African-American subcultures

Black students divide themselves into two main groups. The larger one has no name but is associated with "middle class" characteristics, a kind of "black Frat." Both males and females within this group "dress for success." The boys affect what they call the "GQ" look. This consists of cords or jeans like the Frats, but unlike them, the black males may wear slacks and "baggies" (stylish, full-cut pleated trousers). Black males alternate preppy clothing with sportswear, the "jock" look: sweatshirts, jogging shoes, and warm-up jackets. Designer names and high status brand names are also favored, according to informants. African-American females wear the same kinds of designer clothes as white Frat females. However, the former tend to wear slacks more often. According to the female black students we spoke to, they also like to wear fashionable tops such as lacy collared blouses (the current style). According to black informants, this group prefers popular "soul music" – artists like Michael Jackson and Diana Ross. They also dislike the music of white groups preferred by the Stoners and Punks.

Black students, like the whites, distinguish themselves by how they wear their hair, in addition to clothing styles. "Unprocessed hair" is worn as either a short or long "Fro" Afro). "Treated hair" can take one of several forms. Currently, the most popular style of hair among both males and females is straightened curl. The hair is processed first and straightened, then a loose curl is put back into the hair. This is a somewhat complicated process and is usually done in a salon; however, some treatments are done at home. Finally, hair can be braided in a number of different ways. In short, and according to informants, the largest group of black students consider attention to hair styles a very important aspect of appearance. This sentiment was not expressed by the majority of whites or Chicanos.

The other group of black students are called "Thugs" (or "Gangstas"). Thugs are lower-class blacks who are perceived as not trying to be fashionable by the majority of black students. One black informant characterized them as "wearing clothing that was not in style," but now their inner-city look is quite fashionable among all non-Frat students. Thugs wear street clothes: sports caps that are often worn backwards, basketball sneakers, T-shirts or see-through tops, Levi's or baggie pants, and often a "crip" coat (a short jacket distinctive of ghetto gang members). Thugs listen to "gangsta-rap" music, which has recently also become very popular among white suburban students. Thugs are associated with wearing earrings and hanging a bandana out of their back pocket to signify gang allegiance (red for "bloods" and blue for "crips"). They often get into fights with both white and black students and, even if not fighting, are generally rowdy. There are both female and male Thugs. They tend to dress alike and have a kind of black Punk anti-fashion bond. Female Thugs wear their hair short or braided, while the males also cut it short and avoid the "Afro" look. According to one black informant,

Thugs are disliked by other blacks who stereotype them as "low class," "dirty," and "stupid." Finally, when compared to whites, both groups of blacks have a conspicuous absence of clothing which references rock music, a similarity they share with Chicano students.

Mexican-American subcultures

Mexican-Americans, or Chicanos, are the fastest-growing ethnic group in California. Most information about the differentiation among Chicanos was obtained from white and Chicano school counselors. Chicanos divide themselves into three subgroups on the basis of their degree of assimilation into mainstream US culture, how well they speak English, and how familiar they are with US culture. One group is comprised of recent immigrants. They wear polyester clothing which is looked down upon by most of the other students regardless of ethnicity. They speak little English and keep a larger spatial distance between themselves and other groups. A second group of Chicano students is competent in English. They are much like the large middle-class group of blacks, except they sometimes wear polyester clothing. This more assimilated group does wear designer fashions and subscribes to many of the same values as the Frats do . The females tend to wear shoes with high heels, a rarity among other groups. They wear their hair straight and cut either long or short. They also tend to wear brighter colors than other students. According to one non-Chicano informant, such colors are looked down upon outside this group. Both blacks and whites disparage the Chicano's use of bright colors and polyester. As in the case of blacks, and in distinction to whites, middle-class Chicano students do not wear clothing referencing rock groups.

   The final subgroup of Chicanos are the analogue of the black Thugs. They are reputed to be gang members. The boys are called "homeboys" or "Cholos" and the girls "homegirls." Cholos all wear their hair alike in a distinctive style: combed straight back and cut short and square around the neck. Sometimes they shave their heads completely. They wear bulky cotton/polyester pants called "Dickies," or khakis, which they taper severely at the bottom, and tennis or "earth" shoes. Sometimes they wear undershirts as tops, but they also prefer heavy wool flannel plaid shirts called "Pendletons", a manufacturer's name. Some white students wear ventilated work or golf caps displaying a logo of some kind; when Cholos wear these caps, like the Thugs, they put them on backwards or with the bill flipped up. The homegirls tend to wear jeans or khakis with satin baseball jackets or other sportswear. Homegirls also have a distinctive hairstyle. They wear their hair long and cut straight in the back. The hair on each side of the face is then curled back over the ears. Homeboys and homegirls are born in the US and speak English and Spanish with varying degrees of proficiency. Whereas Thugs are seen as "lower class," Chicanos consider homeboys and homegirls not in terms of class, but rather as a group which rejects assimilation. Like the Thugs, Cholos have an oppositional subculture. Finally, unlike other Chicanos, this group strongly identifies with a particular type of music – "Oldies." They dislike popular music and listen only to radio stations that play songs from the 1950s and '60s.

Analysis

Considerable differentiation occurred among the students at Central High School. This was evident in appearance and the clustering of groups in space. Each of the ten groups subscribed to a unique style of dress, although some groups, such as the Frats and main group of blacks, blended styles from several sources. Stoners, Punks, Thugs, Cholos, and Frats, in particular, dressed distinctively. In these observations, groups that dressed the same, ate together and therefore socialized together; the one exception may be the Goody-Goodies who did not appear enough times at lunch court to be studied adequately. The distinctions between these groups is illustrated in table 9.1.

Appearance alone, however, was not a sufficient factor to differentiate the separate groups. Race and ethnicity also played a role. In fact, this distinction seemed to predominate. For example, although many black and Chicano students might qualify as Frats by their dress, blacks, Chicanos and whites all sat separately. Furthermore, while Cholos, Punks, and Thugs all shared a similar anti-middle class, anti-fashion ethic, they never interacted and kept a significant spatial distance from each other. Thus, it can be concluded that race and ethnicity are the principal ways in which these high school students differentiated themselves for social reasons. The most isolated group was the recent Chicano immigrants, who did not even interact with other Chicanos. In all cases, space was used to separate groups through the mechanism of clustering.

The second factor of differentiation was some version of hierarchical status within and sometimes between each main group. In the case of blacks, the main factor was class. The black majority, which had no

Table 9.1 A comparison of subgroup characteristics among high school students

Group	Characteristic appearance	Gender	Ethnicity/race	Characteristic activity	Music preference
Frats	Preppy look	Mixed, more women	White	Suburban, middle-class activities	Top 40
Stoners	Long hair, rock T-shirts	Male	White	Taking drugs, going to rock concerts	Heavy metal
Surfers	California beach wear	Male	White	Surfing, going to the beach	Top 40
Punks	Punk, Mod, or Skinhead fashions	Mixed, more males	White	Taking drugs, going to new wave clubs	Maximum rock and roll, New Wave, ska
Goody-Goodies	The Nerd look	Mixed	White	Studying	Unknown
Black (majority)	Modified preppy, styled hair	Mixed	Black	Suburban, middle-class activities	Soul, disco
Thugs (or Gangstas)	Short hair, street clothes, sneakers	Mixed	Black	Gang members	Funk, rap, soul, break-dancing
Chicano (majority)	Polyester, modified preppy	Mixed	Mexican-American	Suburban, middle-class activities	Top 40, salsa
Cholos, homegirls	Straight hair, pegged pants, khakis	Mixed	Mexican-American	Gang members	Oldies
Immigrants	Polyester	Mixed	Mexican	Speaking Spanish	Unknown

specific name, distinguished itself from Thugs, whom it considered lower class. The Thugs were looked down upon by fellow black students because they did not subscribe to middle-class attitudes, such as striving for academic success. Thugs, in turn, were anti-middle class (i.e., anti-white and anti-black) in their physical appearance, use of ghetto slang, adherence to the attitudes of gangsta-rap, and aggressive behavior.

According to informants, whites differentiated themselves by class less than blacks or Chicanos did. Middle-class white students did not disparage lower-class whites as middle-class blacks did lower-class blacks. Middle-class black informants told us that black and Chicano students, regardless of class, considered white Frats to be a kind of economic elite. Minority students expressed resentment that white Frats were "special" – i.e., that they received more attention and prestige from school officials or other groups. Yet, white Frat informants did not perceive themselves in that way, although they did view themselves as belonging to a higher socio-economic class than non-white students. If anything, Frats tended to feel that Goody-Goodies were considered special by the school administration, because they were most concerned with academic success.

Finally, Chicanos also distinguished amongst themselves in a hierarchical manner. However, their differences were essentially cultural. The majority ascribed a lower status to Cholos and recent immigrants, with the latter valued least. This was not specifically class related because Cholos, like the majority, were from assimilated Chicano families. The latter differed from the majority on the basis of culture because of their anti-middle class attitudes. Yet, homeboys and homegirls did not identify with the Mexican culture of recent immigrants. They have fashioned their own counterculture symbols and values.[14] Consequently, as our school counselor informants advised, Chicanos differentiated amongst themselves principally on the basis of cultural rather than class distinctions.

Whites distinguished amongst themselves principally by leisure activities and the subcultures that went along with them. Stoners and Punks were tied most directly to the rock music scene. They differentiated between themselves on the basis of strongly guarded musical tastes, with the Stoners tending to like heavy metal, and the Punks, New Wave music. In contrast, Surfers associated themselves with the leisure activity of surfing and its subcultural attitudes. While a specific type of music was also linked with this activity (surf music), it was not as strong an organizing influence as music's role in the two white groups above. With the exception of the Punks, these groups can be viewed as extensions of life-style preferences among the white adult population.

Stoners, Surfers, and Punks are all associated with subcultural forms that exist throughout California and possibly elsewhere,[15] and which include adults as well as adolescents.[16] Their presence in Central High implies that mass consumption markets which attempt to dominate preferences have only a modest effect that is most successful among Frats. While certain mass marketed commodities are used by the other white groups, they are more impervious to fashion and change. Furthermore, Stoners, Punks, and Frats are not only subcultures in this high school, they are also present in schools across the country. Hence, there is a geographical uniformity to alternative adolescent subcultures which counters the mass market desire for constant change. Furthermore, the main subcultures – preppies, Stoners, and Surfers – represent subcultures that have been around since at least the early 1960s. These canonical adolescent subcultural forms exist across time and space. A Stoner student can move from one end of the country to another and probably find Stoners at the new school. Group identification is strong and the ideology of these subcultures is relatively well defined to allow reproduction over time and across space.

These results place the claims of postmodernists in a less sanguine perspective. Certainly Harvey's and Jameson's assertions regarding the superficiality and eclectic pastiche of rapidly changing fashions does not fit the jealously guarded taste differences that are both historically defined and spatially invariant among high school students.

To be sure, the Frats are dominated by the ever-changing Top 40s record market and this requires a certain acceptance of fashion cycles. However, Frats also look very much like preppy students of the 1950s and their conformity to popular music styles reproduces middle-class, preppy behavior of the past. Other subcultural or counter cultural groups also display a consistency of consumer choice that indicates the presence of an active ideology which guides selection criteria. These ideologies have been relatively invariant across time and space since the 1960s.

Black and Chicano oppositional subcultures are equally as strong and consistent. Cholo life is a venerable institution in Southern California, as are Chicano-oriented "oldies" radio stations. The presence of historically grounded, canonical subcultural forms among high school students replicates the same kind of structure exhibited by English adolescent subcultures, even if the forms themselves vary between the two countries. Teddy boys, for example, are experiencing a third generation in the UK.[17]

If there is anything "postmodern" about high school subcultures, then, it is not their domination by hyperreal simulation. It could be observed, however, that the sheer number of distinctions among the students represents a kind of postmodern cultural "hyperdifferentiation".[18] This is similar to the kind of remark that could be made about the new fabric of the urban built environment as it gets worked over by a variety of styles all different in appearance. However, in the case of the high school, cultural differentiation has been common since at least the 1960s when the counter culture brought ideological and appearance diversity to school populations. The apparent eclecticism precedes the postmodern. My problem with critics who claim a certain postmodern specificity for the present living and working arrangements of the built environment, which I believe is a bogus one, is the same with mass culture observers who read in a "postmodern" quality to subcultural life without awareness of the historical, contextual, or constitutive, basis for adolescent subcultures.

Furthermore, familiarity with the students themselves, which this case study accomplished to a degree, results in an appreciation for deeply held subcultural differences. Thugs, Cholos and Stoners are sincere about their jealously guarded ideological differences with the mainstream. Even Frat status symbols are not superficial signifiers, but substantial sign vehicles that indicate the quest for prestige and wealth and identification with upward mobility. The apparent postmodern recycling of styles, implosion of tastes, pastiche of postures constitutes only one aspect of adolescent life. The postmodernists are only partially right. There is another side to these subcultures that is grounded in deep-level meanings, systems of signification that are also modes of intentionality and communication, expressive symbols of historically and spatially invariant signifieds, and, in short, a decidely non-postmodern, tribalized subcultural life.

In sum, Thugs, Stoners, Surfers, Punks, and Cholos are well-defined subcultures with an articulated sense of values, language, behavior, and appearance that differs qualitatively from the mainstream lifestyle of the middle class. Cholos and Thugs remain separate from other Chicanos and blacks respectively because of their reputation as gang members. Like the Punks, Stoners, and Surfers among the whites, these groups close themselves off by their refusal to dress and behave as middle-class students. The Thugs, Cholos, and Punks have the most in common, although they would never acknowledge such a fact, because all three are countercultures with a reputation for violence and extreme anti-middle class sentiments.

A final finding is the relative absence of gender as an important distinguishing factor. This result is counter to the findings of some researchers of grade school children.[19] Only two subgroups, the Stoners and Surfers, are comprised exclusively of one sex. Within the other subcultural groups, males and females tend to dress alike. This unisex convergence is most extreme for Thugs. Cholos also have their female counterparts, although the homegirls, unlike the female Thugs, dress with subtle feminine distinctions while affecting the Cholo look. Why do the two groups identified as proto-gangs integrate by gender? Male teenage gangs have long been known to cultivate an affiliation with female counterparts. This is so because women play important roles in gang activities, such as carrying weapons or drugs for males. Thus, females from less affluent family circumstances may identify with their male counterparts more than with middle-class females. Yet, the Punks are also integrated by gender, unlike the Stoners and Surfers. At present, Punks are the most fashionable of these three white counterculture groups. Consequently, membership in the Punk subculture may have more to do with current cultural trends which attract students to a clearly defined deviant status, despite its violent reputation. This is in keeping with the analysis of white student groups which finds them structured by mass culture leisure activities, rather than concern about racism (Thugs) or assimilation (Cholos). In effect, while each of these groups is an extension of radical and ethnic subcultures in the society at large, influences from the latter penetrate and structure interaction among whites more so than other groups. Since whites are the majority in the society, this is less surprising than at first glance.

Conclusions and Additional Questions

The presence of this dense array of separate student groups raises some interesting questions. Recent material from other schools in southern California indicate that similar groups exist elsewhere.[20] Why and how are these particular types formed? Some of the groups are relatively recent and are associated with current fashions such as the Punk or preppy looks. Yet others, such as the Stoners or Surfers, have been around for some time. Why is this so? What is it about the latter two that not only contributes to their longevity as a subculture but also structures the interaction of a new generation of high school students? Finally, why is rock music such a potent differentiator among whites? To what extent do mass cultural marketing publics help structure the behavior of adolescents?

Two inferences can be drawn from this study. First, since both the adolescent and adult worlds are heterogeneously organized into sub-cultures, it can be assumed that the latter penetrates the former to varying degrees. However, it would be a mistake to suggest that youth subcultures are mere extensions of the adult world and popular culture. Rather, cultural innovations from student groups also influence the larger society, especially with regard to fashion, language, and music. This is notably true of the influence of countercultural forms associated with adolescents, Thugs, Cholos, and Punks. Thus, cultural influences must by viewed as flowing between all levels of society. Second, racial and ethnic distinctions are the most powerful way in which students differentiate amongst themselves, while class is important primarily in the case of blacks. This does not mean, of course, that class plays no role in other groups, only that its effect is not readily apparent and subgroup members do not talk about interactions in these terms to us. It is possible that Stoners, Surfers, preppies, and Punks among whites come from different socio-economic strata, but they are more readily distinguished on the basis of leisure preferences.

This study suggests that mass cultural forms provide sign vehicles for the expression of subcultural difference, but we have not explained why certain cultural products within each racial/ethnic group help structure certain subgroups and not others. Finally, there are strong countercultural expressions present in all three groups, whites, blacks, and Chicanos. To what extent are these anti-mainstream sentiments carried over into post-high school life? At least for the students observed in this study, perhaps maintaining distinct cultural expressions was a potent way of organizing social interaction. College students and adults in society appear much less diverse. What happens to adolescents when they get older that makes them conform? Finally, it is worth asking how other industrial societies, such as those in England, France, or Poland, differ both with regard to the importance of cultural subgroups as the organizing referent for social interaction and with regard to the extent of social differentiation based upon subgroup differences among different age groupings.

Notes

1   R. Peterson, "Revitalizing the Culture Concept," *Annual Review of Sociology*, 5 (1979): 137–66.
2   G. Fine and S. Kleinman, "Rethinking Subculture: An Interactionist Analysis," *American Journal of Sociology*, 85 (1979): 1–15.
3   Ibid., p. 1.
4   Frederick Thrasher, *The Gang* (Chicago: University of Chicago Press,

1927 [1963]); Howard Becker, B. Geer, E. Hughes and A. Strauss, *Boys in White* (Chicago: University of Chicago Press, 1961); Bennet Berger, "On the Youthfulness of Youth Cultures," *Social Research*, 30 (1963): 319–42; J. Bernard, "Teen Age Culture: An Overview," *Annals of the American Academy of Political and Social Science*, 338 (1961): 1–12; Albert Cohen, *Delinquent Boys* (Glencoe, Ill: The Free Press, 1955); J. Coleman, *The Adolescent Society* (New York: The Free Press, 1961); David Matza, "Subterranean Traditions of Youth," *Annals of the American Academy of Political and Social Science*, 338 (1961): 102–18; H. Remmers and D. Radler, *The American Teenager* (Indianapolis, Ind.: Bobbs-Merrill, 1957).

5   G. Mingham and G. Pearson, eds, *Working Class Youth Culture* (London: Routledge and Kegan Paul, 1976); Working Papers in Cultural Studies, *Resistance through Rituals* (Birmingham: University of Birmingham, 1975); W. Partridge, *The Hippie Ghetto: The Natural History of a Subculture* (New York: Holt Rinehart and Winston, 1973); M. Brake, "The Skinheads: An English Working Class Culture," *Youth and Society* 6 (1974): 179–200; S. Larkin, *Suburban Youth in Cultural Crisis* (New York: Oxford University Press, 1979); Dick Hebdige, *Subculture: The Meaning of Style* (New York: Methuen, 1979).

6   Hebdige, *Subculture*.

7   David Harvey, *The Postmodern Condition* (Oxford: Blackwell, 1989).

8   Fredrik Jameson, *Postmodernism, or the Cultural Logic of Late Capitalism* (London: Verso, 1992).

9   Jean Baudrillard, *Simulations* (New York: Semiotext(e), 1983).

10 D. Crowe, *Fast Times at Ridgemont High* (New York: Simon and Schuster, 1981).

11 Gilda Haber, "Spatial Relations between Dominants and Marginals," *Social Psychology Quarterly*, 45 (1982): 219–28.

12 See, for example, *Seventeen*; L. Birnbach, *The Official Preppy Handbook* (New York: Workman Press, 1980).

13 Brake, "The Skinheads"; Hebdige, *Subculture*.

14 Luis Plascencia, "Low Riding in the Southwest: Cultural Symbols in the Mexican Community," in *History, Culture and Society: Chicano Studies in the 1980s*, edited by G. Keller and M. Garcia (Ypsilanti, Mich.: Bilingual Press, 1983).

15 Crowe, *Fast Times*; Hebdige, *Subculture*.

16 J. Irwin, *Scenes* (Beverly Hills, Calif.: Sage, 1977); Partridge, *Hippie Ghetto*.

17 Hebdige, *Subculture*.

18 Stephan Crook, Jan Pakulski, and Malcolm Waters, *Postmodernization: Change in Advanced Society* (London: Sage, 1992).

19 For a similar study that deals with grade school, see B. Thorne, "Girls and Boys Together . . . But Mostly Apart: Gender Arrangements in Elementary School," in *Feminist Frontiers III*, edited by L. Richardson and V. Taylor (New York: McGraw-Hill, 1993), pp. 115–26.

20 Crowe, *Fast Times*.

10

Unisex Fashions and Gender Role Change

Gibbon tells us of the Roman emperor Elagabalus, who exhausted the traditional means of living to excess available to heads of the empire, put on women's clothing and forced a Roman senator to marry him. In a comparable occurrence, Simmel[1] notes the royal antics of Elizabeth Charlotte of the Palatinate, a sister-in-law of Louis XIV, who wore men's clothing and dictated fashion at the French court for a time by requiring all the palace women to follow her lead and by coercing the males to conduct and dress themselves as women.

These are examples of transvestitism – the wearing of clothes produced for the opposite sex. Through the arrogance of power such deviance can be acted out. Most of us, however, find laws and everyday social norms constraining greatly our gender role appearance. For example, a male transvestite wearing a dress is liable to be arrested. As Gregory Stone[2] has indicated, sex differences are forcefully regulated by the personal evaluation, social judgments, and expectations governing "appropriate" dress. This fundamental activity of gender socialization through clothing styles comes to constitute a gender-based "universe of appearance" for the individual and society. The process of gender role socialization in all its aspects uses appearance as a visual vehicle.

Social norms regulate the body.[3] While much of this normalization is subtle, the regulation of appearance in societies usually is not. Fashion or dress is comprised of material objects that articulate with the body to create sign vehicles that help signify a variety of cultural codes. One of the strictist divisions is gender. In fact, there is little question that the social distinction male/female as manifested in clothing is a primary one. It may, in fact, be added to other structural binary oppositions, such as Lévi-Strauss' raw/cooked and Durkheim's sacred/profane, as a fruitful analytical antipode. In a historical review, for example, Crawley[4] maintains that sexual distinctions in dress are a universal aspect of all cultures. As a general category of socialization, therefore, gender appearance is a powerful mechanism for organizing, integrating and enforcing patterns of social interaction.[5] In this sense transvestism is a phenomenon which negates the fundamental male/ female distinction and its social order. This suggests its consideration by society throughout history as an anti-social act.[6]

   This chapter explores further the male/female dress distinction. It does so by examining the phenomenon of unisex – the borrowing or blending of gender-specific fashion styles produced for both sexes. Rather than the negation associated with transvestite acts, unisex in- volves a resolution of gender differences which still preserves the tension of the social distinction and stops short of one sex dressing totally in clothes made for the other. My thesis is that contemporary unisex phenomena (circa 1970s) are not only interesting social acts in their own right, but that unisex is the social vehicle associated with the gender role change observable among middle-class women from the Second World War to the present. The discussion proceeds in two stages. First, I shall explore briefly the social processes governing appearance and gender role distinctions in modern society. Second, I shall examine the phenomenon of unisex and use a structural analysis of fashion changes in the post-war period to demonstrate the associa- tion of unisex with gender role change. In both cases the material objects of clothing constitute a system of sign vehicles that help to regulate the important social division of gender relations.

Gender Roles and the Social Order

It is clear that in our society women have been ascribed a weaker social position than men. Dress is one way that gender status differ- ences are signified and enforced.[7] For this reason the importance of gender-specific clothing in male-dominated society compels us to examine more closely the socialization mechanism of appearance. The mere act of wearing women's clothing situates and validates the fe- male's subordinate role. While it may be supposed that men's cloth- ing would also signify their dominance, this relationship is not as strong. This is so because of the dual nature of super- and subordi- nation. Once the lower status is accepted by women, male dominance is validated. One social manifestation of this ascription involves the harsh social response elicited by male transvestites, because they threaten the implied control of a social order in which women are expected to do most of the symbolic work in status role dress dis- tinctions.[8] In contrast, women dressing in men's clothing have been accepted generally as bohemians, such as the Victorian writer George Sand; as fashionable celebrities, such as Marlene Dietrich, Katharine Hepburn and Madonna; or trivialized as lesbians.

The male-dominant social order is structured by two additional factors related to dress. The first concerns the representation of occupational roles by clothing. Until quite recently, women dressed either for domestic work or to show that they did not have to do such chores.[9] House dresses, aprons and bandanas were some of the everyday clothing worn by most women. In contrast, men's clothing signifies the varied work roles of individuals who participate in a labor market. The traditional businessman's suit, for example, has its design origin in the austere Puritan uniform adopted by the bourgeois Protestant aesthetes of Cromwellian England.[10] Until the 1950s capitalist accumulators following in this spirit could be spotted by the vested suit of somber black or brown which they wore, just as the workers signified their "calling" and social status by their job-specific uniforms.

Second, the male/female dress distinction is signified by the shapes, colors, and fabrics of clothing itself. There is evidence to suggest that class/status differences in our society continue to be represented symbolically by dress distinctions and, in addition, that women continue to do most of this work, despite the growing complexity of the present social order.[11] According to one analyst, for example, the two basic forms – dress and pants – have clear sexual connotations. The former emphasizes the pelvic region and the maternal function. Historically, women have used various devices such as hoops, crinolines and pinched waists to emphasize their shape, as well as using the bodice, corset, or the present-day brassiere to accentuate the breasts. In contrast, pants represent masculine characteristics. (See figure 10.1.)

The longhose which superseded the Barbarian trews and preceded the modern trousers emphasized most effectively the male attribute and social quality of energy and activity as represented by lower limbs, the organs of locomotion.[12] Such contrasts exist in fabrics and colors as well. Men's fashions are dominated by coarse, heavy material, such as corduroy and wool, and by somber colors. Women's fashions still reflect a preference for light fabrics, such as crepe de chine and cotton, and are available in the entire spectrum of color.

Unisex and Gender Role Change

The male/female social order of industrial society can be defied in appearance by transvestite negation. In unisex, the tension of the

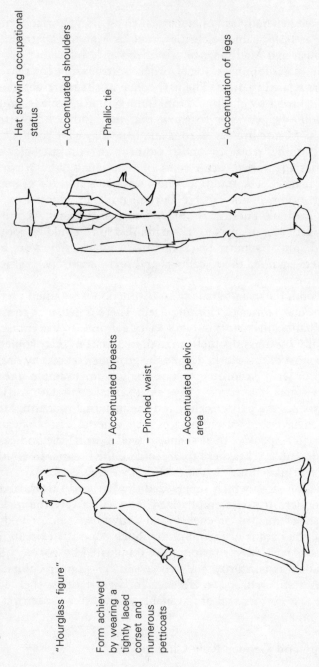

Figure 10.1   The female and male icons

"Hourglass figure"

Form achieved
by wearing a
tightly laced
corset and
numerous
petticoats

– Accentuated breasts

– Pinched waist

– Accentuated pelvic
  area

– Hat showing occupational
  status

– Accentuated shoulders

– Phallic tie

– Accentuation of legs

distinction remains but is reduced. The borrowing or blending of gender-specific fashion forms associated with unisex, therefore, involves a process of symbol exchange and communication about the dress code and the social order it represents.[13] This process uses appearance as a sign vehicle to communicate gender status differences. During the progressive development of the capitalist system in England and America there has always been a close connection between the dominance of the male bourgeoisie and the reaction against it utilizing the vehicle of appearance. Unisex phenomena have been present for quite some time. Before tracing the modification of male superordinate status in the fashions of contemporary society, let us examine briefly several earlier instances.

Dandyism or the Flaneur

Because of the expected fluctuations in women's appearance and fashions, unisex clothing first achieved notoriety as a male-initiated event. In England during the 1800s, non-violent social change had enabled the members of the aristocracy to retain wealth and social significance despite the rule of the bourgeoisie. Some of the young males belonging to this upper class, including the infamous Beau Brummel, became known as "dandies," "Flaneurs," or "Dudes."[14] The dandies showed their disdain for the Victorian businessman by flaunting their lack of need to work, by becoming the paramours of wealthy middle-class women, and by dressing in a flamboyant manner. They adopted elements of feminine apparel, such as ruffled shirts and stylized hats, and also carried these forms to extremes by exaggeration and embellishment.[15] Gradually, dandy fashions spread across Europe to the aristocracy and bohemians who wished to demarcate their social distance from the vigorously productive but blandly dressed capitalist entrepreneurs and their exploited, uniformed workers.

The fashion revolt against the Victorian industrial order eventually also inspired female unisex. This was most notably connected with the turn-of-the-century women's suffrage movement.[16] Amelia Bloomer and her followers agitated for the right to vote and wore bloused pants or "bloomers" under their knee-length skirts, resolving the male/female dress opposition in a below-the-waist layered look. This kind of accommodation is typical of changes in gender dress styles; that is, the contentious nature of male–female relations is manifested in the way alternative sex-typed objects of appearance are borrowed, blended, and modified by both women and men.

Why women and pants?

In the 20th century, as the industrial order became stabilized before
the Depression, acceptable styles of appearance reinforced the male/
female dress opposition. Bohemians, dandies and suffragettes seemed
to die out. Paris haute couture designers, however, kept women's
unisex alive among the bourgeoisie in a stylized manner. Along with
the right of vote, several women were beginning to have careers and
one, the female French designer, Coco Chanel, was frequently pho-
tographed wearing pants in her more active social role. By the '20s
couturiers such as Paul Poiret, Chanel, Patou, and Le Long introduced pants for women and popularized what they labeled the
"garçonnes" look – tailored suits, white silk shirts, and men's ties.[17]
     It was not, however, until the 1930s that the man-tailored look
acquired limited social acceptability in this country. At that time
women such as Marlene Dietrich and Katharine Hepburn achieved
"star" status and chose to validate their success and independence by
wearing pants and suits designed for them. While this mode of dress,
especially as worn by Dietrich, may have bordered on transvestitism
in the manner of George Sand, it was not. The look was unisex:
fashioned by Parisian women's designers; tailored for women with
feminine touches, such as attached clasps instead of belts; and considered "chic" by the female fashion world even if few women would
wear it. (See figure 10.2.)
     Prior to the 1950s, therefore, most men conformed to the dress
code signifying male dominance, while women flirted with unisex
phenomena in a stylized form that was, in part, the creation of Parisian designers. This reflected the growing change in the female role
beginning with the suffragettes and continuing with the few women
who achieved public careers. The specific attainment of social acceptability for women's pants was a highly significant event. As we have
indicated, it remains a unique act of freedom available to women
relative to men in our society. In sharp contrast to male dress limitations, women can avail themselves of two fashion worlds and a
continuum of appearance alternatives, from man-tailoring to total
"cloying femininity".[18] Men cannot cross-dress to skirts with the same
impunity. In fact, male cross-dressing, as indicated above, is a much
more serious matter, because it jeopardizes the male-dominated social
order.
     Pants, therefore, provided the basic unisex vehicle which reflected
the increasing social independence of middle-class women. The unisex aspects of fashion fluctuations in womenswear from 1900 to 1950

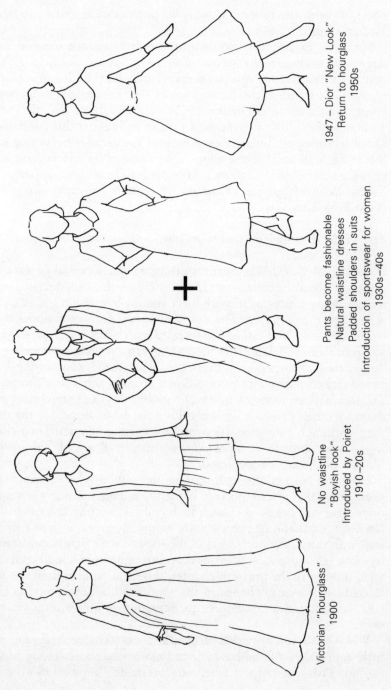

Figure 10.2 Fashionable womenswear, 1900–50

1947 – Dior "New Look"
Return to hourglass
1950s

Pants become fashionable
Natural waistline dresses
Padded shoulders in suits
Introduction of sportswear for women
1930s–40s

No waistline
"Boyish look"
Introduced by Poiret
1910–20s

Victorian "hourglass"
1900

contrasts with the relative stability in menswear, as shown in figure 10.2 and figure 10.3.

Symbolic exchange between both genders did not develop on a large scale until after the Second World War. It was at this point that conformist patterns of appearance were defied by both sexes. Unisex phenomena signified the breakdown of the male/female dress opposition which occurred in the 1960s counterculture and the 1970s women's liberation movements. In order to support this contention, I shall examine clothing styles in each of the decades beginning with the 1950s, and analyze the appearance alternatives and fashion code exchange using socio-semiotics. My conclusions will be supported by fieldwork investigations of the use of fashion by career women in New York City.

The 1950s: Conformity and rebellion

Post-Second World War America brought about a period of maturing capitalist social organization. In the 1950s fashions associated with the emerging white-collar work force and the burgeoning middle class were highly conformist. There was little variation in clothing worn from day to day and fashions associated with work were also used for social occasions. Adult males became "organization men" wearing the same Brooks Brothers or J. Press grey flannel suits and herring-bone tweed jackets along with button-down collared shirts that comprised the standard uniform of upwardly mobile Ivy League college students. Women played a limited role in the labor force, for the most part working for the growing corporations as secretaries. Their clothing was as uniform as menswear, consisting of a dark shirt, white blouse, and pearls or pin jewelry.

Conformity was also enforced in the public schools which had dress codes that were especially harsh toward girls wearing pants and boys wearing blue denim jeans. Such codes resembled the sumptuary laws of the Middle Ages by strictly enforcing appearance as a sign of status. In this case, adolescents in the society were rigidly constrained by both age and gender identification through grade school codes. As we discussed in the previous chapter, this rigid regulation of the adolescent body was to change in the 1960s with a breakdown in code enforcement and a consequent proliferation of subcultural clothing styles.

While the fashion worlds of men and women were separate, with little appearance alternatives, unisex phenomena arose among adolescents as a nascent spirit of rebellion (foreshadowing the 1960s). When

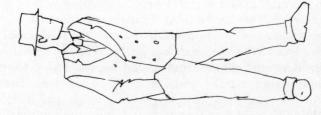

Soft shoulders
Single breasted
Three button
1950s

Padded shoulders
Wide lapels – wide pants
1920s–40s

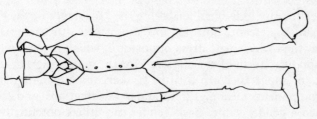

Figure 10.3 Fashionable menswear, 1900–50

High button suit
1900

not in school both boys and girls wore denim jeans. The latter rolled up their cuffs to display the thick, white socks known as "bobby socks", while the former's use of denim identified young males with the outlaw motorcycle gangs and "juvenile delinquents" achieving notoriety during the period. The wearing of denim by both sexes became the ultimate violation of high school dress codes and signified rebellion to the conformist adults who were concerned with the behavior of youth. During the 1950s wearing Levi's was an instant sign of rebellion and was responded to harshly by school officials.

To an extent the male/female dress opposition was minimized by adolescent fads during school hours as well. Gender-neutral unisex forms such as "penny" loafers and the exchanging of class rings, "ID" bracelets, and high school sweaters were additional modes of reaction against enforced gender separation through appearance.

Women engaged in unisex dressing through the medium of pants which were worn in leisure hours associated especially with suburban living. Females could choose from several popular styles: above-the-ankle "Capri" pants; mid-calf "pedal pushers"; or mid-thigh "Bermuda" shorts. For the most part, however, school, work, and social occasions required sharply drawn appearance alternatives in the 1950s.

I shall demonstrate the growth of appearance alternatives in the syntagm of fashion and their relationship to the phenomenon of unisex by utilizing the following notational scheme. Female appearance or "form of the expression" will be designated by a plus sign (+), male appearance or "form of the expression" by a minus sign (−), and gender-neutral styles or "form of the expression" worn by either sex will be designated by a zero (0). We can then break down aspects of appearance for any individual analyzing the "substance of the expression" − hair, top, waist, bottom, and shoe styles, for example − according to the male/female dress opposition, which is the denotative and connotative "form of the content" for the gender sign in society.

Aspects of appearance can then be broken down, paradigmatically (i.e., by components meaningful for apparel distinctions) and each can be assigned a gender value. Each gender can utilize potentially three sexual signs in our scheme. One would signify clothing in the style traditionally associated with that gender. A woman wearing a dress, for example, would be assigned a bottom gender-valence of plus (+) in this case. A second alternative would signify a clothing form associated traditionally with one sex, but styled and marketed for the opposite sex, such as pants for women or flower print shirts for men. The former would be designated by a minus gender-valence (−), while the latter would be assigned a plus (+). Finally, we must consider in our scheme clothing which can be worn by either sex as socially acceptable according to prevailing norms, such as penny loafers or denim jeans. Such forms will be signified by a neutral gender-valence (0).

Using such a scheme, which is structured both paradigmatically and syntagmatically according to dress distinctions, we can then identify unisex phenomena as consisting of one of the following two alternatives. One gender can borrow a form of clothing from the opposite sex and thus switch gender-valence, or unisex can be signified by the wearing of a gender-neutral style. Judgments of valence are made on the basis of social acceptability for each period under consideration. Our classification of alternatives and their gender-valences for the 1950s is illustrated in table 10.1.

As we can see from table 10.1, in the 1950s unisex phenomena occurred with limited frequency. Minimal appearance alternatives were created by adolescents in the unisex form of gender-neutral styles. De-emphasis of gender differences in the 1950s was associated with youthful rebellion and this is a highly significant point for later stages. Switching of valence occurred through short hairstyles and pants or leisure wear for women. In this way, females could take advantage of the minimal freedom available to them in male-dominated society. By wearing pants women could *double* their clothing combinations relative to men. The latter were "locked in" by the requirements of

Table 10.1   1950s appearance components and alternatives

Gender valence	Hair	Face	Fragrances	Neck jewelry	Top	Arm or finger jewelry	Waist	Bottom	Shoes
Female									
(+)	+	+	+	+	+	+	+	+	+
Unisex									
(−) (0)	−					0		−	0
Male									
(−)	−	−	−	−	−	−	−	−	−
Unisex									
(+) (0)	−					0			0

the dominant code. Hence, pants were a powerful sign vehicle of women's liberation.

Table 10.1 makes an added distinction with regard to males. Their faces are self-evidently gender-specific because of sexual differences in facial hair, however disguised by soap and razor. Nevertheless, if men so desired they could exercise a degree of freedom from the majority by emphasizing or de-emphasizing facial hair. Thus in the "clean-cut" era of the 1950s men, such as the beatniks, rebelled by growing beards. Beards are designated by a double minus (– –).

The 1960s: The counterculture

It was not until the 1960s that the drive towards the relation of male/female dress distinctions became as strong for men as for women. This coincided with the formation of the college-aged counterculture that emphasized equal participation in activities and an ongoing dialogue between men and women. "Sexual freedom" and women's rights, if not fully realized, were early elements of the political protest movement. The general agreement among both genders of a rejection of adult values and their society included the adoption of adolescent outfits of rebellion, especially blue jeans, army surplus jackets, workshirts and workboots on an everyday basis. These were masculine in form and by the middle sixties politically involved youth of both sexes began to resemble each other in overall appearance.

At this time young males de-emphasized their social role by engaging in gender-neutral behavior, such as refusing to cut their hair in any style, thus giving them an unkempt, rebellious look. In fact, a major gesture of rebellion among males was simply moving away from the normative male version of appearance through the growing of hair length. Gender-neutral fragrances such as patchouli oil and gender-neutral "love beads" or Indian turquoise were also worn by both sexes. The masculine blue jeans themselves evolved into a gender-neutral unisex style called "bell bottoms" which were to be worn along with boots by both sexes. Bell bottoms were pants with a slightly flaired skirt at the bottom, thereby combining male and female attributes. Although overall unisex appearance in the middle sixties relied on the rebellious masculine form, the period witnessed as well the introduction of several gender-neutral unisex fashions which served to de-emphasize the male/female distinctions.

The progressive development of the counterculture in the late sixties shifted to a psychedelic phase which moved beyond the drab outfits of the earlier period. For the first time, gender-specific styles were exchanged as men visibly borrowed clothing and fabrics from women's fashion in a *reciprocal* relationship. Long hair became worn by men in "pony tails" or braids. Flower print shirts made of women's house dress fabrics were worn by men, complementing the sentiments of the "flower power" generation. The feminine aspects of counterculture male clothing were largely inspired by the Carnaby Street fashions tailored for the working class Mods in England. Their Edwardian clothes revived dandyism and its stylized, effeminate mode of dress.

By the 1970s, counterculture dress had developed into a highly creative activity which utilized a large variety of clothing elements and fashion inspirations. Antique, recycled clothing, T-shirts, army surplus, western wear and Carnaby Street fashions provided the wide availability of assorted apparel that facilitated maximum self-expression and minimal conformity. Both genders "mixed and matched" these elements in rather flamboyant costumes which were worn every day and included fragrances, capes, leather fringes, beads, turbans, rings, and bells. This system of signification for the counterculture stood in sharp contrast to the clothing available in the adult world, which retained its conformist and separatist character.

Women's fashions from mass culture clothing industries also were affected by change. During this period major fashion designers promoted the feminine miniskirt. As in all other periods, females could avail themselves of such feminine-oriented forms as well as indulging in counterculture rebellious behavior, such as refusing to wear bras. Males, in contrast, were sharply divided between "hippies" and the easily identifiable proponents of the status quo in the Vietnam years.

During the counterculture period, a marketing form also developed which catered to the denim and antique clothing needs of unisex youth. Bell-bottomed pants, T-shirts, boots, and used clothing were sold to both sexes in establishments patterned after the small Paris fashion shops called "boutiques." Both men and women availed themselves of the same changing rooms in these boutiques, breaking down the traditional barrier between male and female clothing departments in stores. These kinds of unisex stores are prevalent even today. Finally, "unisex" itself emerged as a word or specific signifier in the 1970s lexicon to define hair styling salons which serviced the demanding needs of male/female long hair. This loss of gender-specificity in hair developed through several stylized expressions, such as the shag or layered look. As late as the 1980s hair salons could still be found advertising "unisex" cutting techniques. These counterculture changes are illustrated by table 10.2, and figures 10.4 and 10.5.

Table 10.2   Counterculture appearance alternatives, 1967–1972

Gender valence	Hair	Face	Fragrances	Neck jewelry	Top	Arm or finger jewelry	Waist	Bottom	Shoes
Female									
(+) Unisex	+	+	+	+	+	+	+	+	+
(−)					−		−	−	
(0)	0		0	0	0	0	0	0	−
Male									
(−) Unisex	−	−	−	−	−	−	−	−	−
(+)	+				+				
(0)	0	−	0	0	0	0	0	0	

As indicated in table 10.2, fashion alternatives were increased in almost every area of appearance. Importantly, these developed along the two dimensions of unisex. First, styles were borrowed from the other gender and, second, styles were developed which were not gender-specific. Both of these cases are examples of cultural creation discussed in chapters 8 and 9. In the first case, already existing material objects were invested with new signifieds and became sign vehicles of gender changes. In the latter case, new material objects were created within the context of dress.

Of the eight areas in which change occurred for women, seven involved the use of gender-neutral articles, while four aspects borrowed from male clothing. Of the seven areas in which change occurred for men, each involved a gender-neutral phase, de-emphasizing the male role, and only two borrowed distinctly from women's fashions (see figures 10.4, 10.5, and 10.6).

When compared to table 10.1, fashion changes of the counterculture (i.e., table 10.2) indicate several significant differences between the genders. First, there was a general de-emphasis of male/female dress distinctions during the 1960s with the development of gender-neutral unisex apparel and marketing forms. Second, change for men moved less towards dandyism than in the gender-neutral direction. In contrast, women availed themselves of masculine appearance alternatives in addition to gender-neutral styles. Added to the female fashions present at the same time, the wide range of clothing choices defined

Figure 10.4 Female unisex fashion alternatives

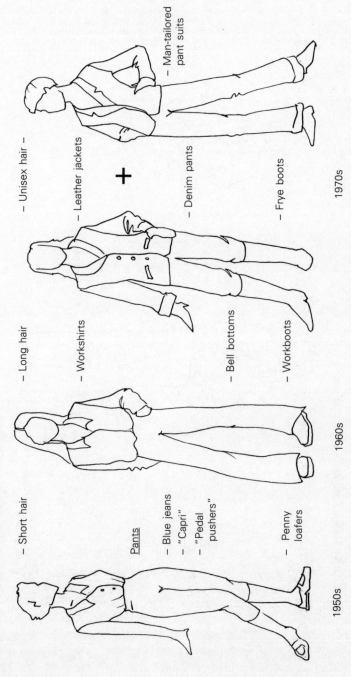

– Short hair –

– Long hair –

– Unisex hair –

Pants
– Blue jeans
– "Capri"
– "Pedal pushers"

– Workshirts –

– Leather jackets –

– Man-tailored pant suits

– Denim pants –

– Bell bottoms –

– Penny loafers

– Workboots –

– Frye boots –

1950s

1960s

1970s

Figure 10.5 Male unisex fashion alternatives

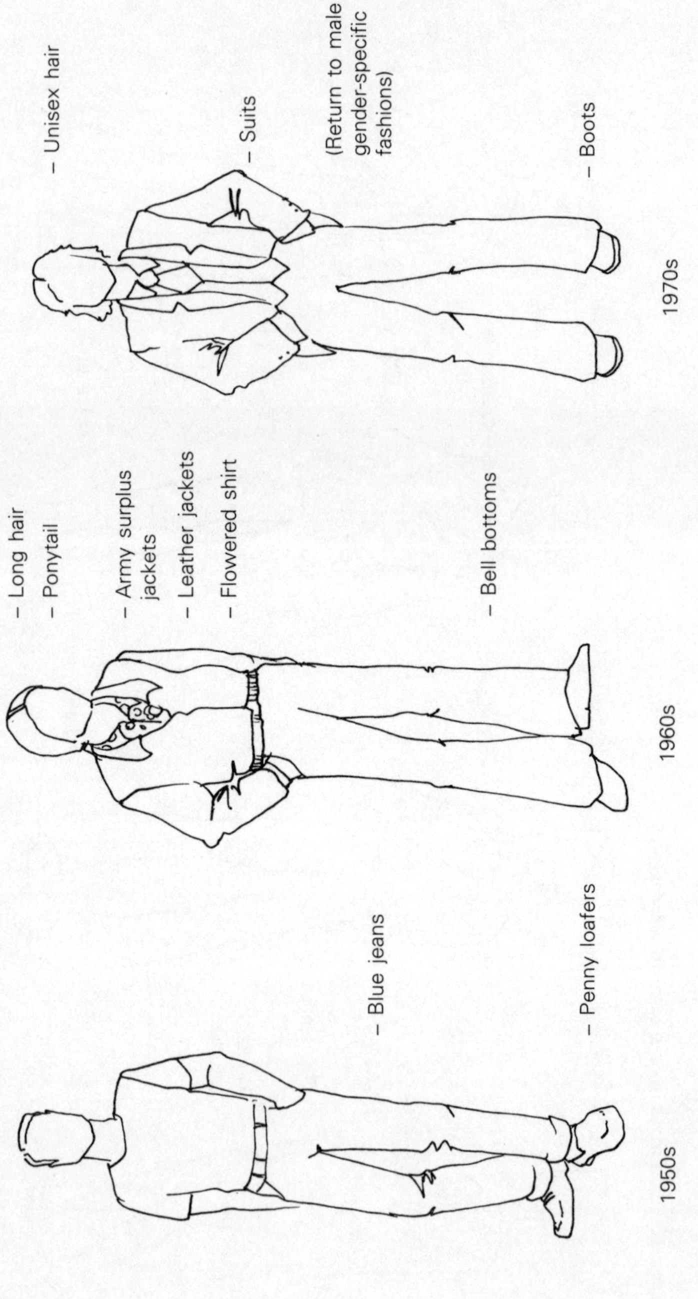

- Unisex hair

- Suits

(Return to male gender-specific fashions)

- Boots

1970s

- Long hair
- Ponytail

- Army surplus jackets
- Leather jackets
- Flowered shirt

- Bell bottoms

1960s

- Blue jeans

- Penny loafers

1950s

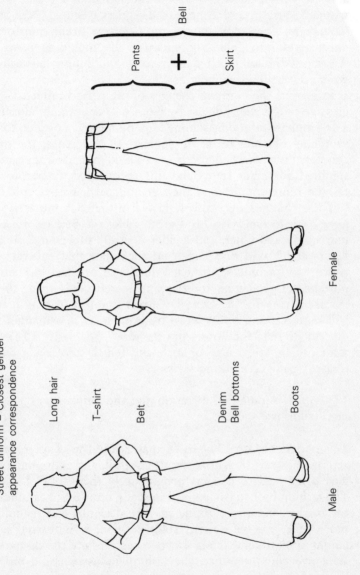

Figure 10.6 Unisex clothing transformations
1967–1972
Street uniform – Closest gender
appearance correspondence

Long hair

T-shirt

Belt

Denim
Bell bottoms

Boots

Male

Female

Bell

Pants

+

Skirt

world of appearance that was broader in scope and freedom for women. Parisian and American designers, such as Yves St Laurent, Courrèges, Chester Weinberg, and Geoffrey Beene transformed these alternatives into "chic" acceptability by including pants, fatigues, American-Indian motifs, miniskirts, and hippie fashions in their womenswear lines as early as 1968.

In general the clothing changes of the period reflected a more aggressive role in the wide use by women of appearance alternatives and a de-emphasis of the masculine look by men, as opposed to the actual switching of roles by both genders. In this sense, the men in the counterculture "backed off" from the rigid masculine appearance which signified dominant status and this encouraged women to engage in fashion representations of their greater participatory role in society.

These changes were also reflected in the rock music world which gave birth to dandyish Mod groups like the Beatles, unisex couples like Sonny and Cher, and gender-neutral "superstars" such as Mick Jagger and David Bowie. Recent rock stars that cultivate unisex or androgyny include Madonna, Prince, and Michael Jackson. The importance of gender neutrality was also reflected during the counterculture period by the everyday street uniform of long hair, T-shirt, bell bottoms, and boots worn by both sexes in a manner making it difficult to tell "the boys from the girls" (see figure 10.4). Much the same can be said today of male and female adolescent Stoners that follow "grunge" clothing styles.

1970–1977: Women's Liberation and the return of man-tailoring

This period, the final one to be analyzed in this chapter, can be characterized as one in which social, political, and economic institutions have attempted to reassert progressively their control over society. The fashion industry depends especially upon a tight orchestration of the market, because clothing may be designed and manufactured as much as a year before it is sold. Fashion, in industrial society and among the affluent, is highly coercive. Despite the disappearance of an active counterculture, the fashion industry could *not* recapture the lead in dictating womenswear choices, sharply contrasting with the well-oiled corporate machine that emerged elsewhere during the Nixon–Ford years. While the number of women who participated in the counterculture remained small, by 1970 every female in the society had undergone a consciousness-raising process regarding their social status. This was reflected directly in the clothing market. In

1970 the industry pushed the "midi" skirt as an answer to the mass-produced mini of the 1960s and the flamboyant counterculture clothing. All fashion leaders and magazines, with the exception of *Glamour*, supported the controlled change in style. The midi, however, became the "Edsel" of the womenswear world with its rejection by consumers across the country.

In the period which followed immediately, it became apparent that unisex sensibility and female gender role change were both still alive and had to be adjusted to by the industry. This was increasingly accomplished in a process which continues to the present day, basically by a broadening of all the available choices open to women in manufactured apparel. On the one hand, no one style is considered today to be *de rigueur*. On the other hand, the industry accepts the concept that fashion can no longer change completely from year to year.[19] Thus, while we could assert that the proliferation of fashion alternatives constitutes a kind of postmodern hyperdifferentiation, it must also be noted that this eclecticism comes as much from a breakdown in the power of image-driven culture over everyday use values as it does from orchestration by the clothing industry of mass market styles.

Unisex phenomena continue to operate in society in association with gender role change. In the case of women, heightened consciousness by consumers has rejected the principle of being dictated to. The industry has retooled its approach by appealing to the subjectively felt needs of females as individuals. In this way, advertising tries to appropriate the ideology of the women's movement. Magazines, designers, manufacturers, and department stores have coopted the signifiers of "women's liberation," if not acquiescing to its politics. Fashion copy and promotion project the message of freedom, independence, and individuality. For example, a 1976 ad for designer clothes stated: "Today's woman reflects an independent mind. And that independence supports the genius of John Kloss. Because she knows, as America's primary night clothes designer, he is committed to making the most of her body in a simple yet sophisticated way."[20]

While such copy merely appropriates the need for gender equality and does not realize it, the fact remains that such appeals are used precisely because women hold such sentiments and consciously feel such subjective needs. In this sense, domination of the market place no longer exists and many women exercise an independent attitude that cannot be taken for granted by the industry.[21] The greater freedom exercised by women in fashioning their appearance is reflected best by the notion of "separates" and the fact that adult females today

no longer purchase entire outfits or "ensembles," but are more in-
clined to buy separate items of clothing. They then use their ward-
robe as a source of self-expression, dressing each day in a creative
exercise by fashioning a mode of appearance which consists of the
wide variety of new and old clothing. The ready-to-wear industry in
the US produces for this market by providing an extensive assortment
of choices for each category of clothing. That is, the pants, skirts,
tops, shoes, hair styles, and fragrances which comprise the system of
fashion have numerous choices in each category which are socially
acceptable to wear and which structure the complex syntagm code of
fashion.[22]

Fieldwork interviews conducted among career-oriented young
women in New York City indicate that many working females enjoy
this dressing activity as a creative means of self-expression. They are
involved in fashion less as consumers, because they must pay for their
own clothing and restrict their purchases, and more as highly selective patrons. They make judgments about what is made available in
conjunction with what they already own and relative to how it will
effectively manage social interaction, and enhance their moods. The
system of dress represents a set of sign vehicles that enable women to
negotiate social interaction. This is often a creative activity. Thus, it
is difficult to claim, as some cultural critics might, that mass culture
holds hegemony over these women. The activity of dressing, while
circumscribed by the persisting social regulation of the body, is characterized by self-actualization and cultural creation, rather than the
passive consumption hypothesized by hegemony theorists (see chapter 8).

In one example, a woman photographer revealed that when she
goes for job interviews she is well aware of the constraints on women
professionals. She chooses distinctive designer outfits or man-tailored
clothes because "I don't want to appear frivolous. I need the gig and
I really want to be taken seriously." In another example, an attractive
model stated that when not working she encountered problems from
men while walking in Manhattan. She managed this unpleasant interaction more effectively by switching to westernwear boots and denim
jeans, along with a leather jacket. The mannish appearance drew less
negative attention from male chauvinists.

By the late 1970s, womenswear persisted in actively following both
aspects of unisex, although gender-neutral styles were progressively
disappearing for both sexes. The major emphasis by the end of this
case study (late 1970s) was on man-tailoring and men's fabrics for
women in addition to the usual alternatives available in feminine-

Table 10.3 Contemporary fashion alternatives, 1973–1977

Gender valence	Hair	Face	Fragrances	Neck jewelry	Top	Arm or finger jewelry	Waist	Bottom	Shoes
Female									
(+)	+	+	+	+	+	+	+	+	+
Unisex									−
(−) (0)	0		0	0	−	0	−	−	0
Male									
(−)	−	−	−	−	−	−	−	−	−
Unisex	−								+
(+) (0)	0	+ (Cosmetics)	0	0		0			0

appearing apparel.[23] Menswear, in contrast, displayed a strong return to gender-specific styles as counterculture de-emphasis of masculinity appears no longer to exist. Males participate in unisex in a more broadly structured way by having become fashion conscious. Presently they have entered the traditional women's world of fashion. In contrast to the situation during both the 1950s and 1960s, there exists a wide variety of apparel items available to men which change fashionably in social acceptance including cosmetics, suits, shoes, jewelry, shirts, and leisure wear. Almost all of this array is fashionable in a second sense, because such commodities are associated with industry designers and labels such as Bill Blass, John Weitz, Yves St Laurent, and Ralph Lauren. Many of these orchestrators of style, such as St Laurent and Blass, were originally womenswear designers who presently produce clothing lines for both sexes. Thus, while men's clothing has returned to a separate status in a specific sense, men themselves have been enticed into the fashion world and participate in its marketing forms as much as women. The contemporary trends are indicated in table 10.3. Feminine styles for men exist only in cosmetics and shoes. The latter recently reintroduced dandy-style buckles. Gender-neutral styles persist in hair, shoes, fragrances, and jewelry, while women appear to be borrowing more from man-tailoring. (See figure 10.5.)

The 1960s counterculture broke down partially the male/female dress opposition code through symbolic exchange utilizing unisex phenomena. Men de-emphasized their dominant role and rebelled by wearing effeminate as well as non-conformist clothing. Women wore the aggressive outfits of college radicals and gender-neutral hippie fashions. This symbolic exchange made use of an incredible variety of apparel choices which fragmented the regimentation of fashion styles typical of the 1950s. This type of fashion interaction was more limited by the 1970s. Men returned to gender-specific clothing, and fashion code communication about the male/female distinction appears one-sided in favor of women. In part this reflects the persistence of male dominance and the appropriation of feminine sensibilities among men by their participation in the commercial fashion world. In contrast, women continue to communicate their desire for equal status through the vehicle of unisex clothing and its 1976 form of man-tailoring.

In the 1970s women displayed their dual freedom by drawing upon a separate feminine fashion world with its exclusive womenswear designers such as Kenzo, Mary McFadden, and John Anthony. Simultaneously, however, they pursueed the need for man-tailoring in a vigorous way. One reason for the vital popularity of the latter in 1976 fall lines was the progressive participation of women in the "man's" world of careers. Copy for an ad placed adjacent to an Ann Klein double-breasted pinstripe woman's suit said, "This is what feeling self-assured is all about – serious suitmanship – right down to the last perfect detail. All I need now are extra pages for my appointment book."[24] Thus, while equal gender status has not been fully realized, the desire to attain it persists among women. Unisex clothing will continue as well to be an important way in which such symbolic sentiments are communicated.

Notes

1   Georg Simmel, "On Fashion," *American Journal of Sociology*, 62 (1957), 541–58.
2   Gregory Stone, "Appearance and the Self," in *Human Behavior and Social Processes*, edited by Arnold Rose (Boston: Houghton Mifflin, 1962), pp. 86–118.
3   Michel Foucault, *Discipline and Punish* (New York: Vintage Press, 1979).
4   Ernest Crawley, "The Sexual Background of Dress," in *Dress, Adornment and the Social Order*, edited by Mary Ellen Roach and Joanne Bubolz Eicher (New York: John Wiley and Sons, 1965), pp. 72–5.
5   H. I. Douty, "Influence of Clothing on Perception of Persons," *Journal of Home Economics*, 55 (1963): 197–202; R. Sybers and Mary E. Roach, "Clothing and Human Behavior," *Journal of Home Economics*, 54 (1962): 184–7.

6 Otto Fenichel, "The Psychology of Transvestitism," *International Journal of Psycho-Analysis*, 11 (1930): 211–27.

7 For some time in the past, studies of the relation between fashion and the regulation of appearances, especially with regard to gender, were written by men such as Thorstein Veblen (see below). Recently, however, this topic has resurfaced as part of feminist literature and some excellent studies have been published: Juliet Ash and Elizabeth Wilson, eds, *Chic Thrills* (Berkeley: University of California, 1992); Lois Banner, *American Beauty* (New York: Alfred Knopf, 1983); Diane Barthel, *Putting on Appearances* (Philadelphia, Pa.: Temple University Press, 1988); Alison Lurie, *The Language of Clothes* (New York: Random House, 1981); Anne Hollander, *Seeing through Clothes* (Berkeley: University of California, 1993); Elizabeth Wilson, *Adorned in Dreams: Fashion and Modernity* (London: Virago, 1985).

8 E. Bergler, *Fashion and the Unconscious* (New York: Brunner, 1953).

9 Veblen has indicated that one way in which conspicuous consumption has operated for wealthy men is through the clothes worn by their spouses. The time-consuming participation of wealthy women in the haute couture world of fashion, often involving several trips a year to Paris, was a distinctive mark of the leisure class. See Thorstein Veblen, *The Theory of the Leisure Class* (New York: New American Library, 1953); "The Economic Theory of Women's Dress," *Popular Science Monthly*, 46 (1894): 198–205.

10 Rene Konig, *A la Mode: On the Social Psychology of Fashion* (New York: Seabury Press, 1973).

11 Bernard Barber and Lyle S. Lobel, "Fashion in Women's Clothes and the American Social System," *Social Forces*, 31 (1962): 124–31. See note 7, above.

12 See Crawley, "Sexual Background of Dress," p. 74.

13 The semiotics of fashion is explained in: Roland Barthes, *The Fashion System*, translated by M. Ward and R. Howard (New York: Hill and Wang, 1983); Umberto Eco, *A Theory of Semiotics* (Bloomington: Indiana University Press, 1976); M. Gottdiener, "The Semiotics of Fashion," in *Encyclopedic Dictionary of Semiotics*, edited by Thomas Sebeok and P. Bouissac (The Hague: Mouton Publishers, 1986, 1994).

14 C. M. Franzero, *Beau Brummel: His Life and Times* (New York: John Day and Co., 1958); see also Walter Benjamin, "On Some Motifs in Baudelaire," in *Illuminations*, translated by Harry Zohn (New York: Schocken Press, 1969), pp. 155–200.

15 Konig, *A la Mode*; Simmel, "On Fashion."

16 R. E. Riegel, "Women's Clothes and Women's Rights," *American Quarterly*, 15 (Fall 1963): 390–401; see also Roach and Eicher, eds, *Dress, Adornment and Social Order*, note 7, above.

17 *Women's Wear Daily*, March 3, 1976, p. 5.

18 Roach and Eicher, eds, *Dress, Adornment and Social Order*, p. 214.

19 Information on the "midi" was obtained from an interview with an

editor of *Vogue*; information on fashion industry changes was obtained from an interview with a fashion critic for the *New York Times*.

20 *The New York Times*, July 11, 1976, p. 6.

21 At this point it is appropriate to mention briefly a word about the notion of cultural control in late capitalism (see chapter 8). Several mass culture critics support the view that industry control is total and that all needs are fetishized and appropriated by the system. In this sense, subjective acts under capitalism are within the dominating or hegemonic closure of the profit motive and choice is merely an illusion. This "one dimensionality" may exist, for example, in the movie industry, which has limited participation in production; however, it does not characterize the situation in fashion. The incredible variety of clothing choices, marketing outlets, home sewing patterns, and fabric shops represent a qualitatively independent sphere of production and consumption possibilities for appearance.

Baudrillard, among postmodernists, would simply not care about these possibilities, since they all can be viewed as manifestations of sign value differences. However, the importance of appearance as a mode of self-expression and development of subjectivity has been widely demonstrated (see note 7, above). As indicated in chapter 8, it is far better to conceive of this activity as the interplay among use, exchange and sign values, rather than the reductionism of Baudrillard. As Theodore Adorno has pointed out in his critique of Veblen, the dialectical tension between real subjective needs and objective dominating society *always* exists. Even the pursuit of desires through commodity purchases represents a personalized response to a world in which culture is progressively mechanically produced; see Martin Jay, *The Dialectical Imagination* (Boston: Little, Brown and Co., 1973); Fredrick Jameson, *Late Marxism* (London: Verso, 1990).

22 For a discussion of the syntagm and paradigm as it relates to the analysis of dress, see Barthes, *Fashion System*, chapter 1.

23 It is interesting to note that man-tailored clothes for women today use heavy, coarse, masculine fabrics as well as men's styling. The linings, however, are made of soft fabrics such as cotton or satin which are traditional feminine ones. In this way women's man-tailoring has a hidden, feminine touch. This unseen dimension representing the outside vs. the inside of clothing is extended in the phenomenon of unisex by undergarments which have retained gender-specific fabrics and styling, although men's underwear has progressively become articulated with fashion in recent years and include color and style differences.

24 *The New York Times*, July 11, 1976, p. 31.

11

Recovering Lost Signifieds: Cultural Criticism in a Postmodern World

Postmodernists such as Baudrillard celebrate the liberation of signs from dependency on well-defined signifieds. In part, this is viewed as a liberation from the strict confines of normative, foundationalist doctrines which themselves have historically led to tyranny and repression so many times. In part, too, this liberation celebrates the demise of bourgeois ideology which disappears in the "black hole"[1] of omnivorous and voracious capitalist consumerism. The outcome of postmodernist cultural production has meant for many a liberation from the canons of tradition and the creation of a certain space within which free expression and free association can reign.

In chapter 8 I argued that culture in late capitalism doesn't quite fit the reductionist vision of postmodernists. Mass culture involves a three-way relation between use, exchange, and sign values. The extraction of the latter by mass culture industries who produce commodities for profit most often involves the stripping away of deep-level signifieds, or contextualized use values, and the marketing of the gutted shell of meaningful signs as images. The latter constitutes the elements of culture that bother postmodernists most, but free-floating signifiers represent only one aspect of culture. There is also an authentic sector that involves everyday practices which can manifest resistance.[2] One important feature of the dynamic relation between subcultures and the dominant culture industry is the way the latter requires the everyday cultural production, or the signifying practices[3] of the former for its own commodity production. Reversing that process and reclaiming the stripped-away signifieds becomes, then, a type of cultural criticism, just as it may also protect us from the imperialistic demands of the dominant culture industries.

Postmodern critics, however, are not completely wrong. While all forms of authentic culture are not automatically coopted by the hyperreal image-inducing and -mediating process of the culture industry, there is ample evidence to suggest that image-driven culture affects individual self-expression and the grounds of meaning in daily life. Mass cultural production diverts our ability to place deep-level understandings on the images that are constantly valorized for us by that industry.[4] In particular, there remains an often implicit acknowledgement that postmodernism, more so than previous cultural modes, subverts the desire for authenticity in everyday life.[5] It is, in fact, the enemy of authenticity, posed as it is to pounce on any cultural form and strip its deep meanings bare for the benefit of handling a decontextualized and easily manipulatable signifier as some new image or facade.

We can respond to this process by restoring lost signifieds and reacquiring the meaning of things. This type of cultural criticism and resistance depends not only on examining the meaningful basis for individual action, but on the recovery of previously abandoned or marginalized group contexts. Cultural criticism involves recontextualization and a return to authentic cultural forms through the discovery of lost signifieds which counteracts the superficial consumerist culture of postmodernism that privileges image, appearance, and disembodied signifiers.

This chapter concludes this book with two examples of cultural criticism as cultural exploration and discovery that reflect the sensibility advocated by the above perspective, rather than being exemplars of the method itself. The first concerns the quest for roots and the second involves the difficult task of reading subcultures from popular rock music.

The Quest for Roots

Alex Haley's monumental accomplishment, *Roots*,[6] ranks as the singularly best example of how individuals can counteract the negating qualities of modern and postmodern consumerist culture as they affect self-identity. Haley crystallized the politics of authenticity for its most disadvantaged group, African-Americans. It moved the signifier "Africa" away from its abstract nature as some vague, heterotopic "promised land" in the discourse of black nationalists, such as Marcus Garvey or Malcolm X, and recontextualized in great detail the African experience of black Americans. The "Africa" of Alex Haley is a multidimensional signifier with polysemic signifieds invoking a sense of history; a rupture with the past; a specific place, location, village, spot on the global geopolitical grid; a culture, a cultural diversity; an origin; and finally, a "home." Black Americans now possess this "Africa," thanks to Haley, and this sign's ability to recontextualize daily life rather than the abstractions of the past, of the "back to Africa" days, of the decontextualized ideology of separation and nationalism.

Recontextualization of personal history and the cultural politics of identity has its postmodern side in enabling a proliferation of polysemic frames of reference for social interaction. This multiplication of personalized, subjectivized conceptions of social interaction and its multicultural politics may be the down side of the search for authenticity. Yet, the quest for an authentic past is decidedly non-postmodern from the individual's point of view. It represents empowerment, spiritual and emotional grounding, existential cohesion, and the contextualization of personal history and identity – all of which work against the hyperdifferentiation and superficial aspects of consumer culture characteristic of postmodernism. We are not simply one self one day and another the next, not simply the product of marketing schemes and a self imputed by the dominant culture of hypercommodified capitalism; instead, as Haley showed, we can possess a grounded, empowered self based on a historical account which operationalizes our individual signifieds around which an authentic self can be constructed.

For Haley, the discovery of roots began as an earnest and organized quest. For most of us, the recontextualization of identity occurs through accidental or serendipitous encounters that provide some missing information to the great puzzle of personal background, if this mystery is confronted at all. When the confrontation with the past occurs by accident it can have great power in reconceptualizing personal identity.

In 1993 the Pintig Cultural Group of Chicago performed the play *Alamat*. Its story underscores the importance of cultural politics as the recontextualization of lost signifieds through the encounter with personal history and localized space, as described by a newspaper account:

> "Alamat," the ambitious work of a young playwright named Rodolfo Carlos Vera, is the story of Pat (Tony DeCastro), a college educated Filipino American who comes of age during the Vietnam War era, but only comes to terms with his heritage after he brings his father's body home to the Philippines for burial. For Pat, his father, Gadiaman, was always the pathetic loser, an alcoholic hopelessly trapped in the past and treated like

a second-class citizen in American society. What the young man discovers, however, is that he is a descendant of the Kalinga tribe, an indigenous people of the Cordillera mountain region renowned for their skill as warriors and their fierce determination to remain free of outside authority. Through an ambitious use of flashbacks that interweave the myths and realities of the Kalingas with scenes from Pat's life and his conversations with his saintly, storytelling mother, a whole century of experience comes to light.[7]

For Haley and Vera, the recontextualization of identity involves a physical journey which extracts the individual from the context of this society and inserts her/him in the different reality of some antecedent culture. This physical journey, or the encounter with a material milieu or space, is an important part of the search for self-identity. Without it, the reworking of signifieds by the dominant culture which becomes convoluted and highly multivocal over time cannot be truly untangled. Put another way, only the individual's physical and spatial encounter with the culture of origins enables the personal epiphany of self-awareness to work its existential magic and re-integrate the lost signifieds with subjectivity. This is so because self-realization and identity formation take place within a material as well as ideological context. The former dimension, the valorization of material artifacts and locations as the setting or props of identity, is ignored by theorists of the self. Instead, they rely almost exclusively on the idealist, psychological, and cognitive aspects of this process (see below). Socio-semiotics, as discussed in previous chapters, corrects the privileging of the mind in the discourse of culture, and prefers to articulate the balanced relation between the psychic and the physical, or ideal and material factors in the production and consumption of culture.

We are never simply a product of culture. We are what we have made ourselves in response to personal experience, the valorization of the artifacts of our own milieu, and the mediation of the image-making interpretations of mass media. This formation of the self usually privileges the present or most contemporary experiences. But we are always something more – a historical product of the specific experiences of individuals who are now dead but who integrated their own experience with the culture within which they were born. Cultural criticism as the politics of authenticity, as the recontextualization of self-identity, underscores this personal search for lost signifieds which often entails physical travel and the re-insertion into a different cultural milieu as a way to find historical roots and re-contextualize the self through an encounter with a separate material reality.

Case Study

If postmodern culture works against realizing an authentic self, as some suggest (see next section), that might explain why the search for roots has become important to all social groups, not just African-Americans. One form this takes is through spectacular associations. That is, often people will claim that some long-dead ancestor was a member of royalty. This is a practice I find common among English and German descendants living in America, but I have also encountered people who claim descent from tribal chiefs and princes, famous rabbis, or historical and sports figures. I cannot say much about the relative truths of these claims. All of this symbolic work, however, reflects the quest for cultural capital and the valorization of the family name in the face of society's persistent devaluation of the individual. Other efforts at grounding family history are reflected in the construction of family trees, including the monumental archiving project on family descent being carried out by the Mormons. There are even shops in suburban malls that have commodified this desire and sell family crests and annotated histories, which in cases other than common Anglo-Saxon names seem quite suspect.

I began an investigation into my family tree quite by accident. My father was an orthodox Jew from the section of Hungary that is now part of Russia, not too far from the Hasidic community of the Satmar, although his family belonged to the Misnagdim (anti-Hasidim). When he settled in the Bronx, New York, he chose to live within walking distance of a synagogue. This temple was orthodox and had a well-known rabbi. My religious identity at the time was formed through my experiences within this environment where most of the people my parents interacted with were Hungarian Jews and also belonged to this temple, although my immediate neighborhood was predominantly Puerto Rican/Italian and possessed a multicultural social environment. I received a substantive Jewish education and a bar mitzvah; I socialized at the temple with people my age, and participated in the religious services. In short, the social and religious space of this corner of the Bronx reproduced an authentic Jewish identity within myself and other children my age, despite the multiculturalism of the South Bronx, although it did not reproduce the experience of orthodoxy in Hungary. In addition, that religious identity, while substantive, was only one aspect of my sense of self, which also included being a part of the South Bronx, Puerto Rican/Jewish/Italian working-class milieu.

While growing up I understood myself to be an Ashkenazic Jew – i.e., a Jew belonging to the cultural grouping of the population that was dispersed among the European nations. My father worshipped in an Ashkenazic synagogue, our Jewish neighbors were Ashkenazim, and at Hebrew School we were taught the Ashkenazic variant of Judaism and its culture. In addition to the many multivocal, polysemic subgroupings of Jews with geographically distinct cultural variations, Jewish culture is split along two overarching lines: Ashkenazic and Sephardic. The latter are said to descend from the Jews of Spain and North Africa who remained for centuries members of Near Eastern societies and, later, the Islamic societies of the Muslim expansion. Sephardic and Ashkenazic cultural differences are substantial and include strong distinctions in the practice of rituals, world outlook, everyday demeanor, and relation to religious life.

When I was 19 I took a trip to Israel in order to visit relatives and work on a kibbutz. Before I went, my rabbi in the Bronx asked me to deliver a valuable package of documents to the head of a yeshiva in Jerusalem. He wrote a letter of introduction for me, but it was in Yiddish, which I could not read.

While in Jerusalem I found this particular yeshiva, with great effort, and presented the package from my rabbi. I had just come from the kibbutz and was dressed in shorts and work boots and was obliged to borrow a skull cap in order to enter the yeshiva. The rabbi accepted the package and said that the letter introduced me to him. My last name, "Gottdiener," means "servant of god" in German. He then looked at me and said, "Do you know who you are?" I did not know what he meant by that question, because it seemed so stupid. He appeared to be threatening me in some strange way. He sensed that I did not understand and said, "Do you know what your name means?" I responded that I did. He then told me that I could not know, if I were dressed the way that I was and had come to see him. I responded that I had just come from the kibbutz, but he said that I did not understand. Then he just stared at me. I became very uncomfortable and turned to leave. In fact, at that moment I thought of running from that place and his presence.

"Your name in Hebrew is 'Ovadia,'" he said. "That's a name that is usually reserved as an honorary title for Sephardic rabbis." I remember this moment well. I simply could not relate to what he was telling me. I thought of running again. And then the rabbi did a strange thing. He reached out and grabbed my hand. "Where did you get this ring?" he asked. When I was 13 my father had given me a pure gold ring that he wore which he said belonged to my great-grandfather. Many of its features had become worn over the years, but I could make out distinguishing marks. The bottom part of the ring consisted of someone's initials, while the top third was taken up by a crescent moon design with the tips of the moon pointing up. I told the rabbi about the origin of the ring. He asked me if I knew what that symbol was. I didn't. It was now so uncomfortable for me talking to this man that I could not stand being there another moment. I excused myself and left quickly.

The encounter with the rabbi was very disturbing and I remember it vividly to this day. I needed to travel only a little ways in the city of Jerusalem to identify the symbol on my ring which I had already worn for several years. It was the same crescent moon hung from below that adorned all the buildings in Israel dating from the Turkish era. I saw this sign on the top of mosques and carved into stones on the side of buildings. Later I noticed that many Arab countries used the crescent symbol on their national flags, but only the Turks had it positioned in the same way as on my ring. "Was I a Muslim?" I thought. "An Arab? A Turk?" I did not think so, but I was confused. Certainly my family background involved more than the typical Ashkenazic roots which I had taken for granted until the encounter with that particular rabbi in Jerusalem who had been able to interpret the signs for me. Out of that instant an entire universe of material culture and symbolic forms located in the Middle East suddenly became personally relevant.

In subsequent years the mystery of family history surfaced from time to time in my consciousness, although it was never a specific interest to which I devoted full attention. I remembered, for example, that while my father was alive he had exhibited a peculiar behavior during the High Holy days. My congregation in the Bronx was Ashkenazic but there was a significant community of Greek Jews who lived in the neighborhood. On the occasion of the High Holy days, the Greeks would hold their own service in the basement of the building. My father, who was extremely knowledgable in the ways of the Ashkenazic synagogue service, would, nevertheless, slip away for hours at a time to the Greek service. He had said that he enjoyed it more than the main service because it was closer to the way he had prayed back in Hungary. Greek Jews are Sephardic.

Was my family originally Sephardic? I do not know for sure. The Holocaust has burned a black hole in the place of where most European

Jews' family roots would be. I never knew my grandparents, since they perished in the camps, and have no information on their ante-cedents, not even names. Since I know little about my direct ances-tors, I can only guess who they were from the sparse clues of personal experience. I know, for example, that the synagogue service of Hasidic Jews is supposed to be similar to that of the Sephardim. However, it was told to me clearly that my family was anti-Hasidic (Misnagdim), so my father's preference for the Greek service could not have been based on a Hasidic past. More probably, my father's family was origi-nally Sephardic, hence the last name, Ovadia. Greek Jews came from Turkey, as did many Sephardic Jews, because they were welcomed by the Ottoman Sultan in the 1500s after the Spanish Inquisition and expulsion. For several hundred years, Turkey also controlled parts of Hungary. It's a best guess that quite a few Sephardic Jews spread out to the peripheral borders of the Ottoman Empire, including my fa-ther's section of the Carpathian Mountains. Eventually, they may have intermarried with Ashkenazic Jews. That's all I can say without more facts. If I want to know more, there are a number of sources I can turn to, such as books that help Jews overcome the lasting dam-age of the Holocaust and forced conversions on family genesis[8] and the genealogical services of the Bet Hatfusoth (Diaspora Museum) in Tel Aviv. The enigma of cultural identification is embodied by my great-grandfather's ring and its own enigma of origins. This object, which signifies Turkey, not Judaism, holds the key to the mystery. I am bound by this object and the riddle of its signifying practice which can no longer speak and explain "Why?"

I possess a generalized Jewish identity, having grown up in the United States, with which I am quite comfortable. But when I travel to Israel, with its strong distinctions between Sephardic and Ashkenazic cultures, between European Jew and Arab Jew, I do not really know who I am.

Identity and Materiality

Postmodern culture is said to undercut the basis of self-authenticity, to "de-center" the self, and replace identity formation with a media-driven, moment-to-moment self-presentation.[9] As we have seen, self-formation is dependent on a mutually reinforcing process that links materiality and symbolic processes of interaction and valorization. In contrast, much of the sociological literature conceives of self-formation solely as a cognitive process that privileges mental states, even if it also is said to be dependent on social interaction. Material culture enters into this process principally as the props which are utilized to promote staged identities;[10] hence, the process by which meaning is imputed to objects is conceived of by privileging thought. For the case of sociologists, when it comes to the question of identity and self-formation: we think, therefore we are. Such Cartesianism does not exclude the important role of emotions and psycho-biological or somatic states, but it does exclude an exploration into the relationship with significant material artifacts that are essential to self-identity within the discursive situation.[11]

This privileging of the mental over the material also characterizes postmodern literature. It is within this context that the self becomes problematic. In fact, while the rest of postmodern cultural change is received lukewarmly by scholars, because they seek relief from the industrial orchestration of culture, it is precisely the postmodernists who have been alarmed at the effect of contemporary culture on the self. Although the literature is filled with statements regarding just what an alleged postmodern social order can do to the individual, it is best to return to the original remarks of Jameson, since these have a specificity that can be backed up by theory.

For Jameson, a culture that exhibits the fast pace of constantly shifting, valorized signs is also a culture that constantly undermines the individual's staging ground for the construction of identity. Postmodernism engenders a breakdown of the symbolic integrating mechanisms; we no longer have the capacity to organize our experience of culture in a coherent and meaningful manner, because the basis of meaning is constantly undermined.[12] As Jameson observes, the subject

> has lost its capacity actively to extend its pro-tensions and retensions across the temporal manifold, and to organize its past and future into coherent experience, it becomes difficult enough to see how the cultural productions of such a subject could result in anything but "heaps of fragments" and in a practice of the randomly heterogeneous and fragmentary and the aleatory.[13]

The above discussion and its case study were meant to show that, while there is this tendency to undercut the grounds of authenticity, the individual is capable of rediscovering lost signifieds and re-integrating aspects of the self. Furthermore, whereas much of the literature implicates the mass, image-driven culture as the villain that obstructs self-integration, the case study suggests that the quest for a foundation to self-identity may be hampered more by large historical events and movements of population across the globe than by the effects of mass media. This is always a matter of degree, but identity depends a great deal on origins, including those of family, religion, race, and ethnicity. These origins are dependent on certain material contexts, principally location and a cultural milieu which contains localized artifacts. Disruptive events deriving from either the relative fate of personal history or global forces affect greatly the resources that connect any individual to his/her origins, including the material objects of cultural heritage which embody specific signifying practices.

Postmodern observers, in keeping with the one-sided view of that topic, claim that identities based on origins have become problematic because of "deterritorialization": the eradication of localized cultures by the homogenizing, superficial, image-dominant culture of global advertising, global media forms, and global technologies of communication.[14] As some observers suggest, "The rapidly expanding and quickening mobility of people combines with the refusal of cultural products and practices to 'stay put' to give a profound sense of loss of territorial roots, of an erosion of the cultural distinctiveness of places."[15]

These observations are accurate as far as they acknowledge a particular tendency of contemporary life. But they go too far, like other postmodern ideas, in their reduction of all experience to the control of global, mass culture. The imputation of hegemony to the homogenizing power of global media, deriving from the theoretical specification of postmodernism as a cultural "dominant",[16] privileges the process of sign production and ignores the material dimension. In this case, such ideas are fallaciously *a-spatial*. They neglect the role of space – i.e., a material milieu – as manifested in localized differences which include valorized artifacts, local institutions, and symbolic modes of interaction. The experience of identity remains a combination of fragmentation and symbolic leveling that derives from the media and, simultaneously, the unending search for authenticity which is as dependent on material artifacts, institutions, and localized space as it is on cognitive processes of self-integration. In fact, the latter cannot proceed without the former.

The experience of deterritorialization, which is produced by postmodern culture, can be offset as a homogenizing tendency by the recovery of lost signifieds that have the power to restore difference. The individual capacity to resist, however, is hampered by the larger historical forces of change, including wars, forced conversions, and large population migrations, which have altered the geo-cultural landscape

of the globe. As the above case study suggests, resistance and recontextualization, like fragmentation, deterritorialization, and simulation,
never achieve closure or domination, and the quest for authenticity
must contend, instead, with an ironic and imperfect world that is
as dependent on chance, localized encounters, as on other forms of
experience.

Recovering Rock Music Subcultures

In chapter 9 we saw that rock music is closely intertwined with other
expressive symbols of adolescent subcultures. Successive waves of
innovative music within the rock idiom have also been generated by
specific subcultures. As discussed in chapter 8, innovations, such as
reggae, are discovered and marketed by the mass media industries
who also strip away deep-level signifieds in the process of popularizing new musical styles. Cultural criticism of the rock industry can
reverse this process by rediscovering and recontextualizing popular
music. We can work backwards, so to speak, from the reggae of
UB40 to the reggae of Marley and, further, to Rastafarian practice
which also explains "dub," "rock steady," "rap," and all the expressive symbols of reggae lyrics.

In my classes on the Sociology of Culture, for example, my students by the 1990s almost universally knew what reggae music was
and could identify it when played in comparison with other kinds of
popular music. Virtually none of them, however, had a personal
understanding of either Rastafarian culture or the common expressive
symbols of reggae lyrics which reference that culture. They did not
know what these symbols meant other than being global referents to
reggae.

Exercises in the rediscovery of lost signifieds can help students
(and any individual) recontextualize their own cultural milieu and
enable them to gain a better appreciation for rock music as a source
of expressive, subcultural symbols.

Case Study

I enjoy rock music and have followed it closely since the 1960s. During
the late 1970s the innovations of hard rock from the 1960s had died
out and the disco craze had taken over. Because I hated disco, I was

consigned to the limbo world of consumer marginality where I was presented with the prospect of feeding on sixties nostalga and the tired recordings of aging psychedelic rock stars. The popular success of *Saturday Night Fever* and *Disco Duck* seemed to mock me.

One day in 1977 I wandered into my neighborhood record store to browse. I asked the clerk if there was anything new or interesting and he told me to check out a recent arrival from England that was an anthology record. I found the album. It was called simply *The Roxy London WC2: (Jan–Apr 77)*. Inside was the following sparsely written liner note: "On January 1st 1977 The Roxy opened exclusively for the New Wave. There was nowhere else for most of the groups to play. We promoted the music until April 23rd, and enjoyed it (A. Czezowski, R. Jedraszczyk, B. Jones)."

The album back cover had some very strange photographs with bizarrely dressed people looking definitely non-disco. I bought the record immediately.

At home as I played the music I experienced the kind of epiphany that comes when you are exposed to a powerful new cultural form for the first time. Jameson calls this overwhelming sensation the "hysterical sublime" and surely it is of this quality. The music is totally new. It is beyond your cognitive capacity, yet you try to orient yourself to its contours or boundaries in order to grasp the structure. No comfort is given through the solace of familiarity and the reproducible artifact of mass commodity marketing. Instead, the shock of innovation and difference is encountered and previous cognitive frames must be jettisoned in order to grasp the new aesthetic.

Much later I came to understand that this new music was called "Punk." That label, however, only meant for me a way of denoting the innovation, not of understanding its dynamics or mode of origin. Nevertheless, the antidote to disco was now at hand. On that particular album I especially enjoyed the music of X- Ray Specs, Wire, and, my personal favorite, The Buzzcocks. I searched for more Punk to buy, but was at a disadvantage during this point in 1977, because I didn't know exactly what to look for. There were no marketing signposts at the record store. No one I knew had any familiarity with the music. Punk was an unchartered domain.

Late in that same year a friend of mine, who was a hair cutter, returned from a trip to England with blue spiked hair and heavy eyelid makeup. She looked very much like the people on the back of the Roxy album. She had not heard of Punk rock, but was very enthusiastic about the changes that were occurring in the way people dressed and wore their hair among the Brits in London. As a cutter,

the new styles opened up many possibilities for reworking her customers' hair and coloring. I did not realize it at the time, but I was
witnessing the marketing of Punk during its early stages.

My hair cutter friend was kind enough to give me a newsletter/
pamphlet which she had obtained at the most important boutique
pushing the new fashion. Called simply "Sex," it was located on the
King's Road. This printed material, published by Glitterbest of Oxford St, London W1, also contained pictures of the same kind of
people as the Roxy album. Three quarters of the front cover was
taken up by a photo of a girl with a haircut that was flat on the top
with grease-stiffened wings on the sides. Her heavy eye makeup consisted of exaggerated eyebrows that curved around the sides of her
face and deep shadow above the eyes. Her left ear was pierced several
times, with the innermost hole holding a half-inch chain, on the end
of which dangled a plastic human skull. She had a small-link chain
around her neck which was anchored by safety pins sticking through
a dark sweat band, also around her neck. Her blouse consisted of
black and white stripes. Above this girl was printed the headline of
the newsletter, which read in large red letters, "Anarchy in the UK,"
and then underneath it, "Sex Pistols" in smaller red lettering that
looked like it was cut out from a magazine with different type faces,
as in a ransom note.

I had no idea what was meant by the "Sex Pistols" but the word
"anarchy" had a specific connotation as the last mutation of an important part of the 1960s student movement, especially in France. I
wondered if there was any connection between the latter and this
strange and exciting newsletter. Looking inside I saw other photos of
people in the new fashion. There were also pictures of rock bands in
concert. On one page was an overlay of a newspaper clipping on top
of photos of a band playing. The clipping was from *Music Week*,
October 23, 1976. It said, "Sex Pistols join 'establishment,'" and then,
"EMI quick on the draw for Sex Pistols." The rest of the clipping was
unreadable and I had no idea what it all meant. In fact, with the
exception of one page, the entire pamphlet was indecipherable to me
and I could not tell whether it was promoting a band or some new
subculture, although it fit in with the new cultural changes I had seen
recently.

On the one particular page that was significant to me, there was a
title: "How to improve your mind." It then said, "There is only one
criterion. Does it threaten the status quo?" The rest of the page was
devoted to several photo comparisons between a picture of a bureau-
crat in a suit, the British Concorde, and a girl dressed in the new

fashions. This simple coding device represented, to me, the apotheosis of late 1960s student anarchism, and a way to produce a new, oppositional subculture that promised unbounded anarchy. For a short time in the late 1970s, principally in England, it did just that.

It is not possible to understand a culture without knowledge of its code. This is especially true for countercultures that seek some oppositional split with dominant society. Back in 1977 I pieced together from the above experiences that (a) some wonderful new kind of music was being played in England, and (b) that some new fashion ideas were developing that totally changed the way people looked. I did not know at that time that the two movements were connected. The only frame that seemed familiar to me was the use of the concept "anarchy" and the way the programmatic statement regarding how to improve your mind used the concept as an oppositional device contra bourgeois, straight European culture. This was a simple but powerful coding device for producing a counterculture.

In 1968 France underwent a social upheaval known as the "events of May," the "upheaval," or the "Explosion."[17] Students and workers had joined together to demand change. Millions of people went on strike and major universities were taken over. For a time it seemed that the radical left parties would assume control of the society. Instead, they splintered and the communists threw their weight into a deal with the sitting, conservative administration of De Gaulle that effectively ended the organized worker opposition. Within this milieu an important student organization had operated to push certain ideas that rejected the old ideologies of communism and socialism from a left point of view. Decidedly anarchistic, they called themselves the "situationists," and for a time derived inspiration from leading French intellectuals who had abandoned communism in the 1950s, such as Henri Lefebvre.

I was not in France during 1968 but admired the events of May from afar. I wanted to know more about what had happened, especially since student politics in the United States after the summer of 1968 had taken a very bizarre and frightening turn which left me alienated from the major student organizations. I decided to visit Paris in 1969, as a way of revitalizing my own attachment to social change despite the moribund downturn of the American "new left." During this time I was introduced to the ideas of the situationists and their political movement, the Situationist International.

Because there was nothing comparable to this anarchist organization in the US that I was aware of, I simply filed away the information regarding what I had learned about situationism, on my return to the States. I was left intrigued, not with the particular activities of the situationists, but with several of their ideas as inspired by philosophers such as Nietszche and, most especially, Henri Lefebvre, whose books I began to devour. Back in the States I pursued academic work, as did many others of my generation.

And then, almost ten years later, I discovered some of the situationist ideas percolating again through this bizarre new subculture. Shortly thereafter, the band the Sex Pistols broke onto the American scene. Their album was heavily promoted in the US, as was their song, "Anarchy in the UK" (all very familiar today to followers of rock). The lyrics of the lead song are as follows: "I am an antichrist. I am an anarchist. Don't know what I want, but I know how to get it. Wanna destroy all the passersby, cause I wanna be anarchy."[18]

Aside from the signifier "anarchy," the song didn't make a lot of sense to me, except for the phrase "I know how to get it" and later on "I use the best, I lose the rest" which was directly out of situationist ideology.

The mystery of Punk's origins remained with me until 1985. I only had a working hypothesis: a connection between the verses of "Anarchy in the UK" and the situationists. During 1985 the British group The Clash made what would be their very last American tour. I was a big fan of The Clash. One of my students was working security for the California leg of their trip. Through him I arranged also to work security for the concerts and thereby obtained the much valued "all areas" backstage pass. At the very first concert I worked, in Santa Barbara, I had arrived early for the soundcheck and was surprised to find Malcolm McLaren standing around. McLaren was the originator of the Sex Pistols, as is well known now.[19] At that time he was marketing himself as a solo act using sampling and other pre-rap Jamaican DJ gimmicks with a song called "Buffalo Girls." I went over and introduced myself. I told him I only had one question to ask but it was very important to me. For years I had been trying to figure out where the ideas about anarchy that had inspired the Sex Pistols had come from. My hypothesis was that they were somehow related to the situationists. I asked Malcolm if he had ever heard of them. He said, "Of course! I was in Paris at the time as an art student." No revelation now, but a critical one for me back in 1985.

Recovering lost signifieds

All of this is very much old news today. Several highly detailed and important accounts, such as Greil Marcus' *Lipstick Traces*[20] and Jon

Savage's *England's Dreaming*,[21] document the close connection between Paris in 1968, the situationists, and the Sex Pistols. What's
remarkable is the way these influences fashioned a completely innovative subcultural response that included a third generation of rock
music in the 1970s (after the rhythm and blues of the 1950s and the
hard rock of the 1960s). In 1993 the overtones of Punk are still po-
tently influential in the grunge sound of bands such as Nirvana and
Pearl Jam.

It is also remarkable that all these antecedent connections took a
long time to piece together for those writing in the popular press, as
evidenced by the Marcus and Savage books which just came out recently. The new code was so potent that it spawned cultural change
for almost 20 years. Yet, how little of that code or its deep-level signifiers were ever really understood? Confrontation with the cultural
change of Punk still provokes mystery. According to Marcus,

> Connections between the Sex Pistols, dada, the so grandly named
> Situationist International, and even forgotten heresies are not
> original with me. In the early days of London punk, one could
> hardly find an article on the topic without the word "dada" in
> it: punk was "like dada," everybody said, though nobody said
> why, let alone what that was supposed to mean. References to
> Malcolm McLaren's supposed involvement with the spectral "SI"
> were insider currency in the British pop press, but that currency
> didn't buy anything . . . Still, all this sounded interesting . . . even
> if I'd never heard of the Situationist International. So I began to
> poke around, and the more I found, the less I knew. All sorts of
> people had made these connections, but no one had made any-
> thing of them – and soon enough my attempt to make some-
> thing of them led me from the card catalogue at the university
> library in Berkeley to the dada founding site in Zurich, from Gil
> J. Wolman's bohemian flat in Paris to Michele Bernstein's sev-
> enteenth century parsonage in the south of England, from Alex-
> ander Trocchi's junkie pad in London back to books that had
> stood on library shelves for thirty years before I checked them
> out.[22]

In the 1980s I was using Dick Hebdige's *Subcultures*[23] in my class
on mass culture to teach American students about the importance of
the recovery of lost signifieds in the understanding of rock music.
Hebdige's book details the role of British working-class subcultures
in promoting different aspects of the music scene in the UK. His

descriptions of Mods, Teds, Skinheads, Rastas and Punks are unparalleled in their insights, but he fails in explaining the meaning of Punk. As Marcus observes in another context, above, Hebdige doesn't discuss "how." He could not decipher the code of Punk like we all could for the Rastafarians or Mods.

The journey from Hebdige's account of the UK subcultural scene in the late 1970s to the Marcus and Savage books represents the time required to understand the gesture of Punk. It is a trip that moves from the broadly based description of UK rock subcultures in Hebdige to a finely grained accounting of the creative moments of Punk as a significant historical event during the 1970s. I cannot help but be impressed with the length of the Marcus and Savage books, the one 496 pages, the other 602 pages. All this time, since the 1970s, the need had been there to recapture the lost signifieds of Punk, to explain exactly why, how, and when. That need was finally satisfied at last only in 1992 and in a monumental way.

Hebdige

The recontextualization of Punk is not self-evident. It requires the recapturing of localized experiences, such as the Paris of 1968, chance encounters like the presence of McLaren in Paris, and the general decline of the English economy and culture in the 1970s. It also requires an appreciation for the primed desire for difference and modes of rebellion among adolescents, the power of cultural creation through fashion and rock music, and the disseminating powers of image-driven, mass culture.

Writing in the late 1970s shortly after the events of the Sex Pistols took place, Hebdige paints with broad strokes. He discusses the "gloomy, apocalyptic" and economically troubling atmosphere of the 1970s. He shows how punk rock emerged through a voracious eclecticism that synthesized diverse, but innovative strains: glitter-rock, the "proto-punk" of New York groups like the Ramones, the innovative sounds of the London pub scene, reggae and "northern soul." As he suggests,

> Not surprisingly, the resulting mix was somewhat unstable: all these elements constantly threatened to separate and return to their original sources. Glam rock contributed narcissism, nihilism and gender confusion. American punk offered a minimalist aesthetic, . . . the cult of the street and a penchant for self-laceration. Northern soul . . . brought its subterranean tradition

of fast, jerky rhythms, solo dance styles and amphetamines; reggae its exotic and dangerous aura of forbidden identity, its conscience, its dread and its cool.[24]

Although he does not mention it at the time, the music which came to be identified with Punk was subversive in a particularly significant way. It undermined the polished, audience controlling efforts of the record producing industry. Punk was essentially anti-commercial, despite its commercial aspirations which were subsequently revealed by later studies of the phenomenon. It gave expression to anarchy in the music industry because it allowed for innovation, minimalist recording techniques, and an unpredictable market. In fact, it was the apotheosis of anti-commercialism and the breakdown of the performer/audience distinction, just as situationism was the consummate expression and aestheticization of deviance.

Hebdige also describes vividly how the new sound attracted an equally eclectic way of dressing that helped propel the Punk attitude into a fully fledged subculture. Specific mechanisms of eclectic bricolage were deployed to cut and paste, slice apart and reform, and staple or pin together diverse elements into new fashions. As he observes,

> Punk reproduced the entire sartorial history of post-war working class youth cultures in "cut up" form, combining elements which had originally belonged to completely different epochs. There was a chaos of quiffs and leather jackets, brothel creepers and winkle pickers, plimsolls and paka macs, moddy crops and skinhead strides, drainpipes and vivid socks, bum freezers and bovver boots – all kept "in place" and "out of time" by the spectacular adhesives: the safety pins and plastic clothes pegs, the bondage straps and bits of string which attracted so much horrified and fascinated attention.[25]

Out of this chaos of fragmented, sampled forms, a Punk sensibility emerged as the unifying mechanism. Indeed, without a mode of integration around some central metaphor, we could not speak, the way Hebdige does above, about this radical eclecticism as "Punk." We would only have, instead, a disconnected melange of different, fragmented cultural self-expressions, much like the way postmodern popular culture is conceptualized by promoters of that term. There was, however, a powerful integrating mechanism operating during the 1970s, but writing at that time, Hebdige could not specify it.

Marcus

Greil Marcus' book differs from Hebdige's because of the way the former plunges the depths of anarchist tendencies throughout western European culture and relates those gestures to Punk. Marcus, quite rightly, focuses the first part of his book on the activities of Malcolm McLaren and the Sex Pistols. He shows how McLaren wedded his knowledge of situationism and the *enrages* student group of Paris, 1968, to the sale of clothing. Wanting to broaden the market for his boutique items, he promoted a rock band of dubious musicianship as the standard-bearers for the new look. McLaren turned situationist ideology into a commodity, first through fashion, and then through rock music. Marcus shows how Punk, as the commodification of anarchism, succeeded beyond anyone's expectations.

In an effort to understand McLaren's inspiration in more depth, Marcus devotes the remainder of his book to a history of the artistic margins exemplifying the spirit of anarchism. He connects the present with the 1950s efforts of a small group of Parisian artists – Guy Debord, Asger Jorn, Michele Bernstein, and others. Then he reaches further back to other lost signifieds – to the Dada movement at the turn of this century, to Lettrism, Surrealism, and then, going as far as he can, he travels back to the 1960s and 1970s with the situationists. Marcus plumbs the anarchist code refashioned from politics to aesthetics as situationism, as an aestheticization of politics. He shows how McClaren moved that aesthetics back from politics and fashioned it into a popular and commercial teenage idiom which involved the marketing of hair styles, records, and clothes. Suddenly, we know more than we may have cared to about the lost signifieds of Punk.

Savage

After Marcus, Savage's 1992 book could have been anti-climactic. But it is not. Marcus recovers the historical signifieds and re-contextualizes situationism. Savage returns to Marcus' starting point, Malcolm McLaren, but never leaves. Malcolm's act was the articulation of commodification with situationism as a popular culture gesture. Savage provides us with a blow-by-blow accounting of McLaren's accomplishment as rock and subcultural entrepreneur. We start in December 1971, in a small shop at 430 King's Road, London, and end in May 1979 with the victory at the polls of Mrs Thatcher's Conservatives. Savage provides us with every conceivable detail. He retells when and why certain decisions were made, who was there at the beginning, middle and end, what was said, and why. The essence of Punk, the particulars of its lost signifieds, are now valorized forever. At the very end of the book Savage cannot resist the temptation to write Punk's epitaph:

> Punk was beaten, but it had also won. If it had been the project of the Sex Pistols to destroy the music industry, then they had failed; but as they gave it new life, they allowed a myriad of new forms to become possible. When Punk entered the music and media industries, its vision of freedom was eventually swamped by New-Right power politics and the accompanying value systems, but its original, gleeful negation remains a beacon. History is made by those who say "No" and Punk's utopian heresies remain its gift to the world.[26]

With Marcus and Savage, it is now even possible to become lost in the abundance of material on Punk's system of signification. The cure to the postmodernist gutting of signs may be difficult to absorb all at once, but we have the necessary example – cultural criticism as the rediscovery of lost signifieds. I return, therefore, to a material artifact, which early observers, like Hebdige, or Marcus and Savage, may not have had in their possession – the pamphlet from my hair cutter friend, which was a form of publicity for the Sex Pistols, contained the encoding instructions that organized the Punk response to mainstream culture. This subversive document may not have produced that subculture alone, but it was part of a discourse that did. As the recent books by Marcus and Savage demonstrate, it has taken almost 20 years to piece all the parts of the puzzle together.

"Against an idea, even a false one, all weapons are powerless."

Notes

1   Jean Baudrillard, *Simulations* (New York: Semiotext(e), 1983).
2   Michel de Certeau, *The Practice of Everyday Life* (Berkeley: University of California Press, 1984); Henri Lefebvre, *The Critique of Everyday Life* (London: Verso, 1989).
3   Dick Hebdige, *Subcultures: The Meaning of Style* (London: Methuen, 1979).
4   M. Real, *Mass Mediated Culture* (Englewood Cliffs, N.J.: Prentice-Hall, 1977); Robert Goodman, *Reading Ads Socially* (New York: Routledge, 1992).
5   Kenneth Gergen, *The Saturated Self* (New York: Basic Books, 1991); Michael Schwalbe, "Goffman against Postmodernism: Emotion and the

Reality of the Self," *Symbolic Interaction*, 16, 4 (1993): 333–50; Lauren Langman, "Alienation and Everyday Life: Goffman Meets Marx at the Shopping Mall," in *Alienation and the Individual*, edited by F. Geyer and W. Heinz (New Brunswick, N.J.: Transaction Press, 1992).

6 Alex Haley, *Roots* (New York: Doubleday, 1976).

7 Hedy Weiss, "'Alamat' Takes Fascinating Look at Stuff of Legends," *Chicago Sun Times*, October 12, 1993, pp. 4, 61.

8 Arthur Kurzweil, *From Generation to Generation* (New York: Schocken, 1982); Rabbi Malcolm Stern, *First American Jewish Families* (New York: KTAV Publishing, n.d.); for Sephardic Jews, Kurzweil suggests writing to The Judezmo Society, Brooklyn, NY 11235.

9 Gergen, *Saturated Self*; Langman, "Alienation"; Douglas Kellner, "Popular Culture and the Construction of Postmodern Identities," in *Modernity and Identity*, edited by Scott Lash and Jonathon Friedman (Oxford: Blackwell, 1992), pp. 141–77.

10 Erving Goffman, *The Presentation of Self in Everyday Life* (New York: Anchor, 1959), *Interaction Ritual* (New York: Pantheon, 1967); Schwalbe, "Goffmann against Postmodernism."

11 For examples of this idealist approach within the context of contemporary concerns about postmodernism, see Anthony Giddens, *Modernity and Self-Identity* (Stanford, Calif.: Stanford University Press, 1991); Lash and Friedman, eds, *Modernity and Identity*.

12 The theoretical basis for Jameson's concern involves linkage with the work of Lacan, also a position of the *Tel Quel* group and, hence, the adoption of the orthodox line that self-formation is a process of discourse or language. As such, blockages in the formation of identity arise as breaks in the signifying chain – an idealist and reductionist position which makes the individual only a text, but one that is not much different from Freud or the sociology of Mead and symbolic interactionists to which Lacan's approach owes a great debt.

13 Fredrick Jameson, "Postmodernism, or the Cultural Logic of Late Capitalism," *New Left Review*, 146 (1984): 30–72.

14 A. Gupta and J. Ferguson, "Beyond 'Culture': Space, Identity and the Politics of Difference," *Cultural Anthropology*, 7, 1 (1992): 6–23; C. Kaplan, "Deterritorializations," *Cultural Critique*, 6 (1987): 187–98; R. Radhakrishnan, "Ethnic Identity and Post-structuralist Difference," *Cultural Critique*, 6 (1987): 199–220.

15 Gupta and Ferguson, "Beyond 'Culture,' " p. 9.

16 Jameson, "Postmodernism."

17 Henri Lefebvre, *The Explosion: Marxism and the French Upheaval* (New York: Monthly Review Press, 1969).

18 Paul Cook, Steve Jones, Johnny Rotten and G. Matlock, "Anarchy in the UK" (Los Angeles: Careers Music, Inc., 1977).

19 Greil Marcus, *Lipstick Traces* (Cambridge, Mass.: Harvard University Press, 1989); Jon Savage, *England's Dreaming: Anarchy, Sex Pistols, Punk Rock, and Beyond* (New York: St Martin's Press, 1992).

20   Marcus, *Lipstick Traces*.
21   See Savage, *England's Dreaming*, for more details.
22   Marcus, *Lipstick Traces*, p. 19.
23   Hebdige, *Subcultures*.
24   Ibid., p. 25.
25   Ibid., p. 26.
25   Savage, *England's Dreaming*, p. 541.

Index